FIELDING
TRAVEL GUIDES

FIELDING'S HOT SPOTS

Travel in Harm's Way

Fielding Titles

Fielding's Alaska Cruises and the Inside Passage
Fielding's America West
Fielding's Asia's Top Dive Sites
Fielding's Australia
Fielding's Bahamas
Fielding's Baja California
Fielding's Bermuda
Fielding's Best and Worst — The surprising results of the Plog Survey
Fielding's Birding Indonesia
Fielding's Borneo
Fielding's Budget Europe
Fielding's Caribbean
Fielding's Caribbean Cruises
Fielding's Caribbean on a Budget
Fielding's Diving Australia
Fielding's Diving Indonesia
Fielding's Eastern Caribbean
Fielding's England including Ireland, Scotland & Wales
Fielding's Europe
Fielding's Europe 50th Anniversary
Fielding's European Cruises
Fielding's Far East
Fielding's France
Fielding's France: Loire Valley, Burgundy & the Best of French Culture
Fielding's France: Normandy & Brittany
Fielding's France: Provence and the Mediterranean
Fielding's Freewheelin' USA
Fielding's Hawaii
Fielding's Hot Spots: Travel in Harm's Way
Fielding's Indiana Jones Adventure and Survival Guide™
Fielding's Italy
Fielding's Kenya
Fielding's Las Vegas Agenda
Fielding's London Agenda
Fielding's Los Angeles Agenda
Fielding's Mexico
Fielding's New Orleans Agenda
Fielding's New York Agenda
Fielding's New Zealand
Fielding's Paradors, Pousadas and Charming Villages of Spain and Portugal
Fielding's Paris Agenda
Fielding's Portugal
Fielding's Rome Agenda
Fielding's San Diego Agenda
Fielding's Southeast Asia
Fielding's Southern California Theme Parks
Fielding's Southern Vietnam on Two Wheels
Fielding's Spain
Fielding's Surfing Australia
Fielding's Surfing Indonesia
Fielding's Sydney Agenda
Fielding's Thailand, Cambodia, Laos and Myanmar
Fielding's Travel Tool™
Fielding's Vietnam, including Cambodia and Laos
Fielding's Walt Disney World and Orlando Area Theme Parks
Fielding's Western Caribbean
Fielding's The World's Most Dangerous Places™
Fielding's Worldwide Cruises

FIELDING'S HOT SPOTS

Travel in Harm's Way

By
Robert Young Pelton,
Coskun Aral, & Contributors

Fielding Worldwide, Inc.
308 South Catalina Avenue
Redondo Beach, California 90277 U.S.A.

Fielding's Hot Spots: Travel in Harm's Way
Published by Fielding Worldwide, Inc.

FIELDING WORLDWIDE INC.

PUBLISHER AND CEO	**Robert Young Pelton**
GENERAL MANAGER	**John Guillebeaux**
OPERATIONS DIRECTOR	**George Posanke**
ELEC. PUBLISHING DIRECTOR	**Larry E. Hart**
PUBLIC RELATIONS DIRECTOR	**Beverly Riess**
ACCOUNT SERVICES MANAGER	**Cindy Henrichon**
PROJECT MANAGER	**Chris Snyder**
MANAGING EDITOR	**Amanda K. Knoles**
COVER DESIGNED BY	**Digital Artists, Inc.**
COVER PHOTOGRAPHERS —	
Front Cover	**Robert Young Pelton/Westlight**
Back Cover	**Coskun Aral**
INSIDE PHOTOS	**Robert Young Pelton/Westlight, Coskun Aral, Jim Hooper, Anthony Morland, Peter J. Willems**

Inquiries should be addressed to: Fielding Worldwide, Inc., 308 South Catalina Ave., Redondo Beach, California 90277 U.S.A., ☎ *(310) 372-4474*, Facsimile *(310) 376-8064*, 8:30 a.m.–5:30 p.m. Pacific Standard Time.
Website: http://www.fieldingtravel.com
e-mail: fielding@fieldingtravel.com

ISBN 1-56952-166-2

Printed in the United States of America

Letter from the Publisher

Travel is often confused with vacationing. This book will let you peek over the abyss into areas where few people venture. The contributors may hide behind labels like photographer, writer, adventurer, mercenary or tourist but these vocations are simply excuses to visit the most extreme regions of the world. So sit back, relax and enjoy travel in harm's way. (Oh, thought you might want to know that according to accident statistics, your home is the most dangerous place in the world.)

RYP

Robert Young Pelton
Publisher and CEO
Fielding Worldwide, Inc.

THE AUTHORS

Robert Young Pelton

Pelton, 42, has led an adventurous life. His interest in adventure began at age ten when he became the youngest student ever to attend a Canadian survival school in Selkirk, Manitoba. The school was later closed down after the deaths of a number of students. Pelton went on to become a lumberjack, boundary cutter, tunneler, driller and blaster's assistant in addition to his more lucrative occupations as a business strategist and marketing expert. On his time off, his quest for knowledge and understanding have taken him through the remote and exotic areas of more than 60 countries.

Some of Pelton's adventures include breaking American citizens out of jail in Colombia, living with the Dogon people in the Sahel, thundering down forbidden rivers in leaky native canoes, plowing through the East Africa swamps with the U.S. Camel Trophy team, hitchhiking through war-torn Central America, setting up the first video interview of the never before photographed *taliban* leaders in Afghanistan and completing the first circumnavigation of the island of Borneo by land as well as numerous visits to and through war zones. It is not surprising that his friends include shepherds, warlords, pengalus, mercenaries, nomads, terrorists, field researchers, sultans, missionaries, headhunters, smugglers and other colorful people.

Stories about Pelton or his adventures have been featured in publications as diverse as *Outside, Shift, Soldier of Fortune, Star, The New York Times, Los Angeles Times, Class, El Pais, The Sunday London Times, Der Stern, Die Welt, Washington Post, Outpost,* and hundreds of other newspapers around the world. He has also been featured and interviewed on the BBC, NBC, CBS, ABC, Fox, RTL, CNN, CBC, and is a regular guest on CNN.

Not much slows Pelton down; he has survived car accidents, muggings, illness, attacks by the PKK, African killer bees and even a plane crash in the central highlands of Kalimantan. He attributes his numerous arrests and detainments to his hosts' need to get to know him better. Despite these minor setbacks, Pelton still faces each dangerous encounter with a sense of humor and an irreverent wit.

What makes Pelton's travels unusual is that they are his vacation. He wrote *DP* because he couldn't find an author who would.Unfortunately since he now devotes his time to writing and updating *DP*, he is fond of cursing and yelling "It's not an adventure, it's a job! He doesn't quite know what he will do for his holidays now.

Pelton's approach to adventure can be quite humorous. Whether it's challenging former Iban headhunters to a chug-a-lug contest, calling the *taliban* a bunch of women to their face, loading expedition members' packs with rocks, indulging in a little target practice with Kurdish warlords in Turkey or filling up a hotel pool with stewardesses, waiters and furniture in Burundi during an all-night party, he brings a certain element of fun and excitement to dangerous places. As we go to press Pelton is off on a DP tour of duty in Algeria, Egypt, Pakistan, Afghanistan, Tajikistan, Kazakhstan, Myanmar and Papua New Guinea, winding up with a visit to the rebels on Bougainville. He freely admits that he will also visit England, Germany, Australia, New Zealand, Singapore, The Solomons and Tahiti; "just so I don't lose my perspective, or my tan."

Pelton is a Fellow of the Royal Geographical Society in London and author of *Borneo,* and *The Indiana Jones Adventure and Survival Guide* for Fielding Worldwide. Pelton lives in Los Angeles California.

Coskun Aral

Coskun Aral, 41, was thrust into the spotlight as a young photojournalist when he was caught aboard a Turkish 727 hijacked by terrorists in 1980. He risked his life to cover the hijacking from the inside. He survived the deadly shootout and his career was launched. Since then, Aral has made a living covering dangerous and forbidden places. His accomplishments range from being one of the few people who have photographed Mecca to being on first-name terms with a number of the major warlords. Aral has seen and done many things but has never lost his love for humanity.

His special relationships with some of the world's most dangerous people make him uniquely suited to contribute to this book. As a photojournalist, he has covered wars on the front lines in Afghanistan, Azerbaijan, Bosnia, Cambodia, Chad, Iran, Iraq, Kuwait, Liberia, Libya, the Philippines, Nicaragua, Northern Ireland, Panama, Romania, Sri Lanka, Bosnia and many other areas. He is also the only ten-time participant of the Camel Trophy and has participated in a number of scientific and endurance expeditions.

Aral was the only reporter in the world to interview the hijacker of the TWA plane in Beirut airport in 1985, and he spent more than 10 years covering the war in Lebanon. He covered the Gulf War from downtown Baghdad and has two *TIME* covers to his credit, as well as numerous magazine features. His adventures for *DP* as well as other topics are currently featured in his hour-long show, *Haberci* ("The Reporters,") on ATV in Turkey. He lives in Istanbul, Turkey.

The Contributors

Sedat Aral

Aral (coauthor Coskun's younger brother) has been a "hot spot" photojournalist for more than 12 years. He has covered Afghanistan, Azerbaijan, Bosnia, Chechnya, Georgia, Iran, Iraq, Lebanon, Malaysia, the Philippines and Syria, as well as news stories in his native Turkey. He has worked internationally for news agencies including Reuters and Sipa Press and works on assignment for *TIME*. Currently he is a special assignment reporter for the Sabah Media Group in Turkey. He can no longer enter Iran by official routes, having been deported twice for taking photographs. He has had his life threatened in Tunceli for photographing burnt Kurdish villages in the region closed to the press, and has been seriously beaten by police after photographing armed attacks on unarmed protesters. Aral lives in London, England.

Wink Dulles

Wink covers the Far East for *DP* and for other Fielding books. He has spent hard time in Cambodia, Thailand and Vietnam, traveling by motorcycle. Dulles covered the elections in Cambodia and the subsequent breakdown of order in that besieged country, being in-country at a time when few foreigners dared. After the first edition of *DP* was published in 1995, he was "invited" back to Cambodia by the government to attend a personal tongue-lashing for his contribution to *DP*. Wink's other notable talents are being mistaken for Mel Gibson and playing a mean guitar. He even arranged the extraction of ABC journalist Ted Koppel from Cambodia. Articles on Wink's adventures have been published in *Newsday, National Geographic Traveler* and *Escape* magazines. In February 1996, Dulles guided the first American motorcycle tour of Vietnam and is still trying to ambush Khun Sa in Yangon for a foursome on the golf course. Dulles is the author of *Fielding's Vietnam, Fielding's Southern Vietnam on Two Wheels* and *Fielding's Thailand, Cambodia, Laos & Myanmar.* Dulles lives in Bangkok, Thailand.

Martin Gilmour

Gilmour was born in Scotland and served in the Royal Ordinance Corps of the British Army. A member of the French Foreign Legion for six years, he divided his time as a parachutist, sniper instructor, combat diver, and infantry corporal among other duties. He was also team leader for an International Rescue Committee in Rwanda. Gilmour is now a resident of New Zealand

Jim Hooper

Hooper is a freelance journalist based in the U.K. Wounded twice in Africa (obviously before he had a chance to read *DP*) Hooper is known for showing up where few other people dare. He is the coauthor of *Flashpoint! At the Frontline of Today's Wars* (with Ken Guest) and *Beneath the Visiting Moon*, a documentary account of his six months with a counterinsurgency unit in Namibia. During the war in Angola, Hooper accompanied UNITA forces on guerrilla operations against Soviet and Cuban-backed government forces. He also spent considerable time with the contract soldiers of Executive Outcomes in Sierra Leone. He has covered conflicts in Bosnia, Chad, Sudan, South Africa and Uganda. His meticulously detailed articles and way-too-close-for-comfort photos have appeared in a wide range of publications including *Jane's Intelligence Review*, *The Economist* and *The Sunday Telegraph* of London. Hooper lives in Hampshire, England.

Jack Kramer

Kramer has been sent to the world's most dangerous places on assignment for *TIME*, *Business Week* and *PBS*. He began his career by covering the civil rights movement in the Deep South during the mid-60s. In the late '60s, he went from covering the battles at home to experiencing and reporting on some of the bloodiest fighting of the Vietnam War, from Cam Lo to Khe Sanh. Later, his beat was the turbulent Middle East, including the Six-Day War, Sudan and Eritrea. He worked as a television producer for PBS on "Behind the Lines" and was *Business Week's* Cairo bureau chief, covering Saudi Arabia, the Gulf States and Iran. He covered Iran before, during and after the revolution and then restarted the defunct *Beirut Daily Star* in 1984. Kramer has covered Kenya, Rhodesia (Zimbabwe), Tanzania, Laos, Thailand, Tunisia, Turkey, Syria, South Africa and the Somalia crisis. He has traveled with the Innuit in northern Canada and with the Polisario guerrillas in Morocco. He is author of *Our French Connection in Africa*, a major investigative report published in *Foreign Policy* and *Travels with the Celestial Dog*, a historical analysis of the 1960s. He lives in Washington, D.C., with his wife and their two children.

Rob Krott

Krott, 34 is a former officer and paratrooper who attended Harvard (anthropology). His military career has earned him various awards and decorations from ten foreign governments. Besides his anthropology pursuits (with Richard Leakey's Koobi Fora Project) he finds time to organize parachute jumps for ex-spec forces and paras around the world and cover conflicts as a correspondent. He is a rare blend of intellectual, soldier and adventurer. He has been on the ground in El Salvador, Guatemala, Sudan, Uganda, Somalia, Bosnia, Myanmar, Cambodia and Angola and continues to work in, or travel on assignment to, the world's most dangerous places. He has served with three foreign armies and lived with a number of rebel groups including the SPLA, and the KNLA in Myanmar. He continues to spend a considerable amount of time in Asia, Africa, The Balkans and Latin America. He is a columnist for *Behind the Lines: The Journal of Military Special Operations* and is a senior foreign correspondant for *Soldier of Fortune*. He has been published in *Harpers, Explorers Journal and New African*. Krott has an an affliction similar to Wink's. Rob is often mistaken for Chuck Norris in his travels. He is hoping some day to be confused with Robert Redford. He keeps *DP* honest with his multipage corrections, illuminations and anecdotes. He lives in Olean, New York.

Anthony Morland

Morland was born in York, England, and grew up in London and Rome. He began his journalism career in Geneva and now works as an AFP correspondent for Agence France Presse in Abidjan, Ivory Coast. Morland resides in England.

Roddy Scott

Scott, 26, graduated from Edinburgh University and began his career as a journalist for a magazine in the Middle East. Scott says he went to one of those pseudo-military schools in his youth and thinks author bios are all bullshit anyway. His work speaks for itself. He seeks out the least visited or most dangerous spots and then manages to pick the world's most dangerous people to be his travel companions. He has traveled through Sierra Leone with the RUF rebels, The Bekaar valley with Hezbollah, Northern Iraq with the PKK, and other journos in gun-crazed Albania. He continues to write articles for a variety of newspapers and magazines including military and consumer publications on current affairs. He conducts radio interviews for *BBC World Service* and *Radio France International.* Scott lives in Ankara, Turkey.

Peter J. Willems

Peter J. Willems is a freelance journalist who spends much of his time in the Middle East and Central Asia.

TABLE OF CONTENTS

INTRODUCTION

This is a book of stories written by my friends, associates, fans and readers of *Fielding's The World's Most Dangerous Places (DP)*, and yours truly. Many of us have traveled together, some of us have never met face to face, but we all share a love for adventure. We have an urge to leave our everyday lives and dive headfirst into the black abyss that can lead to high adventure. In doing so, some of us work as journalists, mercenaries, explorers, writers, photographers and stringers in a thinly veiled attempt to add a sense of purpose and industry to our adventures. But even the clever masks of our professions do not hide our real purpose. We travel to places others fear to tread. We choose to, and we each go because in a way we have to.

When I first wrote *DP* I tried to find a writer who could capture what it is like to travel in these places (and to provide extensive nuts and bolts information to keep travelers safe) but could not find a single person who would take on the task. Undaunted, my desire led me to compile what became *Fielding's The World's Most Dangerous Places* (affectionately called "DP" by its readers), the world's only guide to the world's least salubrious areas. When the book was near completion I realized that all the facts and background in the world could not truly communicate the humor, pathos, hope, despair and enlightenment these journeys convey. So I went back to work to create and gather simple stories of what it is actually like from the authors' perspective. I asked my friends to write honest narratives detailing how we got in, what we did and what we saw. I think the results are unusual and dramatic in their candor and simplicity.

The book has been a success, consistently outselling most, if not all, of Fielding's more levelheaded guides to saner regions and pursuits. Booksellers who once asked "Why would anyone buy a book on places no one wants to go?" are now making mini-Everests of DP and happily promoting the book as "the next big thing." The press reacted favorably and lauded our frank, dark and sometimes brutal description of the world's worst places for travelers.

Aside from the hundreds of positive reviews that define DP as "one of the oddest and fascinating travel books to appear in a long time" *(New York Times),* the inclusion of narratives created a problem: What do we do with our stories when a country is dropped or a newer more relevant story replaces it?

Thus, *Fielding's Hot Spots* was born. Sort of a Valhalla of past volumes or an Elysian Fields for old tales twice told.

Now wait one minute you say, how can you pass off these adventure stories as a collection of travel tales? You might say it's comparable to renaming and republishing great adventure tales along the lines of: *What I Did on My Summer Vacation by Marco Polo.* Despite the current fad for publishers to focus on tales of misery and ineptitude, we simply tell our tales and you decide whether you want to be angry, relieved, giddy, nervous or sick. We don't have a spin or even an underlying message other than we want you to *see the world with your own eyes,* only then can you truly learn.

Travel is usually defined as the movement from one place to another. I tend to think that travel is an inward and an outward journey where geography matters little. These stories are proof of this perception. They are also honest-to-God travel stories. In every single case the author chose to get on a plane, a camel or a canoe and head into harm's way. The fact that some of my friends try to make ends meet by selling accounts of their journeys or their photographs is secondary. In many cases even an amateur accountant could tell you that adventure is definitely not a paying job.

So understand that each story is a travel tale. As you vicariously journey with us, you will get to be amused, depressed, hijacked, liberated, shot at, blown up, shocked, saddened and enlightened without any of the suffering that we have endured.

—RYP

bia _____

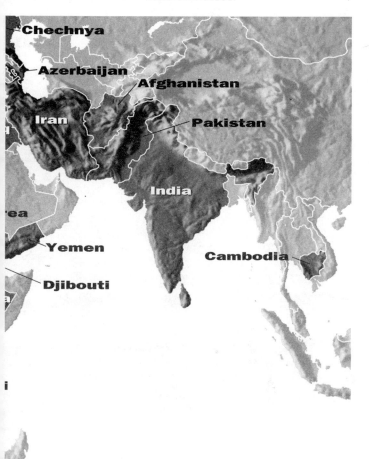

Chechnya

Azerbaijan

Afghanistan

Iran

Pakistan

India

ea

Yemen

Cambodia

Djibouti

i

AFGHANISTAN
In the Lion's Lair

Back in 1983 Coskun, then a young Turkish war photographer wanted to earn his spurs. Unlike the other journos who hung around Hekmatyar's headquarters near Peshawar, Coskun headed into the steep frozen valleys of the Panshir where a young man (now the Minister of Defence for the Afghan Alliance) named Shah Ahmad Massoud was leading a band of fighters far from the CIA and Pakistani Secret Service in Peshawar. Massoud has been fighting for the last 18 years of his life and is still fighting the taliban from his base in the Panshir valley.

An expedition into war-torn Afghanistan has developed in Paris. Three French doctors from Médecins sans Frontières decide to go to the Panshir Valley headquarters of the Afghan resistance. In addition to myself, two other journalists will join us: Philippe Flandrin, a Frenchman, and the Iranian-born photographer Reza Deghati. Deghati wants to go to east Kabul to meet the monarchists of leader Mahaze Melli. Flandrin will continue to Baktia outside Kabul to locate the Hezbe-Islami and their leaders, Yunus Khales and Abdul Haq.

We fly to Peshawar to meet the *mujahedin* organization. The Hezbe-Islami propose to bring us into Panshir, but we prefer to trust the people from Jemiaate-Islami, because this time they control the Panshir region. The leader of this organization is Muchai Barzali. The trek will cover about 450 kilometers and is expected to last one month.

The three doctors will bring in food and medicine, and the guerrillas will provide protection. We wait until March for the snow to start melting. We will climb the 4500-meter-high mountain of Hindi Kuch. On the other side, we are expecting jeeps to be waiting to provide us with transit to Peshawar. But after the long, grueling trek, we will find no jeeps.

The trip begins on March 10, 1983. We dress like Afghans because we are crossing tribal country. I bring along three cameras. Flat-footed and out of shape, I am always behind. Our convoy moves at night to avoid the Russian helicopters. Despite our stealth and our altitude, the group is often attacked by Soviet gunships. I have brought along some dry fruit to supplement the meager rice rations. As our food supply dwindles, I discover there is nothing in the countryside with which to replenish our supplies. Once in a while, we come across a small tea shop in the villages.

In my fatigue and hunger, I make the mistake of taking a leak while standing up. An Afghan spots me and the alarm goes out. Muslims always squat to urinate. The group decides that I'm a Russian spy and that I am to be shot. Our body-guards come to my rescue and argue that Turkish Muslims always stand to piss, and that I am a true Muslim. The argument rages on; our explanation finally prevails. It is a close call. One of our convoy is not so lucky, and the cause for his execution is even more ridiculous. A young man is shot to death in the backyard of a village house because the hairs on his arms are not pointing in the correct direction. If he had been cleaning himself five times a day in preparation for prayer, the hairs on his arms would have been pointing toward his hands. The sentence is passed by the leader of our column and he is shot out of sight of the others.

It is frigid in the mountains. Sometimes we have to cross ice-cold rivers fully clothed. I am amazed that I do not freeze to death. I am starving. I dream of greasy hamburgers and crisp french fries.

On the last leg of the journey to the Panshir Valley, we ride in a truck. The truck hits a land mine and rolls over, launching a piece of a metallic ladder into my jaw and knocking out three of my teeth. I lose a lot of blood and am saved only by the doctors.

We finally reach the Panshir Valley and set up a makeshift hospital. Wounded rebels are carried in, some from two to three days away. There is no anesthetic; bullet wounds are washed out with tea. During Ramadan, a Muslim fast lasting 40 days, the Afghans would not give blood, so I and the doctors give blood, depending on the blood type necessary.

The man named Massoud, "The Lion of Panshir," is the reason for our trip. The rebel leader has asked for medical help and the doctors come at great personal risk. Massoud and I became friends. Massoud was educated in the Lycée Istiqlal (a French high school) in Kabul. Now a resistance leader, he was considered to be very clever and was always on the move. He needed medical help because his men were dying slow, agonizing deaths from gunshot and shrapnel wounds. The doctor Gilles will accompany us. We take the injured back to Pakistan in a convoy. Since I am the least injured member of the group, I will be the leader. As a token of the rebels' appreciation, I am given a horse. I use it to help transport the wounded. When we arrive back in Pakistan, we are detained because we carry no identification papers. Finally, we are permitted entry.

I traveled back to Afghanistan two more times to cover the *mujahedin*. Gilles returned to Paris, and shortly afterwards committed suicide.

—**Coskun Aral**

Sex, Drugs & Rock'n'Roll

The taliban are led by a group of mullahs from Kandahar. Their form of strict sharia or Islamic law is designed to remove the Western influence and to combat the evil deeds of warlords. But Afghanistan will never be one homogenized country under the taliban, or anyone, as photographer Peter J. Willems found out in December of 1996.

I was unloading my luggage from a Flying Coach after pulling into Kabul when I heard a call to prayer coming from a mosque across the street. I flagged down a taxi and was still loading my luggage when three Toyota 4x4s came screaming around the corner, slamming on the brakes in front of me. Half a dozen *taliban* soldiers jumped out of each truck and ran toward the mosque. They started beating, kicking and dragging men who were missing prayer into the mosque. I pulled out my camera and started shooting what was going on. Suddenly, four of the soldiers saw what I was doing, turned, and ran toward me with sticks and AK-47s held in the air. I bolted to the taxi, dove into the back seat, and heard sticks pounding the rear of the car as we pulled away.

The *taliban* militia made a promise to bring law and order to Afghanistan by establishing an Islamic state running on strict Islamic law. It appears to me that their promise has been carried out. The crime rate in Kabul has dropped to almost nil. But not only are the laws coming out of the *taliban* mullahs' interpretation of Islamic law, but the rules for enforcing the laws are decided by the *taliban* soldiers themselves. They have their own set of rules and they change sporadically, usually on a whim.

I was walking through the Farshga bazaar when I saw a boy at the top of a traffic tower with a bruised and swollen face that was painted black. While the *taliban* soldiers surrounding him were laughing hysterically, he was beating an empty gas can with a stick and crying: "The one who does something like me will be punished worse than what is happening to me." Another witness told me later the real meaning: "They only beat *me*; if they catch *you* they will cut off your hand." He was taken to a "police station" where the soldiers could punish and keep him in jail as long as they wanted to. He was caught stealing a jar of purified butter.

I started moving away from the tower when I heard a big explosion in the center of the bazaar. I ran to where the terrorist bomb went off, believed to be planted by *mujahedin*, and found dead bodies and many people injured among bits and pieces of carts, boxes, meat, and sheepskins scattered across the open market. Within a flash, *taliban* soldiers came running in, swinging clubs and firing their AK-47s in the air to chase people away from the scene. They were beating people, trying to help the wounded and desperate vendors who were bleeding from where they caught shrapnel, but trying to collect their goods in a hurry to evacuate. Those who were in the bazaar were attacked by a terrorist bomb set by the *mujahedin*; they were then attacked by the *taliban* soldiers who had promised to bring safety and protect the innocent.

Another afternoon when I was getting a briefing at the UN office on their mine clearing operations, Dostum's planes came in and dropped several bombs two blocks away from the office. I scrambled to my feet after being blown to the ground and ran to the bomb site. I started taking pictures of people being dragged from what used to be houses when an AK-47 struck me across my back with full force. I stumbled forward and another *taliban* soldier grabbed my camera, threw it on the ground and kicked it. I saw soldiers all around hitting, pushing, and kicking me like I was a hacky-sack.

Luckily, one threw me in the direction of where my camera was sitting. I scooped it up, saw an opening, and ran from the turban thugs. What a fool I was thinking that the *taliban* soldiers would assume that a journalist taking pictures of innocent victims would help prove their enemy is evil to the bone—which is what they believe about Dostum. Instead, it was attack the journalist for no particular reason.

On my way to the front-line north of Kabul, I was stopped four times at checkpoints. After I was ordered back to the city each time, I would get out of the car and talk to the soldiers about their recent success and what would be the results if they took the whole country. That earned me a cup of tea and freedom to move on to the front. Near the front I stopped to chat with soldiers sitting on a Russian T-52 tank. We got along well, and they invited me to get into the tank and take a look inside. As I was peering down the barrel through one of the "windows," I heard someone yelling as he was climbing up the side of the turret. I poked my head out of the hole and saw an AK-47 four inches from my nose. I crawled down the side of the tank cautiously and passively and listened to my translator standing near the tank interpret what the soldier was screaming while his gun was still trying to impale me. "If you come back here again, I will kill you!" As we drove away I was a bit thankful because an AFP veteran, Terrence White, told me what happened to him when a *taliban* soldier didn't like what he was covering. The soldier said in all seriousness: "If you come here again, I will fuck you, *then* I will kill you!"

If I was betting on what the *taliban* soldiers would do next, I would be broke in a day. They have little compunction to enforce law and order. But the topsy-turvy make-up of Afghanistan gets even better when you're in *mujahedin* territory, and the stakes get higher.

I was in the trenches surrounded by *mujahedin* soldiers at Dar Alaman front-line in August, 1996 just before the *taliban* rolled into the capital. We were drinking tea, but shells came whistling in sporadically that sent me to the dirt. I soon noticed that the soldiers kept moving in to get closer and closer to where I was sitting. They were pointing at my camera and my hair whispering and smiling at each other. I quickly realized that I had to do something fast because I had suddenly become a target of the *mujahedin*, not the *taliban* artillery. I jumped up quickly to put them offguard. I raised my camera, made movements to get them to pose for a portrait, and climbed out of the trench to position myself as far away as possible to take the picture. Right after I took it, I waved and smiled to say "thank you," turned and ran to the last checkpoint.

My interpreter looked excited as he ran up to greet me. "You're back! You're back!" he yelled.

"You're right, I didn't get hit," I said, assuming that's what he meant.

"Sir, I didn't expect you to get injured by the *taliban* shelling. I didn't go with you because the *mujahedin* have no laws. They could have taken your camera, your money, and used you to please them. Then they would have used you for target practice. Nobody would have cared."

After we left the front and I was eating lunch at the Kamdeesh restaurant in Shar-i-Nau, one of the few areas in Kabul that was not leveled during the civil war, an aged Afghan sitting next to me told me an ugly story. "One night *mujahedin* soldiers came to my neighbor's house in a jeep. My neighbor has a beautiful fifteen-year-old daughter," he said tears rolling down his face. "The soldiers burst into the house, took my neighbor's daughter and turned her over to the commanders at their command post. They kept her and used her for one week. Finally, the commanders let her go and the soldiers left her on the doorstep. She and her family were shamed for life."

In December, after I moved into the *mujahedin* areas in the north, I had an interest in the Baglan province. An Ismailia warlord, fighting with the *mujahedin*, is the leader of the region and is famous for having bizarre quirks while keeping his forces intact and keeping his factories, power stations, and mines working, which is a rarity in Afghanistan. During the four hour drive from Dostum's stronghold to Puli Xamri, the Baglan stronghold, we were stopped a dozen times. The *mujahedin* demanded a payment for us to continue. My interpreter, Idrees, who learned the ropes by traveling with journalists in the past, told the soldiers that I was a foreign diplomat. After looking me up and down, they waved us on.

But at the last "checkpoint," the *mujahedin* dragged us out of the car, held us at gun point, and ordered a strip search. I couldn't even find the first button on my shirt to undo, while Idrees, acting very relaxed, sighed and started talking while unzipping his pants. "General Said Jaffer will be really angry when we don't show up for our appointment with him in Puli Xamri. As you know, he will throw a fit and send out a search party." I was standing there only in my pants near the Hindu Kush in the dead of winter freezing to death while the soldiers gathered in a huddle to decide what to do. They came back and growled at us to collect our clothes and get out of their sight.

Said Jaffer Nadiri, the Commander and Governor of the Baglan province, was educated in England and the United States. His father was in prison while the Afghani government backed by the Soviet Union was in control. Less than ten minutes after the interview started in his living room, the 32-year-old leader held up his hand to stop me asking another question and demanded in fluid English, "What do you drink? Vodka? Whisky?" He caught me offguard. "Well? Tonight we should have a drinking-fest in my guest house."

He led me from his living room to a guest house the size of a high school gym. There was a swimming pool, heated in the winter, with pool and ping-pong tables, a sauna, and a bar we were headed for. As we walked into the bar, I was jettisoned out of Central Asia. There were Bon Jovi, AC/DC, and bikini posters on the walls, a full bar on one end and a Sony stereo system on the other. "Sex, Drugs, and Rock & Roll!" he barked and laughed as he poured us our first drink. He ordered one of his servants to put on Pink Floyd and started reminiscing. "I watched *The Wall* ten times when I got a copy. Excellent movie! But when I asked one of my men to copy the video for a friend of mine, he accidentally erased it. Ha! Ha! I had him strip, lay down on the floor face down, and beat him with a horse whip until I was satisfied."

After our third drink, three commanders came in for a nightcap, After they had taken a few shots of vodka, the tall, bulky commander next to me jumped up, picked me up and screamed in broken English, "You spy! You spy!" The other two ran over and pinned me against Bon Jovi a foot off the ground while the first one frisked me (looking for a tape recorder). Said Jaffer came to my rescue and ordered the commanders to leave after one more shot. As they were leaving, a servant came in with a large chunk of hash that looked like a cow paddy on a silver tray. Said Jaffer pinched off a small piece and held it out for me saying, "Anyway, it's hash time! Sex, Drugs, and Rock & Roll!"

—**Peter J. Willems**

ALBANIA

The War Against the Sky

The need for instant global news coverage has created a new swarm of journalists who descend on chaotic places that promise high rating, breaking news stories. Getting into Albania was easy, getting around was not. DP's Roddy Scott was there in March of '97 to see the fun firsthand. Coskun was there earlier and provided much of the tape used by CNN. Like I said, it was crowded. The aftermath is that the government estimated that between a quarter of a millon and a million weapons were stolen.

At least the taxi mafia are having a good time of it. The hordes of foreign journalists flooding into Southern Albania, as the country descends into chaos and anarchy, are being charged as much as $300 a day for the privilege of being chauffeured around, the equivalent of several months wages for the average Albanian. Equally swift to rise to the challenge are the speedboat mafia. For those journalists wanting to slip into the south of the country via the Greek island of Corfu, the 30 minute ride is a mere $500.

And it is by speedboat that I make my entry to the southern port of Sarande a week or so after furious mobs had stormed military armories for weapons and taken control of the city. The collapse of a series of pyramid investment schemes with government connections and the loss of most people's life savings left civilians in the south in a state of incoherent anger. With one other foreign hack, I climb into the small speedboat that has arrived in the harbor of Kassiopi, in the northeast of Corfu, under the watchful eyes of Greek commandos there to ensure that the Albanians bring none of their usual trading wares across with them on their way to pick up journalists, illegal refugees, guns, drugs etc., the normal everyday exports from Albania.

For half an hour or so we bump our way across the sea, hitting troughs that almost throw me out of the boat, until we reach the calm of the coastline which we hug until drawing into Sarande. Given the TV reports that have been coming out of Sarande the town is quiet—with only the occasional burst of gunfire coming from a distant quarter. After a quick coffee we decide to travel up to Gjrokaster, a 45 minute drive and the most recent town to fall into the hands of the so-called 'rebels'—in reality little more than mobs of enraged civilians. Confronted with this anger, the police and army would generally just pack their bags and head for home.

Leaving the town, we pass the wreckage of a car in which only days earlier a hapless policeman was burned alive. Two old Soviet T-55 tanks form part of the roadblock which signals the end of the town and leaves us free to continue on our journey. Apart from the sporadic roadblocks that have been set up by a variety of local village militias, the dominant feature of the Albanian countryside are the thousands of concrete bunkers and machine gun positions that were erected by the Stalinist dictator Enver Hoxha, for the day that Albania would be invaded.

Gjirokaster, when we arrive, is alive with the sound of gunfire. The din is deafening as pistols, AK-47s and 12mm machine guns release bullets into the air in what has been termed 'Albania's war against the sky'. I decide that there is little to do but wander around and take a few pictures. The town itself is pleasant and old with its typically Balkan cobbled streets. I discover the unpleasant side to the town almost immediately. Walking down one of the gently inclining streets I notice a man approaching.

From 30 yards away it is more than obvious that he is almost—but unfortunately not quite—paralytically drunk. He is also in charge of an AK-47, which he is firing into the air. On seeing me he staggers in my general direction, and to my dismay, decides to stop firing in the air and point his gun straight at me. I give him the kind of smile that any dentist would recognize straight off, while my legs go weak at the knees. It's a pity, I can't help thinking as I watch him lurch towards me with glazed eyes and his finger on the trigger, that there aren't any manuals about dealing with drunks in charge of an AK-47—I could use one. On reaching me he drunkenly reaches up to try and take my watch from my left hand, and it is only then that I realize that I have raised both my hands above my head, although I can't remember doing so. Since he is much smaller than me I quickly lower my arm to let him have easy access to my watch and hope he doesn't get the bright idea to take my cameras as well. My wallet is in my back pocket, and I wonder if I can persuade him to accept Visa or MasterCard in lieu of cash, if only because credit cards are useless in southern Albania and without cash, I am sunk. I suspect he might prefer cash.

Somewhat to my relief, however, two other locals arrive on the scene and gently take the drunk—he still hasn't managed to get my watch off—and lead him away from me. I watch nervously, silently cheering every step they take him; but drunkenness has a determination all of its own. The weapon taken from him, he makes his way back to where I am standing; and instead of wanting my watch decides to hug me while muttering in Albanian. He eventually leaves and stumbles back to his friends while I smile blandly and hope that, with a bit of luck, he might manage to blow his own head off by the end of the day.

Twenty minutes later I reach the town center. It is full of armed and often masked civilians milling around enjoying the freedom that the lack of any state authority brings— gleefully emptying weapons into the air as spent casings rain onto the street. I wonder what the chances are of my eardrums surviving in tact—probably quite slim. Of slightly greater concern, however, is exactly where the spent bullets will end up. None of the gun-toting mob seem to be able to grasp one of the most elementary laws of physics: what goes up must come down. The results are often tragic. More people die from falling bullets than anything else.

I pick up a taxi and it's a Mercedes, probably one of a batch that has been stolen from Greece and given a quick change in color and number plates. The driver offers me a bottle of whisky and I gratefully sit back, take a swig and begin to feel slightly more relaxed as we cruise around town before beginning the search for a hotel.

The hotel is a vast Stalinist concrete monster and for US$10 I procure one of its many freezing rooms. I meet a group of Greek journalists from Skai TV and, after an unsuccessful search for restaurants and food, share a tinned meal with them washed down with some imported vodka. We swap information and chat about the situation generally agreeing that it is one of the crazier places dominating current affairs. The so-called rebels have no coordination or leadership; there are simply vast numbers of angry people with weapons—all of whom want the Albanian President, Salih Berisha, to resign for his association with the disastrous pyramid schemes. I ask if I can share transport costs with them for a while and they readily agree.

We head out of town early in the morning at around 6 a.m.; our destination is Erseke, a small town a couple of hours' drive through the southern mountains which is still under government control. We stop, however, a few miles outside of town. A few cars are coming through the mountain passes and we stop them to inquire about the situation in town. Nothing is happening, we are told. The town is still under the control of the police. But in one of the cars a young man tells us he is the local civilian leader—and informs us that he is going to a small town we had passed through to garner help from outside to lead a rebellion in Erseke. If we go into the town and wait for a couple of hours, he says, he will be back with outside help to eject the police. We cruise the few miles until we reach the edge of town. Four distinctly unhappy looking policemen man a roadblock. I don't have an official visa to be in the country, but the policemen don't ask and wave us through. People mill around in the streets as we drive by, a few make V-signs. We eventually go to a cafe, drink some arak and wait. Looking out the cafe window, I notice that the streets are quieter, there are fewer people, and a solitary policeman drives a police van up and down the streets before disappearing from view. It is as if the whole town is collectively holding it's breath and, like us, waiting.

Cruising back to the original police block at the entrance to town we find it abandoned. The police, rather sensibly, have obviously decided that going off duty might just enable them to collect their pensions—if the government has any money. Not much more than fifteen minutes later, as we sit in the car smoking and waiting, the sound of automatic fire resonates throughout the town. From the far end of town an army truck comes tearing down the main street: there are no soldiers, however, only armed civilians who have come to "liberate" the town.

Within minutes the streets are jam-packed as people crowd around the few guns available to take turns at firing—as usual—in the air. But unlike in the movies, ammunition has an irritating habit of running out and it is not long before someone has the bright idea of looting the local armory that the police have abandoned. En masse the mob heads for the armory and soon carry out everything from boots to boxes of ammunition. To increase the general merriment, someone decides that the whole place would definitely be brightened up somewhat with a touch of pyrotechnics, and smoke is soon billowing from the buildings. It's a complete free-for-all as everyone takes whatever they can carry and smashes anything that is too awkward to pick up. An army jeep is overturned by a jeering mob, after which a man empties his AK-47 into it, causing sparks to fly but, alas, no explosion. With the jeep safely out of commission, the mob turns to a police van. It is quickly overturned and within minutes blazing away. To add to the general ambience, anyone with a gun empties clips of ammunition into the air to celebrate the town's newfound "freedom."

With nothing else left to burn or loot, the rebels have a brief discussion about what to do next and, infused with confidence, decide it would be a capital idea to liberate the next village from the clutches of the government. Piling onto the back of the military truck, they roar off down the road, with us in hot pursuit. But after no more than two minutes of driving, the truck stops on a bend. About 300 meters further down the road I can see an ambulance stuck in a small ditch. "Police," comes the explanation. It seems we have caught up with some of the policemen who left the town earlier, but who must have been cursing their luck at being caught by civilians intent upon spreading the anti-authority revolt. To my amazement, no one seems to know what to do: the 30 or so armed men in the truck (who not so long ago had been firing bullets into the air and shouting anti-government slogans) seem to go into a collective paralysis.

There cannot be more than four or five policemen in the ambulance—which is revving desperately in an attempt to get out of the ditch—yet nobody seems to want to go any farther. Only two or three jump down and sensibly make for the high ground, using the cover of the trees and bushes to approach the van. But even they do not venture too far. The revolutionary fervor has dissipated somewhat.

For the policemen, though, the level of revolutionary fervor may be somewhat academic. Faced with 30 armed, albeit not particularly determined, men with AK-47s they do what any sensible (and more than likely disenchanted) and unwilling wearer of an uniform would do under the circumstances: they surrender. At the sight of a policeman standing beside the ambulance with his arms raised high, a great cheer rises from the mob as they race forward.

On reaching the ambulance, they find only one policeman. He is quickly surrounded by the angry mob. While some try to punch and kick him, others try to protect him, and it is not long before he is bundled into the back of the ambulance. This brief brush with authority seems to have something of a sobering affect on the mob, and the plans for the liberation of the next village are abandoned.

The following day, however, we return. The next village, we are told, revolted without assistance the previous day. Driving on for 40 minutes or so we eventually arrive, but the villagers are in the process of looting the extensive military armory that has been so irresponsilbly abandoned by the police and soldiers. The road to the armory is so bad that we are forced to walk. Already there are numerous civilians returning from the armory, trooping along the wooded road, carrying a vast and varied number of weapons. Over the brow of a hill, I can see plumes of smoke rising.

Approaching the camp, we meet more civilians leaving, all carrying what they can. Up ahead a building is blazing with flames billowing out of a top story window. The scene, once we are inside the perimeter of the camp, is chaotic. There are weapons of almost every conceivable type lying littered around: RPG-7's with warheads, boxes of hand-grenades, rifles, gasmasks, uniforms, even anti-personnel mines.

I watch as young children, no more than ten or eleven, try to load weapons, unaware of how to fit magazines into the rifles, ignorant of where the safety catch can be found. Other children roam around the ammunition dump picking up what they can, supremely ignorant of the weapons they are carrying, and unsupervised by adults. As usual those who don't understand their weapons are firing them continuously into the air without, at least, having to worry about ammunition shortages.

Another group is busy tearing the covers from 20 or so four-barrelled anti-aircraft guns. Outside the camp perimeters heavy machine guns are being belt fed and trained on a concrete bunker placed on an opposite hilltop. Other locals are still in the process of familiarizing themselves with the obviously unfamiliar weapons. "We are here because we are sick of being lied to," a man says. "We want real change in Albania, real democracy." Behind him flames engulf the barracks.

—**Roddy Scott**

AZERBAIJAN

Burning Down the House

Nagorno Karabakh was a dirty little war. The Armenians made a land grab and began one of the largest ethnic cleansing operations this century. Strangely the Armenians complain that they are the victims of the same treatment at the hands of Turks 70 years earlier. The underpaid Russian army added a comic side note as they saw easy money from both sides. It seems that Armenia has been successful in its land grab and removing most if not all Muslims from the stolen territory.

The war had just begun in Azerbaijan. We catch an early morning flight into Baku on a beat-up old *TU-154*. I am with three other journalists and figure we can get past the Russian border guards with a minor bribe. The Aeroflot logo had been crudely painted over, and the plane now is called Azerbaijan Airways. On board are a motley crew: doctors and nurses on their way to the war zone, businessmen looking to set up import-export contracts and men on their way to the cheap sex vacations for which Baku is famous for.

When we arrive, $50 each is all it takes to get our passports stamped. We find a driver outside the airport who will make the 200km trip to Gendje southeast of Baku. This will take us close to the war zone on the Karabakh border. Along the way, we pass hundreds of Russian-made trucks carrying soldiers and tanks. Whatever the Russians had left behind after

Azerbaijan declared its independence is now the official property of the Azeris. Despite Gendje's proximity to the war, the only complaint the people seem to have is how the prices had been driven up by the visiting soldiers and short supplies. That night we find another driver who will take us into the war area. We arrive in Agdam by midnight. The road is rough but, the ever increasing checkpoints make the journey tedious at best. The fact that we are Turkish means that we are among friends. Of all the Central Asian Turkic languages, the Azeri's is the closest to that of the Turks. Our arrival in Agdam looks like a Hollywood director's version of a war zone. It seems that every building is in flames or exploding.We are welcomed by a heavy barrage of Katusha rockets. Our driver is a volunteer member of "the Popular Front" and takes us to their local headquarters, a large house in the center of the besieged town. The place is teeming with soldiers and volunteers. They are talking anxiously on Russian-made walkie-talkies, counting, unpacking and distributing weapons for the front, and what makes it all unusual is that they are all speaking Russian. Even the older Azeris are using Russian, though they speak Azeri amongst themselves.

We are given beds on the upper floor of the headquarters. The fact that we are surrounded on all sides by burning buildings doesn't help us get to sleep. When we find out that the headquarters also doubles as the ammunition depot, sleep is soon forgotten. We listen to each explosion to hear if we will be next. We look at what is in the crates that hold up our mattresses and find that they are packed with grenades and rockets. Though we are worried, we fall asleep and wake a few hours later when a large explosion blows up a sawmill outside our window. We get up and walk the 200 meters to the sawmill to take photos. There is not much to photograph and the intense heat keeps us back. When we go back to our room to try to catch up on our sleep we find a clubfooted soldier in there setting up a radio and fiddling with the dial.

Wanting to get to the front to take some photographs, we arrange for two soldiers to take us there in a Russian jeep about 4.5 kms away. We join a tedious parade of trucks carrying ammunition, rations, men and other journalists. We arrive during an artillery barrage. The Azeris are positioned just below the summit of a hill that faces the Armenian position on another hilltop. The equipment they are using to fight this war is cast off by the Russians, and it is obvious why they don't take it with them. The volunteers manning the artillery are surprisingly young, about 15 or 16; most of them have little idea of how to properly utilize the decrepit tanks and artillery. I watch the teenagers playing around with the colored rings of the mortar shells. Each ring sends the mortar 100-meters toward the target, but if the kids undo the knots that hold the explosive rings around the narrow tails of the mortar shells, they will go off like Chinese Crackers.

I notice what makes the tanks and artillery look so ridiculous. The Azeris had bent the barrels of the tanks into "S" shapes by improperly loading their tanks. The shortage of skilled soldiers and operational equipment had created a market for entrepreneurs. The Russians had kept their presence in Azerbaijan unofficial, but there is an ominous force that looks markedly different. These are the tanks manned by soldiers for hire. These are Russian soldiers who rent out their tanks for $100 a day; the crew cost $50 extra. The white Russian ID number is covered in mud. The comical part is that the same tank will show up on the opposite side a day or two later and shell their former employers.

We stay in our deadly accommodations, becoming indifferent to the explosions around us, even with the knowledge that we will be instantly atomized if a shell lands on our building. The deaf and clubfooted radio operator never returns, and his radio sits in the corner of our room untouched.

The next day we go to the cemetery to see the fighting that is raging where the Azeri cemetery butts up to the Armenian cemetery. We rent a minibus, and, when we arrive, the fighting is fierce and hand-to-hand. Both sides use the tombstones as cover as they shoot at each other and charge each other's position. We try to capture the fighting, while keeping our heads down behind a cemetery wall.

We are surprised by the arrival of the local Armenian commander. Middle-aged with snow white hair, Allahverdi (which translated means "God given") whips out a megaphone and begins shouting orders to his men in Russian. The fighting stops and one of the soldiers with him explains that he is negotiating for the release of 15 prisoners captured the day before. The Azeris are 250 meters away on the other side of the cemetery. The deal is a tanker full of gas in exchange for the prisoners. The answer comes back: "No. We want a tanker full of gas and 12 hours of electricity." A deal is cut and the prisoners are released the next day. We see the prisoners when they arrive at the headquarters building where we are staying. Most are old; they had their gold teeth yanked out and their toes had been broken when they were tortured. The women had been raped, while the young teenagers seem to be in shock and will not talk. The people who had done this had been their neighbors only 15 days before. Now they are sworn enemies.

We have seen enough. This is a dirty, stupid war. We hitchhike our way back to Gendje. We find a plane flying to Baku and ask the fare. It is the cheapest flight I have ever taken— $1. The plane is another ex-Aeroflot junk heap. We count over 80 passengers, not including goats, chickens and luggage. Just before takeoff, the pilot, mistaking us for Russians, turns to us and says, "For $20, I will fly us all to Moscow. Do you want to go now?" We passed.

—**Coskun Aral**

BOSNIA
Tea Before Mortars

Bosnia's proximity to Europe shocked the world and then bred a level of indifference as the horrors faded from TV screens and newsmagazines. Within this war zone people lived and survived completely abandoned by the outside world. Today the world acts as cop, and the region sits simmering but far from peaceful.

It is odd for me to have to cover a war in Europe. I leave Paris with my ears full of the noise made by the French about the need to preserve Dubrovnik's architectural marvels. Nobody seems to care for the Serbs and the Croats, but talk about the ancient city of Dubrovnik and everybody yells about how it belongs to mankind's culture and should be preserved at all costs.

I spend only a week in Yugoslavia, enough to see a horrible war. In Belgrade everything seems normal. Then things start to change as we approach the frontier with Hungary in Zagreb and even more in Ossiek.

I travel to the war with a friend, American journalist Chris Morris. He takes me in his car to Vukovar. We spend three days there amidst the battles. We meet a Canadian mercenary known only as John, the commander of the place. That's one of the features of this war: There are lots of mercenaries. John is a Croatian by origin and commands the Croats.

Our biggest fear is the number of snipers here. John brings us to a mortar position. It is teatime first; after tea the bombing of the Serbs' position resumes, followed by an offensive with mortars made in Germany. The night comes. The situation becomes hellish. It is like the end of the world. We spend three nights in cellars with a Croatian family. The son keeps entertaining his girlfriend who lives nearby, through a walkie-talkie. The girl asks him to give her some cassettes to play on her walkman. The boy turns toward me and I agree to lend him two cassettes. He then proceeds to walk out in the middle of the night under the bombs, but does not come back. Everybody starts worrying. Some people go out to look for him, but they do not come back either.

The next morning we are awakened by shouting and loud sobs. We leave the cellar and there they are—dead bodies. I recognize the boy to whom I had loaned the tapes, and not far from him lies the headless body of his girlfriend. Her head had rolled away after it had been chopped off, either by shrapnel or by some other means.

We leave Vukovar to go to Ossiek. We see prisoners. Lots of them are to be executed.

We receive the news a few hours after our departure that Vukovar has just fallen. There is no story here, just killing and atrocities.The news magazines aren't interested in running more dull grey shots of people being killed.

—**Coskun Aral**

Another War In Europe

The rush of correspondents to Bosnia created the basis for what could be a hilarous but chilling Broadway comedy. It was unique for two other things. Snipers were paid $250 for every journalist they killed, and it was the largest gathering of mercenaries and volunteers in Europe since the Spanish Civil War. All these peculiarities would have deadly consequences.

"*If there is ever another war in Europe, it will come out of some damn silly thing in the Balkans.*"

Prince Bismarck
1815–1898

September 1992

New to the war, we watched silently as the backhoe dug into the garbage dump. When the story began to appear, one journalist backed away in horror, then turned to retch. Eventually, almost 90 rotting corpses lay next to the pit. All Muslims or Croats and many in their eighties, their throats had been cut by Serbs. Had we done our homework properly, of course, we would have known it was a Balkan story already centuries old. Any of those shrunken faces could have been captioned with the same line from Joyce: "History is a night-mare from which I am trying to awake."

####

At a Serb checkpoint, I'm ordered out of the car by five drunken soldiers. One begins slapping me playfully while an-other burns holes in my jacket with his cigarette, all breaking into sly, superior smiles at my sudden efforts to brush out the embers. At their brigade headquarters a white Land Rover bearing the BBC logo and ëTV' in tall, black letters is proud-ly displayed as a war trophy. Resting on blocks, both doors mark the flight of the missile that tore the cameraman-driver to pieces. Serbs 1, media 0 on this front, though just one of the 78 journalists who would eventually die in the Balkans. Today the front lines are blanketed under freezing fog, the white opaqueness pierced with speculative bursts of automat-ic weapons fire. In a farmhouse-cellar-turned-bunker the in-evitable bottle of slivovitz appears and a tank commander asks if I will take a letter to a Croatian friend wounded on the other side. I agree and he writes quickly, translating as he goes along.

To MatÈ Jozaku:

MatÈ, I'm sending you this letter with wishes for a speedy recovery. When I heard you had been injured I took the news very hard. Your old friend, Jovan Jokanovic the shopkeeper, is writing this letter. Your driver's license is still with me; I hope I can personally return it eventually. Both your homes are intact, as are your brothers' homes. Please accept greet-ings from all your old friends on Vlasic.

Jovan Jokanovic

Outside, old friends fire into the fog in hope of killing each other.

####

February 3, 1993

From the Muslim village, a Serbian tank has been spotted 3 km to the west and the defenders race to position their state-of-the-art, anti-armor missile supplied by Iran with CIA connivance. I'm checking my cameras in the command bunker when three bearded soldiers enter and order me out. But these are not from the Muslim Bosnian army, they're mujahedin, avowed enemies of Serbs, Croats and the infidel West. In a nearby farmhouse eight expressionless faces regard me silently. A feeling of malevolence hangs in a room strung with Arabic banners.

Will I accept Allah? The Prophet, I answer carefully, said that those of the Book are exempt from forced conversion. An acne-scarred thug in the corner hisses to his fellow fanatics, "I want to kill him." Why? The thug speaks again, fingers fluttering as his eyes lift toward the ceiling. "So you can greet Allah." But the Prophet directed all good Muslims to protect the defenseless. He snaps the safety down. "I'm going to kill you now," he smiles. "Are you afraid to die?" Their Fundamentalism demands my humiliation, that I beg before the bullet in the head. Deeply frightened, I hold my executioner's eyes and whisper, "Inshallah." Frustrated, the leader grabs my cameras. "You are not welcome here. You will leave these and go." My secular Muslim guide, equally frightened, nods imperceptibly and we walk out alive.

Minutes later I hear the launch of a missile, then an explosion as the tank bursts into flames across the valley. There's an orange flash near the burning tank. I turn to my guide to see him diving for cover. I'm at the bottom of the frozen ditch with him when the Serb artillery shell lands short of us. Rising cautiously, we brush the snow off and step out again. There's a second flash. Back into the ditch. An hour later I'm in army headquarters in Turbe, relating what I've just been through. The Muslim commander pours us each a slivovitz. "Extremists," he shrugs helplessly. Outside, the Serbs are shelling the village. There's a lull and I run for the car just as a rocket slams into the road not more than 50 meters away. When I look up people are running, limping, crawling out of the smoke and dust. I think of the next one on its way. Fuck this for a job, I decide, jumping into Li'l Sue and screeching away in the opposite direction. (The next day the *mujahedin* kidnapped two British mercenaries serving as instructors in the Muslim army. They were taken to the same village, tortured and murdered. I'll never know why I lived and they died.)

February 1993

From an editor's ivory tower came the suggestion that a story might be found in Pale, the Bosnian Serb headquarters. When I mentioned it to the BBC, their first question was: "Soft-skinned or hardcar?" My sotto voice "Softskinned" drew sympathetic tsks from those whose hardcars carried a ton of protective steel and Kevlar. You'll have to run the airport and its Serb and Muslim snipers, they explained, then right at the end. Not left towards Sarajevo, because that's Sniper Alley, the most dangerous stretch of road in the world. I cross to the Serb side, where a soldier hitchhiking to Pale knows a way that misses the airport altogether. We turn onto a narrow country road, then a two-lane highway, where a Serb checkpoint sends us north to a mountain track that skirts Sarajevo. Story done, I retrace the route from Pale: rocky track, then the highway, where I look for the checkpoint. But heavy fighting earlier in the day has sent the Serb military policemen into their bunkers, and I miss the crucial turn.

Come round a curve where a 10 ton truck, tires flat, hulks across the road. I brake to a stop, sure that I've gone too far. Turn the tape player down and look around, seeing fresh debris from mortar shells. A careful six-point turn to avoid the mined shoulders and I'm heading back when a Serb leaps from his bunker, firing from the hip. Out of range and heart pounding, I stop at the first farmhouse to check the way. Straight back the way you came. Are you sure? The door closes. Body armor and helmet snugged, I slash through the gears, eyes switching from road to bunker and back again. No fire when I come abreast of the position, but immediately it's behind shots snap past. I duck my head and floor it, screaming around the truck blocking the road.

And things go from bad to very bad: steel barriers and anti-tank mines. Another AK opens up from the other side. Trapped, I slam to a stop and slowly step out, hands raised as stories of journalists executed by the Serbs flash through my mind. Fifty feet away a soldier curtly motions me forward while another stares down the sights of a Kalashnikov. Unable to think of a better opener than to suggest a solidarity against their enemy, I ask with unfeigned terror: "Where are the Muslims?" He jabs a thumb into his chest and growls, "We're the Muslims. I've just busted two front lines. Dokumenti!" He demands for my papers, and I pass them over reluctantly, for nestled opposite my UN press card is—oh joy, oh joy—my Serbian accreditation. I'm soon surrounded by scowling combatants who, when I finally explain that I'm lost, think it's the funniest thing they've heard all day. All save one, whose slivovitz breath curls my nostril hairs as he wails, "But I almost killed you!" Meanwhile, my Suzuki jeep, Li'l Sue, is idling happily in the middle of the road, Nat King Cole crooning 'Unforgettable' on the tape deck. I'm sent out to move her, but "keep low" they motion, pointing across the road and saying, "sniper, sniper." A sprint and dive through the open door and whip into the side road, skirting another line of mines, then into Sarajevo and a four hour interrogation as a possible Serb spy.

Awake in the freezing Holiday Inn to Serb artillery. In the dining room the warries from the world's heavies are gathering for breakfast. Long silences when shells land close enough to rattle coffee cups. Two Spanish journalists say they're driving out in a few minutes. Please, can I follow? "Si, but you must go very fast." I'm right behind you, amigo. Wrapped in flak jackets and helmets, we blast out of the underground carpark in tandem, squealing up the winding drive and racing flat out through the city, cutting across pavements where the road is blocked by rubble, hammer shifts on the corners to the sound of incoming fire. Skid into the sandbagged UN compound and tag on to the end of a French armored patrol to the Serb lines. A crumbling wall bears WELCOME TO HELL in angry brush strokes, and then it's down Sniper Alley, waiting for the sudden hole in the windshield and praying that if it happens, someone will come back for me. Arrive at last Serb checkpoint, hold breath until across, then on to Kiseljak and the BBC, telling yesterday's story between gulps of scalding tea.

You're one lucky bloke. Day you went over a French photographer was hit in the throat and a Reuters chap in the foot as they were crossing the airport in softskins. Yesterday a French soldier was killed and three wounded by an RPG. I wonder suddenly at my luck in missing the airport, of going through an active front under fire from both sides, of facing the mujahedin in Bijelo Bucje. And the times under tank, mortar, rocket or artillery fire and not a scratch. How much luck are we given? Anyone know the situation between here and Travnik? Pretty nasty because of fighting between Muslims and Croats. Dutch aid driver wounded this morning, and a French TV crew took some hits, but hardcar, so no-one hurt. I try to ignore that sixth sense whispering "Don't do it," and head for Travnik.

Pass through successive checkpoints, Muslim, Croat, Muslim again. At each hastily rigged blockade fingers slip inside trigger guards and muzzles swing towards me. Approach each slowly, hoping they can see PRESS on the hood. Through the last one and the empty road winds along a narrow valley where gutted farmhouses still smolder. I pass a freshly burned out VW. Five minutes later an Opel, windows starred by bullets, blocks half the road. Below the open door something darker than the gray asphalt is congealing in the cold air. My knuckles whiten at the sound of a shot. At me? At someone else? What the fuck am I doing here? Outside Kacuni a British light tank blocks the narrow bridge. What's the situation ahead? Some automatic stuff, and there's a sniper just over there. Firing starts beyond the bridge and the hatch slams shut. Go on, or turn back? Open Li'l Sue's door and rap it twice to hear the tinny ring. She's brought me through 10,000 miles in this lunatic asylum. Probably take me 10,000 more. But not today, and I pull back.

March 1993

From the dark hills a tracer streaks over the snow-covered road and burns into the gathering dusk. Below its path more than a thousand Muslims stagger under the weight of suitcases and bags, the last of a lifetime's possessions. A father draws a small sled, his crippled daughter and her crutches balanced atop what they have been allowed to keep. A second tracer splits the air. It's a reminder of the Serbs' promise to mortar the road if their unarmed victims have not completed the three mile journey by nightfall.

Land Rovers move up and down the road collecting those who have begun collapsing in the snow. In the back of Li'l Sue five people clutch suitcases. In front an old man holds his grandson, a son and daughter-in-law sit on the hood as I edge past a British light tank and its 30mm cannon aimed toward the Serb lines. At the edge of Turbe my passengers step back into the snow. "Where will we go?" one old woman sobs. Another tracer flashes above us, scoring its way into the dark. A convoy of British army trucks looms out of the night to begin collecting the hundreds of refugees still struggling towards safety. Li'l Sue and I are no longer needed. I nose through the mass of dazed and bewildered people, surprised by my tears of anger and relief. My last story, I keep thinking, my last story from this madhouse. I'm alive and I'm going home.

—Jim Hooper

Where Any Idiot Has A Gun

Bosnia was full of volunteers, adventurers and contract soldiers. The calibre of fighting was abysmal and the people who showed up to defend the homeland against the Serbs ranged from criminals to psychopaths. Among them were professional soldiers trying to stop the unchecked slaughter of innocent civilians. Most of these men left.

Another day in Tomislavgrad, much like any other. Two troops are standing at the bar in one of the numerous little Kaffee-Bar establishments and arguing loudly. One is bouncing an old U.S. Army "steel pot" helmet on the bar and shaking his head negatively while the other shakes his head positively and crosses his arms. Now a couple of their buddies are getting into it. Just when it looks like there is going to be *real trouble*, the guy with the crossed arms who's been nodding his head "yes, yes," decides to limber up a little by drawing his Tokarev. Uh-oh. Screw real trouble, this was a *situation*. But wait, amongst all the screaming in Croat, the drunks start to slam wads of dinars down on the bar. Translation: the guy with the Tokarev says the .30 caliber Tokarev pistol bullet will not penetrate his U.S. Army steel pot. Okay, I've seen discussions like this before…argue, make some bets, throw the helmet, flak jacket, etc. in the alley and fire it up. Come back inside. Have some more drinks. No problem. Standard scenario, I muse. More bets are made. Then the guy with the Tokarev cocks the pistol, grabs the helmet, *and plomps it on his head*, and…Oh Shit!…*Ka-Blam*! Redecorates the wall with his brains. Instant Jackson Pollock canvas.

If only he'd asked me, I could've told him.

Some of these Croat civilians, turned defenders of the homeland, have a strange attitude toward firearms. The fact that some of them are even carrying weapons scares the hell out of me. The Muslim and Serb yahoos are no different. Ignorant slivvovitz-swilling pigfarmer gets automatic weapon. Yippee!

Ever wonder what became of the banjo boy in *Deliverance*? They gave him an AK and sent him to Bosnia.

####

One of the kids in Tomislavgrad had an uncle or third cousin six generations removed or some damn thing in New York, Chicago or Toronto (take your pick). Anyway, he writes a letter begging for a bulletproof vest. So in the mail comes a Second Chance ballistic vest. Good quality stuff. Probably about $600 worth of Kevlar. He's so proud of his "bulletproof vest" that he wears it around town. Outside of his shirt. Shiny, bright white cover and all. But of course a few of the boys, jealous no doubt, have been making comments to the effect that it might not be as good as he thinks. This starts to gnaw at the sensibilities, limited as they may be, of our combat fashion victim. One day he's at home sitting in the kitchen showing off the vest to grandma. She thinks it's so nice that her boy Damir or Vlad or Stefan (take your pick) has this nice vest. So attractive too! He takes it off and says, "Here, grannie, you try it on." So the sweet little old 90-some pound Croatian *baka* tries on the vest. (Know where this is going, already, huh?) Grandson has a bright idea as grannie pirouettes, so he draws his Tokarev. *Bang! Bang! Bang!* Hits grannie three times—point blank. She lives. A couple of broken ribs... no problem. Grandson then shows the vest around town to all his buddies. Hey, it worked, and what the hell, the bullet holes weren't a problem. They were in the back.

####

Tom Myers and I roomed next door to each other for six months at Fort Benning in 1985. We were students in the same Infantry Officer Basic Course. After three years in the U.S. Army as a lieutenant he got out and joined the French Foreign Legion for a standard five year contract. When he was discharged, he went to Bosnia and eventually ended up in Tomislavgrad, just after I'd left. There he met Dave, a Rhodesian war veteran, who had left after the political sell-out and went to South Africa where he served in the Recces. As Tom somewhat understatedly said, "He was a bit psycho." Probably because he used to play Russian roulette with a .357. You know, go into a bar, get everybody's attention, whip out a revolver, load one round, spin the cylinder, snap the weapon shut, put it to your head and then: Click! A real macho stunt. Mercenary theatre. Always a winner. Tough way to earn a free drink. According to Myers, "He finally *lost* one day, in a hotel in Split sitting there at the bar in front of God and everybody." Fred Verduin, another American "volunteer," occasionally hung out with the Russian roulette player who wanted Fred to try the game. Fred was tempted, he thought there had to be a trick to it. He found out this was not the case as he was sitting next to Dave that day in the bar in Split.

—**Rob Krott**

BURUNDI

Across East Africa by Land Rover

Adventure comes in many forms these days. The Camel Trophy is a multimillion dollar annual event designed to sell cigarettes. The manufacturer will tell you that all those macho men and machines are promoting Camel clothing, Land Rover vehicles and other goodies, but the organizers and the participants know better. Films, posters and ads of the event are shown in regions where cigarette advertising is banned and the enduring "Man in the yellow Land Rover" is as ubiquitous as the Marlboro man. The event is a unique opportunity to meet like-minded adventurers culled from over a million and a half hopefuls and then to push yourself to the limits as you try to navigate across regions that are considered impassable.

I have come to see Africa as well as to conquer it. The white man's idea of Africa has always been to test his mettle against this daunting land. We will be following the path of fellow Royal Geographical Society explorers, Burton and Speke, roughly tracing an old Arab slave trading route in four-wheel-drive expedition vehicles. Starting in the rough and tumble port of Dar es Salaam, we will travel a thousand kilometers to the source of the Nile, a tiny stream in equally minuscule Burundi. There is a rough track in the dry season, but we will attempt it in the height of the rainy season. If we succeed, we will gain nothing but a sense of accomplishment. If we fail, we will simply join the millions of people who understand that Africa, with all its death, pestilence, disease, hunger and poverty, will always be the dark continent.

As we cruise along country roads, singing stupid songs and dodging potholes the size of small lakes, it feels more like a vacation than an expedition. When we are delayed by overturned trucks or washouts, we amuse ourselves by handing out balloons, baseball cards and candy to delighted children.

As the day progresses, the villages give way to farmland and farmland to grasslands. As evening falls, we wait for the rest of the convoy at the turnoff that will take us onto our first remote trail. A heavy rain begins to fall with a foreboding vengeance; the easy part is over. As the scout in the lead car searches for the path in the tall grass, we watch the villagers stare at us from under the shelter of a giant mango tree.

There is some confusion. Where the road once was, there is now a wall of grass 20 feet high. You can feel the packed ground where a trail has once been. To the right are the remains of a drainage ditch, and along the road a clear area still exists. Step one foot off on either side of the narrow path, and you sink into the bottomless, black mud.

We can imagine the thoughts of the villagers as they watch the long yellow column of vehicles idling at the entrance to what looks like a sea of tall grass. Who are these strange white men? Why are they going down that road?

Our scout keeps searching the wet, sucking mud for an entrance to, or even a trace of, a road, muttering that just three months ago on the pre-scout mission he drove this road at 60 miles an hour. The scout tries to convince himself that the tall grass is an illusion or just a temporary barrier. He has obviously not consulted with the locals, or has a hard time comprehending the growth rate of grass in Africa. Three months ago, in the dry season, the locals would have told him that, yes, there is a definite reason the grass grows so tall here and, yes, there was a road here once but probably only for a few days. We are standing knee-deep at the entrance to a swamp that stretches not for yards, but for miles.

Yes, there is a reason grass can grow 20 feet in three months. We are about to enter the great swamps of East Africa.

Into the Tall Grass

We decide to press forward, despite being faced with an endless sea of swamp and tall grass. The rest of the convoy waits patiently behind, wondering what is going on. This is to be a common pattern over the next few days. At first, we try using machetes to clear the path. As we push deeper and deeper into the swamp, we realize that at this rate using machetes will get pretty old after a couple of days. We wonder what surprises await us in the long grass. There are to be quite a few.

The scout runs ahead to feel the path, while the drivers follow the lead car. We are 20 yards behind the red taillights, leaving enough room in case they need to be towed out of a gully or river. Suddenly, the scout comes screaming toward us, tearing his clothes off while swearing, "Bloody bastards. Get some water, get some water!" His thick accent and apoplectic state make it difficult for us to understand exactly what he wants. Since it is pouring rain, it seems a strange request. It is only after he is nearly naked that we realize he has been attacked by red ants. So we dump half of our precious water supply on him in order to ease the pain.

After our first run-in with African wildlife, we offer to cut trail. We take a more scientific, more team-oriented approach. I assign responsibilities. One person will ride on top with the spotlight, looking for the thin ridge of high grass that identifies the center of the road. We drive blind, sensing the camber of the road through the steering wheel and angle of the hood. I watch out the passenger side for the slight ridge caused by shorter grass that identifies where trucks that have passed in the dry season have slowed grass growth by soil compression. We decide to abandon the machete method and use our Discovery like a bulldozer to smash our way through the green wall of grass.

The Yellow Weed Whacker

The rain increases in intensity. It is nighttime and we are surrounded by a solid wall of grass 20 feet high like an ant walking through a lawn. The powerful driving lights bounce back off the wet grass and illuminate the car like a movie set. What I think is sweat running down my neck is really dozens of inquisitive insects. To say that there are a lot of insects would be an understatement. Not the big fluttery, elegant kind found in Asia but the weird, crawly bugs of Africa. As we slam through the thick, wet grass, bugs of every size and description are flicked through the window and inside the truck.

Soon, car and passengers are a furry carpet of prickly grass and crawling insects. It is a truly special and indescribable feeling to be soaking wet and covered from head to toe with insects of every variety. Hundreds of cockroaches, beetles, flies, mantises, spiders, ticks, moths, crickets, ants, earwigs, grasshoppers and walking sticks are crawling over and through our hair, up our noses and inside our clothing.

Giant praying mantises and walking sticks calmly crawl up our necks to stand next to our head-mounted flashlights and gorge themselves on the gnats, flies and moths that are attracted to the light. Despite our inquisitive friends, we still have to be alert to the other surprises that await us in the endless ocean of grass.

An incredible amount of stress comes from driving at high speed through a 12- to 18-foot wall of grass. It rains every night, swelling rivers, washing out makeshift bridges and deepening ravines. Fallen tree branches suddenly appear like lances straight out of the green wall. Stream beds present themselves quickly and dramatically, forcing us to slam on the brakes to avoid going head over heels into the water. We get our reconfirmation that this has been a road, or at least a bridge when we almost plunge into a 10-foot gap created by two naked bridge supports. We have to drive fast because driving slow means getting stuck, and each river we cross is running higher and faster, swollen by the heavy rains. As night turns to day and to night again, all we see is grass. Fording ravines and rivers offers our only break from the monotony.

We are in a hurry to reach Mikumi to make up lost time. Instead of building bridges and laying passable tracks for the teams behind, we decide to smash through swamps and washouts, leaving a gooey quagmire for those who follow. The rear of the column is getting farther and farther behind—a distance originally measured in hours and now in days. The heavy support vehicles require constant winching through the swamp, until the convoy is no longer driving but dragging itself every inch of the way.

The last time we see the rear of the convoy is at a point on the map where a shallow river crossing is marked. Tonight, or rather this morning, it is a raging river with a 20-foot-high waterfall where the road used to be. We decide to stop and sleep for three hours. As the sun comes up, I walk back to visit with the other teams just pulling in to the rear of the column. They are beginning to show the effects of constant driving and winching, of no sleep and the endless strain of fighting the swamp. In the weak light of morning, large blue crabs scuttle around the two water-filled ruts the vehicles have left behind us, as they hauled themselves through the endless bog.

The Elephant Walk

The tedium of the seamless days and nights is punctuated by rain-swollen river crossings. During one wet and exhausting river crossing, we find an unusually large hole through the trees to winch the trucks up from the river. Once the vehicles are across, we collapse until the dawn comes an hour and a half later. While sleeping on the roof rack in the rain, I hear slow swishing in the grass and wake up to find elephants, obviously quite disturbed to find these metal intruders blocking their path to the river. Eye to eye with these giants, I keep desperately quiet as they slowly thread their way alongside our vehicles and down to the river.

That morning, the car windows are steamed up, the sleeping occupants appearing as if they have been shot dead in their seats, mouths gaping, heads sagging. We realize that we weren't dreaming when we see the huge elephant tracks around the trucks heading down to the riverbank.

We have lost radio contact with the rest of the convoy. At last check, we were four days ahead of the last vehicle. Our fuel indicators have been on empty for the last day and a half. In the last six days, we have slept exactly six and a half hours. Our eyes have given up focusing—they stare straight ahead. We look out through the rain-soaked windshield, hallucinating from lack of sleep. We are traveling up through a pass at night. Huge 50- to 150-foot trees bearing monstrous scars loom overhead. Elephants have ripped branches from the trees, leaving white flesh and jagged skeletons. Illuminated by our eight high-powered driving lights, they seem to dance and move. This is elephant, big elephant, country.

Finally, we emerge from the bizarre forest and re-enter the swamps. We run over what we first think is a giant toad, which turns out to be the head of a very long python. We know it is at least 15 feet long, since we can see only 15 feet at one time. Unharmed in the marshy ground, it slithers back into the grass. Later, we come across the skeleton of an elephant killed by poachers. We take turns taking pictures of each other standing inside the elephant's pelvis. We tie the massive bones to the fronts of our vehicles in a "skull and crossbones" and then decide to take off.

At last, we come to the long-awaited river crossing—the end of the wilderness and the beginning of the road that leads to Mikumi. The water rages under the heavy downpour. Too tired to walk the swollen river, we charge our vehicle across and immediately plunge over the edge of a steep rock ledge and submerge our car for the third time that week. We jump out of the truck and struggle through the heavy current to the opposite bank with the winch line. We hook it up and wait for the driver to pull us across. We wait...and wait. The vehicle is leaning at a grotesque angle. The water is rising and pouring through the open windows. We realize that the driver is fast asleep at the wheel, quite comfortably submerged up to his chest in the raging water. We bang on the hood, and he finally snaps out of it. We winch it out, our fuel running out 20 feet on the other side.

We don't have time to celebrate the fact that we have made it out of the swamps and are only a few miles from civilization. By now, we are zombies as we try to make it to a mission, 20 miles up the dirt track. Instead of a navigable dirt road, we experience a wet and furious roller-coaster ride through lake-sized potholes and muddy cane fields. We don't even notice. We drive straight through, not even caring how deep the holes are. We dive underwater again. By now, we are so wet, tired and cold we are oblivious to everything. We try to stay awake by talking to each other, but we miss chunks of sentences as we doze off and awake mid-sentence. Somehow we get to Mikumi in one piece.

We collapse on the cement floor, only to find ourselves wide awake an hour later and unable to sleep.

Boredom and Death in Mikumi

We have pushed hard for 144 hours (137 hours without sleep), and all we can do now is sit and wait for the others to make it through the swamps. The unforeseen delay and hardship have also depleted their fuel, water and vital spare parts.

A military cargo helicopter on loan from the Tanzanian government is pressed into service to fly the needed supplies to the depleted convoy.

We load up fuel, water and a replacement gearbox and wait in a school yard to load it onto the helicopter. We wait until the sun goes down. Still no helicopter. We find out the details later: Ten minutes after takeoff, it crashed into a mountainside, killing the copilot and seriously injuring the other two crew members. The battered old Huey was exactly 50 percent of the Tanzanian Air Force. Since some of the stuck convoy is a few kilometers from a rail line, we resort to commandeering a rail speeder car for a five-hour trip. The heavy gearbox and diesel fuel are carried in safari style on two poles to the stranded convoy. Later, we regroup and resume our journey.

Out of the Swamps and into the Scrub

We leave the mud and grass of the swamps far behind us and are now traveling through classic East African savannah. The horizon stretches in a virtually unobstructed 360° view, hindered only by gentle acacias and tortured, swollen baobab trees.

Puffy, white clouds form an endless pattern, accompanied by the lazy sound of tsetse flies, as giraffes watch shyly in the distance. Time seems to slow down, and your senses are sharpened. We begin to notice the thousands of purple and yellow flowers that carpet the land. Time passes even slower, as vultures aimlessly circle the convoy. We discover more bleached, tuskless skeletons of elephants killed by poachers. The heat paints swirls on the landscape, creating an Impressionist painting. The cruel African sun draws the moisture out of our bodies. Tiny sweat bees hungrily suck the beads of perspiration from our arms. We figure they are entitled to it.

Our once-soaked clothes are now dry. Our hands become hard, cracked and calloused, the nails and creases packed with black dirt. The hot sun begins to tan our skin and clear up our rashes, grass cuts and insect bites. We are adapting to the hot, dry savannah days and cool, crisp nights. We come to recognize the unique flora and fauna of the spear grass. Thousands of these sharp, barbed weapons are snicked off by the brush guard and embedded in our skin and clothing. However, spear grass pales in comparison to the various types of acacia thorns that grow up to five inches long. Just like porcupine thorns, these light, hollow daggers are everywhere and can pierce right through heavy boots. They become projectiles when they smack through an open window at 40 mph, looking for soft flesh to penetrate.

We also become good friends with the scourge of Africa— the tsetse fly. Built like deer flies with mandibles designed to bite through water buffalo skin, they are vicious. Under constant attack, we smack'em, roll 'em, crush'em—and they just get up, shake their heads and attack again. Well-fed tsetse flies are easier to kill. We catch them on the windows. One smack and—blammo!—they explode in a shower of blood.

We are attacked by African killer bees that swarm out of their nests to rush at us again and again. They will attack even if we pass 20 to 30 meters from their nests. They charge at us in a horde, climbing up our noses, into our shirts. The next day, I feel like I have been beaten with a baseball bat.

We pass through many primitive and scenic areas populated by elephants, warthogs, baboons, giraffes, zebras, gazelles and other savannah animals. In the Selous, we stop to admire a family of elephants playing in the shade of a spreading acacia tree. The bull elephant suddenly takes exception to our intrusion, turning on us, ears flapping, shaking its head and loudly trumpeting its displeasure. After its false charge, it lowers its head like a locomotive and heads straight for us again. As we speed off, the ranger cocks his weathered rifle and only takes it down when the elephant gives up.

Finally, we find a faint trail, which soon becomes a dirt road. We have crossed the savannah and now see the hills and mountains of Central Africa dead ahead of us. Late that night, we pull into the ranger station in Rungwa to refuel, replace tires and sleep. The next morning, we are awakened by a glorious, 20-minute-long sunrise framed by an unusual double rainbow; it's almost as if the heavens are rewarding us for surviving the long journey.

Into the Heart of Africa

Although no signpost marks the spot, there is a distinct transition between Eastern and Central Africa. The soil turns from black loam to red clay; the air turns softer, more tropical—and even the people seem gentler and shyer. It is also darker and more foreboding. The wild, empty panoramas of Tanzania are replaced by the heavily populated, agricultural quiltwork of Burundi. Slipping and sliding through muddy banana plantations, the convoy labors over a mountain pass in dense fog. As we reach the crest, we are dazzled by the brilliant light and spectacular view.

Before us is a wide expanse of shimmering silver, fronting a mountainous wall of rich green. Stretching as far as the eye can see is a massive wall of dark mountains. Soaring above these magnificent mountains are huge, white thunderheads; below is the fabled Sea of Ujijji, now known as Lake Tanganyika, sparkling like a pool of diamonds.

This unforgettable sight has inspired awe in every explorer since Burton and Speke first set eyes on the lake:

"Nothing could be more picturesque than this first view of the lake," wrote Burton. "A narrow strip of emerald green, marvelously fertile, shelves towards a ribbon of yellow sand and bordered by sedgy rushes."

Like Burton, we had endured the swamps, the long, hot savannah, the wild animals, pests, and pestilence. But what had taken him seven and a half months, we have compressed into three weeks.

That night, we celebrate with the locals, among them the president of Burundi and whatever socialites and party animals Bujumbura can muster. Once the politicians and upper crust go home, 20 days of being in the bush with little sleep is erased by adrenaline and alcohol. One by one, the team members start throwing each other in the pool. Soon there are more people in the pool than outside. After we run out of khaki-clad people to toss in, everything else is fair game: Sabena stewardesses, lawn furniture, waiters, pots and pans. Laughing riotously, we pour what beer is left on top of each other's heads and jump into the seething pile of debris and people in the once sedate hotel pool. After the hotel runs out of beer, we migrate to an all-night disco on the shores of Lake Tanganyika.

Still dripping wet, we spend the rest of the night dancing and drinking with the local girls. Most try to stay out of fights with jealous boyfriends, who are determined to see just how tough we are. We didn't come to Africa to prove we were tough; we came here to have a good time.

As the dawn breaks over Lake Tanganyika, the few that can still walk stagger outside to get one last look at this magical lake in the heart of Africa. As the sun rises over the mist-covered mountains across the golden lake, we know we have seen the soul of Africa.

—**RYP**

CAMBODIA
A Ride in the Country

The land that is Cambodia slipped in and out of chaos long before Angkor existed. The influx of tourists to see the great temple complex often leads visitors to wonder what all the fuss is about. Occasionally a few are kidnapped and or executed. Wink Dulles retraced the route of a group of Westerners that were kidnapped to ascertain the danger firsthand.

Is travel in Cambodia safe for foreigners today? The government seems to think so and invited *DP* to see for itself.

In September 1995, in response to a Cambodian government protest over this chapter on Cambodia in the first edition of *DP*, we returned to Cambodia to reassess the country's safety for foreign travelers. Rather than simply take the beaten tourist cow path to Angkor, which—at press time—was secure for tourists (either by air or large speedboat), I journeyed by motorcycle down to Sihanoukville on National Highway 4, the route on which the three Westerners were traveling when they were taken captive and later killed by the Khmer Rouge in 1994. I did this despite being warned by many not to, including the government's tourism minister.

####

As planned, I telephoned Cambodian Tourism Minister Veng Sereyvuth to schedule dinner, and was told by his assistant to meet him the following night at 7:30 at the Cambodiana, Cambodia's queen of hotels and a good place to convince someone that land mines don't maim a thousand Cambodians a month or that Khmers' per-capita annual income isn't below 170 bucks a year.

I rented a Honda Rebel, the Tonka Toy of choppers, and headed back to the Capitol to find a guide. My Khmer is as fluent as my Swahili, and I didn't want to get stuck in the sticks trading my wallet and underwear for smiles with the locals.

I chose the guy who seemed most capable of talking his way out of a hole. He went by the name of "Tall Man". Appropriate, as he was over six-three, making him the King Kong of Khmers. Bony, with wavy, Waldo-like locks, and movie-star handsome, Tall Man had lost both his parents to Pol Pot during the four-year Khmer Rouge slaughter of the Cambodian people during the mid-1970s. His English was excellent.

I met with Sereyvuth the next night at the Cambodiana. He brought along with him a strapping, husky Australian, whose sneer couldn't be seen beneath mustache whiskers spilling over his mouth like stalagtite from the roof of a cave. His name was Trevor. He was introduced to me as an attorney. He looked more like a retired boxer.

"This *Dangerous Places* book has screwed this country," the Aussie said. "You have no idea how much you have pissed this man off." He nodded toward Veng, who seemed to be preoccupied looking at a floral arrangement at a distant table. "He won't tell you this stuff himself because he's Cambodian," Trevor continued. "He won't show his anger."

I was then informed that there were at least seven major projects that had been seriously jeopardized with the publication of *The World's Most Dangerous Places*. "What we need to know is what are you going to do right now to correct this matter?" Trevor demanded.

"I'm here to reevaluate Cambodia's security for tourists," I said. "If it's any safer than it was the last time I was here, I'll report it."

"Listen, my friend," Trevor said. "There's a way of doing things in this country, and there's a way of not doing them. Do not go to Sihanoukville."

"Tomorrow," Veng suddenly cut in, "go to Angkor Wat and have a good time."

The next day, I got a call from Pip Wood, national editor of the *Cambodia Daily*, who wanted an interview because he'd heard I might go to Kompot by train. Foreigners don't go to Kompot by train. Not possessing a death wish, I asked him if it was possible. He said we should ask the Khmers on the paper's staff if they'd make the journey by train.

"It's high in the sky," said Ek Madra, a Khmer journalist.

"What the hell does that mean?" I said.

"There's a chance you'll make it, and a chance you won't." he said.

Foreigners are still not permitted to purchase the discounted tickets for the first three cars of the train, which can only be had by Cambodians. At last check, clerks at Phnom Penh's train station refused to sell any tickets at all to foreigners on any of Cambodia's train routes.

"That's how those guys were hit last year," Martin Flitman, a longtime Phnom Penh-based photojournalist told me. "They were seen buying tickets at the station. Word goes down the line into KR territory. The KR knew those tourists were on the train before it got there. You might be able to make it today, but not if you buy your ticket at the station. Get aboard after Pochentong and you may make it."

I decided the train was out of the question. A death wish I have not.

Kompong Som—or Sihanoukville, the quaintly renamed port of the south—is 220 kilometers south of Phnom Penh. It's at the other end of a marvelously well paved ribbon of asphalt that cuts a swath through the flat rice fields around the Mekong River and winds its way through the Elephant Mountains, before descending into the sleepy seaside port town. Highway 4 is generally considered to be safe for 50 km out of Phnom Penh. The villages flanking its shoulders are large, and psychologically comforting, modern Western-style petrol stations spring from the rice fields every five kilometers or so. As the road cuts into the hills, the villages become fewer and farther between. The Shell stations cease. Rice fields cede the topography to rolling parcels of dense brush, much of the scrub blanketing many of the millions of land mines coated with soil in this Claymore-besieged country. This is Khmer Rouge territory. During daylight on most days, the guerrillas hide in the hills between five and 10 klicks off the highway. At night, they creep to the roadside and lay fresh mines and—along with other groups of thugs, bullies and bandits—stop vehicles and rob motorists.

As the route winds though KR turf, every half klick a small group of soldiers can be seen lounging by the roadside beneath makeshift lean-tos. The small bridges along Highway 4 are manned by troops 24 hours a day. They sleep beneath tarps strung in the trees just off the road. They have the special responsibility of preventing the KR from blowing up the bridges. A number will step into the road, attempting to halt cars for bribes. Few motorists pay them any heed, speeding past. They know they won't have such an escape opportunity at the larger, more fortified checkpoints. At these points, the line of cars and trucks waiting to pay the road "toll" can reach a kilometer long. Until recently, foreigners traveling in taxis were routinely hit up for kickbacks at the military roadblocks. Gratefully, such instances are rare these days.

About 50 klicks from Sihanoukville, Tall Man tapped my shoulder. He had to pee. I saw a bright red "DANGER! LAND MINES" sign off the road and parked the bike on the pavement next to it. Not on the soft road shoulder. There was a way to do things in Cambodia, and a way not to do them.

Three soldiers approached the bike, their automatic rifles slung like purses. They seemed friendly enough. I gave them cigarettes and Mr. DP stickers. Tall Man zipped himself back in and chirped with the soldiers in Khmer. Suddenly, his smile dropped. The soldiers trudged off.

"A child just stepped on a land mine," he said. "About an hour ago. Just up the road."

It started to rain again. I rolled the bike about 50 meters up the asphalt. A small compound of brightly painted hootches on stilts were on the right, just off the road. Tinny, reverbed Khmer mourning music blared from a small loud-speaker. Villagers huddled under one of the wooden dwellings. Beneath an overhang was a circle of people.

I was struck by the blood-soaked blanket covering the corpse, as the circle parted to let me through. An old man, on seeing my camera, removed the shroud and stripped the dead 12-year-old. The child had caught the blast in the groin. His eyes were milky, his tiny hands folded on his chest. He looked as if he had taken a while to die.

The old man was the child's grandfather. He said his grandson had been walking the family cow. The cow had stepped on the mine, then ran off into the forest on three legs. It explained why the boy's legs were fine. He said the mine was planted by some drunken government troops about a month ago.

We made it to Sihanoukville, escaping detainment, arrest, theft, abduction and execution. I got drunk on Thai whisky. The next morning, we headed back for Phnom Penh. I stopped to photograph the village where the youngster had died.

After another 60 kilometers, we came upon a unit of the Cambodian Mine Action Committee (CMAC) tiptoeing on Highway 4's shoulder with metal detectors. The team was led by a young Canadian army captain and supported by Royal Cambodian tanks and armored personnel carriers. A Khmer was slumped asleep behind the wheel of a Nissan pickup. In its bed, a huge Browning machine gun mounted on a turret was aimed toward the eastern mountains. It looked like the "technicals" used by the thugs and warlords in Somalia. Another soldier stooped by the side of the highway, wiping a pair of B-40 rockets. Steamrollers were pressing new asphalt. We had come upon the spot where the KR's diesel and fertilizer bombs had detonated a couple of days earlier. I reported our discovery to the Canadian.

"Thanks for the report," the officer said. "I didn't know there was any action down there. We'll report it to Phnom Penh, and they'll send a team down there to clean up the area soon."

"There's a lot of kids in the village," I said.

"They'll do it soon."

"The old man said government troops planted it about a month ago," I said.

"Unlikely. Probably old. But even we can't tell how long they've been under."

The Canadian had been in-country six months and was charged with clearing Highway 4 from Phnom Penh to Sihanoukville. He'd made it about halfway, saying his team had removed 1800 mines. The kid's mine made it 1801.

—Wink Dulles

Over the Line

Cambodia has seen the deaths of 1.5 to 2 million of its people. It is rare to find anyone who has not lost a number of relatives or friends in the dark years under Pol Pot (Saloth Sar). Just before Cambodia once again erupted into civil war between the two parties (the ousted party was Royalist and aligned with the Khmer Rouge and the other is backed by Vietnam, the sworn enemy of the KR) I took a few days off from an expedition in Borneo to visit Cambodia. Timing is everything since a few months later all hell broke loose.

We went to Cambodia on a lark. These days, Cambodia is not necessarily the most dangerous place in the world, or even a nasty place, but it is an exotic, very inexpensive stop that every traveler to Asia should make. Is it safe? Well, if you stay inside the tourist ruts (literally), don't venture outside the ill-defined "safety" zone and watch where you step, Cambodia can be safe. Cambodia can also be a brutal if you pass through the invisible safety barrier and end up in the hands of the Khmer Rouge. Just remember the advice of your first grade teacher, "Don't color outside the lines."

Cambodia has provided a safe corridor for tourists wanting to visit the great temple complexes around Angkor Wat. Depending on who you talk to, the Khmer Rouge is either a mighty Chinese backed juggernaut, complete with tanks, foot soldiers and tacit support from the Thai generals along the border, or as a rag-tag band of starving anachronisms who have resorted to banditry just to eat. The truth is somewhere in the middle and at both ends of the spectrum.

One tourist can fly into Phnom Penh and Siem Reap on a modern jet, stay in a five-star hotel, and see the temple complex, complete with cold Pepsis, an air-conditioned car and a good meal, followed by an ice-cold beer at one of the many nightclubs the U.N. soldiers used to frequent. Another tourist can find himself kneeling at the edge of a shallow, hastily dug grave, waiting for the rifle butt that will slam into his cortex, ending his brief but adventurous life. The difference between the two scenarios might be 10 km or lingering a few too many minutes along the road.

Despite the kidnapping, execution, injuring and shooting of a number of tourists over the last few years, the government of Cambodia considers its country safe...within certain limits. Those ellipsis can be the difference between life and death here.

When we buy tickets, the Malaysian trained ticket agent for Royal Air Cambodge, a joint venture between Malaysian Airlines and the Cambodian government, is cordial and efficient. We ask whether many tourists come to Cambodia. He thinks we must be very stupid spies and points to the lack of tourists in the check-in area.

We ask, "Is it dangerous in Cambodia?" He looks up and says, "I would say it is a lot safer than Los Angeles," referring to the shooting of Hang Ngor, the Cambodian doctor turned actor who starred in *The Killing Fields*. He had managed to survive Cambodia, only to die on the mean streets of Los Angeles. Killed for a gold locket (that contained a picture of his dead wife) by a member of the Lazy Boys, a street gang made up of Chinese kids. That gold locket was what carried him through the horrors of captivity and his escape; it also killed him. Hang Ngor thought he had crossed over the line, but he never made it.

On the flight in, my sober thoughts about Cambodia are confirmed by the sight of the hard brown country below us. A visual shock after flying over the endless green carpets of Malaysia and Thailand. Cambodia has long been denuded and carved into a patchwork for wet season rice cultivation, interrupted by movie-prop-style sugar palms in random patterns.

When the monsoon arrives, the countryside floods, roads are impassable and the rice fields turn rich green. Food becomes plentiful. There is hope and happiness in the wet season. The dry season is a time of hardship and killing.

The dry season is when the government launches its tank and infantry attacks against the Khmer Rouge, who then retreat into their strongholds near Thailand and their jungle and hilltop hideouts. Slipping away like children chasing pigeons, the KR wait for the rainy season to regroup and infiltrate back to the south. The dry season is the most dangerous time for tourists. It is when food and supplies are at their scarcest for the wandering bands of KR and bandits. It is when the Khmer Rouge must rob and kidnap to raise money to buy supplies or just eat. Many say that members of the KR army simply take off their uniforms and dissolve into the general populace.

The wet season is the most dangerous time for the locals. This is when the KR enters villages to press gangs, farmers, kids, anyone who can carry a gun. Should the young people not be there, the KR promise to come back and kill the entire family if they do not supply a raw recruit. They also carry off rice, building materials and any possessions the villagers have not buried. The wet season is when it is easy to plant land mines and booby traps, which become invisible in the dry season. The villagers are constantly maimed and killed, as they go out to work their fields and paddies during the wet season.

Our flight is full of fat, middle-aged Chinese businessmen with bad haircuts who immediately start gambling and drinking as soon as the seat belt sign goes off. We ask why they are going to Phnom Penh. They all have clothing factories there, we are told. "Cambodia is just like Thailand was ten years ago. Cheap, very cheap."

As the plane comes in for the final approach, I notice the rows of rusty tanks and APCs. Studying the parched ground interrupted by wispy brown bushes and meandering vein-like footpaths, I can't help thinking that Cambodia looks like the skull of someone recovering from heavy chemotherapy.

Upon landing, formalities are brief—$20 in U.S. currency and a visa. The line, the crush of tourists, and the exotic-looking posters of Angkor Wat on the walls makes me feel like I am paying to get into a theme park. Another sick irony makes me laugh—it costs $38 dollars to get into EPCOT, and there are a whole lot less land mines there. On the simple forms we fill out, it seems the government wants to know if we are bringing in any gold bars, ammunition or firearms.

Pushing through the usual Third World crush of touts and taxi drivers, we pause again, these people are only asking for two and three dollars to drive us into town. Obviously, the supply is a lot higher than the demand here. Driving into town, the bullet holes, grass-filled craters and fading scorch marks have all been cleaned up. Phnom Penh is bustling, not a Bangkok bustle, but still busy for a city that once looked like a scene from *Full Metal Jacket*. As if to provide a counterpoint to the death and destruction all around, our driver slows down as he passes a row of small shops with Vietnamese women sitting outside. He points, smiles and simply says, "fucking." This is obviously the standard route into town.

There is still something missing, though. There are very few, if any, people over the age of 45. More than one million people, some say more, were killed in here by Pol Pot and the Khmer Rouge in their attempt to re-engineer society. Today, like Saigon, the post-war generation is gregarious and eager to meet Westerners. The men above 30 are more reticent. Around town, there are men and boys who have been maimed by land mines. They beg, politely repeating, "*Bapa Yam*" (or "please sir, rice"). I also notice that there are no flowers in Cambodia. Their tattered army uniforms and shiny plastic limbs make me think back to Afghanistan.

A few months earlier when we were at the headquarters of the *taliban*, their stairwells and courtyard were full of maimed fighters. The difference is that the tiny Russian mines only took off the foot at the ankle. Here, the legs are gone up to the knee and sometimes higher. Here, the men have prosthetic limbs; in Afghanistan, they gave the wounded a stick to walk with. Here, there has been a different kind of horror. In Afghanistan, the fighters and old men proudly wear their *DP* stickers and T-shirts. In Cambodia, if a soldier or civilian has been through the holocaust, he is more likely to politely hand back the image of the grinning skull of Mr. DP. There are far too many images of real skulls here. I notice something else. There are no birds in Cambodia.

Walking down the main drag in Phnom Penh, we are followed by a Ray-Banned man in a yellow shirt and string tie. He doesn't do his job well, since we repeatedly sneak up behind him and give him a start. Paranoia and posttraumatic stress are just below the surface here.

As all good tourists must, we visit the killing fields as well as the police detention and torture center. It is hard to understand the methodical nature of the Khmer Rouges' killing, as we view black-and-white photos of every victim seated in a posing stool, their paperwork filled out in triplicate.

But then again, does anybody understand what motivates Turks to kill Armenians, Germans to kill Jews, Americans to kill Indians, Jews to kill Arabs, Arabs to kill Christians, Christians to kill Arabs and so on? There are so many skulls, they make murals, maps, monuments and whatever else they can think off. They try to be educational with their macabre building materials, but once again I can't help think what a great pavilion and "audio-anima-horrific" ride this would make. There are still hundreds of thousands of skulls left in the ground to make displays, office buildings or even entire pavilions.

Over 20,000 U.N. soldiers used to keep the lid on this country, but today just about the only remnants are the white Land Cruisers and Toyota pickup trucks of the U.N., repainted with various aid logos. You can see these vehicles parked outside the other remnants of the U.N.'s efforts. Upscale restaurants, air-conditioned massage parlors, cheap whorehouses and surprisingly high-end discos keep Phnom Penh and

Siem Reap hopping late into the night. For a Westerner, a massage costs $5, a night of Cambodian passion, $25. In the bigger dance halls and restaurants, cheap beer is sold by attentive uniformed women who represent and get a commission from their sponsoring brewery. You can't slowly savor a beer here, as your glass is filled past the meniscus level by chatty beer ladies or impatient "go dancing" girls.

We hire a driver to tour the countryside, The hotel we stay in is run by a woman who has hired her ex-husband's old army buddies. Not a difficult thing to do, since most Cambodian men are either in the army or have served in it. We ask the ex-army buddies who hang around the hotel if Cambodia is dangerous. They glibly reply, "Not so much anymore." We ask again, not happy with this pat answer. They pause and say it depends where you go. We ask our driver, who responds: "As long as you visit the temples, it is fine; if you go beyond..." His explanation trailing off, he points to the hills and countryside.

Wink tells him of his trip north of Siem Reap. The driver thinks we are asking if this trip would be dangerous. He replies, shaking his head and laughing at our folly, "No, you cannot do that." Wink explains, that he has already done it. The driver says, "Then you are very lucky to be alive."

We stop at a Thai-owned bank to change money. The manager is equally impressed and amused, as he overhears Wink jabbering away in Thai. He has been here for three months. He cautions us that it is dangerous here. He says, "Do not go out after dark. There are many guns. Men dress up like police and stop foreigners at roadblocks. Do not drive outside of the city. It is dangerous." We ask if anyone has been robbed. He says, "Yes, many people." He warns us to be extra careful. The recent division between the two rulers sharing power is heating up, and he tells us that "the word is out on the street that there may be a coup soon." Aware that three foreigners were sprayed with machine-gun fire when they were mistaken for "white mercenaries," we thank him for the tip.

We ask around town if we can rent bikes or drive up to Siem Reap. Not possible, we are told, for the simple reason that at best you are guaranteed to run into Khmer Rouge roadblocks and be abducted, worst case you will be shot and robbed. No cab drivers will take us. We book a flight instead.

Arriving in Siem Reap, we hire a driver and tell him we want to retrace the route of the American tourist who was injured in a rocket and machine-gun attack just north of the Angkor temple complex. He does not think that is a good idea. "It is too dangerous." He refuses to take us there, so we content ourselves with visiting the temples in the company of reappearing chattering clusters of Japanese, Germans and Thai tourists.

Cambodia is happy. The bus tourists are finally coming back; the temples used to be silent with the occasional back-packer, expat or aid worker carefully avoiding the smaller paths and out-of-the-way complexes. Soon there will be a major development just outside the temples as well as in the nearby city of Siem Reap. This former battle zone is sprouting giant five-star hotels with room capacities in the hundreds, more appropriate for Las Vegas than this tiny county. The red skull signs that signaled areas still full of land mines are mostly gone. The soldiers no longer carry AK-47s (it scares the tourists they tell us). When we ask where the machine guns are, we are told don't worry—there are plenty at the army base. For now, Cambodia is one of the cheapest places to visit. A beer costs $2, a meal in a restaurant goes for about $3—steep, considering we are paying $3 a night for two people in a room. We get our laundry done for a buck. And all of this in U.S. greenbacks.

Hanging around the great man-made lake that surrounds Angkor Wat, we watch the sunset turn the temples' towers to a fiery red. It is hard to believe that the sun has been turning the temples this color for the last 700 years. There are a few bullet holes from where the Vietnamese army once camped out here. All the major statues have been stolen, destroyed or removed by Europeans, the Khmer Rouge or vandals, but there is still an awesome power of solemnity that holds visitors in its sway. The slightly bemused expressions of the great faces of the Bayon are a perfect contrast to the bloodthirsty scenes carved on the friezes that decorate the temple walls.

We strike up a conversation with a member of military intelligence for the Siem Reap provinces. He tells us that two Khmer Rouge generals have defected with military plans. One apparently wanted a Range Rover as part of his retirement package.

A British minesweeper and his assistant are kidnapped by the Khmer Rouge less than a half-day's drive from here. Surprisingly enough, our friend is quite pleased, since one of the goodies one of the generals dropped off at their office was a plan to kidnap a foreigner. The only snag is, they had to make do with a Brit.

Americans are the most favored kidnap victims, followed by British and then French. Yanks bring in an automatic US$10,000 and provide the necessary publicity to give the government grief. We ask him how safe it is. He says, in town, at the temples and in daylight, there is no problem. But 20 km away, there is a battle raging. We also tell him about *DP's* trip by motorcycle around the countryside. He also thinks we are talking in the future tense. He says that would not be a very good idea. We say, no, we already took the trip. He also says Wink was very lucky.

That night back in Siem Reap we go to a nightclub. The sign outside says "no guns or explosives." The music is pure sing-song Khmer played at ear-damaging levels. The Khmers dance to the music in a circular line dance reminiscent of that on a bad TNN show. Wink decides to get up and jam with the band. The audience is dumbstruck and stares open-mouthed for two songs. The dance floor clears out, and the Cambodians don't know if they should clap or cover their ears. Wink finishes up to a round of applause. After Wink sits down, it seems not everyone is thrilled with his impromptu jam session. We are challenged to a fight in a less than sensitive manner. An elbow not once, not twice, but three times in the back—hard. We decide to split. This would not be a John Wayne punch 'em up, but probably a sloppy and quick burst of automatic weapons. As we change venues, the group of surly Cambodian men follows us out into the street. We face off, neither side wanting to be the first to start hostilities. Luckily, our driver pulls up and we drive off.

We stop at another place with the same bad music, same knife-edge tension. Wink sums it up by saying these people are very fucked up. The more genteel would say they suffer from posttraumatic stress, though they aren't even aware of the term here. There is a lot of rage. He echoes a sentiment a Malaysian friend expresses to me on hearing that I would be going to Cambodia: The people here are very quiet and angry—they have seen a lot of death.

We sit with three Cambodian girls, or rather three girls made a hurried grab for the empty chairs at our table. Westerners are big game for these bar girls. Wink keeps talking to them in Vietnamese. In Cambodia, most working girls are divided into "go dancing" girls, women who sit, talk and dance with and maybe sleep with you on request, and "taxi girls," who are simply sex girls. There are also houses where the function of intercourse is emotionally and financially comparable to the drive-through window at McDonald's. Most of the girls are Vietnamese, but these girls are Cambodian. To prove it, they mimic the ancient hand movements and music of the *apsara*, the temptresses seen on the temples at Angkor. Wink is surprised, since most girls who were trained dancers were killed by the Khmer Rouge. Aspiring to more intellectual entertainment, we teach one of the girls a few English words at her request. She tells us that if she learns English, she will get a better job. We find out that what she means is that she can sleep with more Westerners and therefore make more money. She tells us with some pride that one Japanese man actually paid her $40 for the whole night. A curious career ambition.

Sitting outside to avoid the chilling air conditioning and deafening noise inside, we are interrupted as a Cambodian cop comes flying out of the glass entry doors. The girls sitting with us immediately react, jump up, and drag us around the corner and down an alley. They plead with us to "Go, go, run! Please, before you are shot!" Not quite knowing what they are talking about, we walk back to the front, but the girls push us back, pleading with us to run away.

We push past them and are in time to watch the cop being kicked and beaten and then slammed unconscious into the back of a pickup truck. The girls explain that we are lucky (a term we are hearing a lot here). Usually, there is gunfire. They mimic the action of someone firing a machine-gun. They tell us that this week "a man fell down, went to sleep." I laugh. The expression on the girl's face tells me that she is not trying to be cute; she is trying to avoid saying the word "died." She halfheartedly repeats the machine-gun pantomime and tries to make me understand. The sad look in her eyes tells me that I am being far too casual about a very real threat. With a sense of resignation, she says, "This is a dangerous place. You should not be here."

—**RYP**

Postscript

Fifteen months later, Prince Norodom Ranariddh is ousted in a bloody coup by Hun Sen which killed more than 50 people, including three foreigners.

CHECHNYA
Front Row Seats

Sedat Aral is Coskun's younger brother. In an effort to outdo his better known older brother, Sedat has chosen to cover tougher wars in meaner places in his work as a war photographer for news agencies and magazines. Altough his pictures only sell if he can cover the fighting, his attempts to get close to the war are far more interesting. In Chechnya both the Chechens and Russians did not like journalists putting a spin on this brutal oil/drug/religious/clan war. Both Russians and Chechens were kidnapping, shooting, flogging or deporting journalists as well as aid workers. The Chechens won but there were few people who had the guts or stomach to cover their victory.

One can never lead a normal life as a war photographer. As soon as the words "hostilities have broken out in…" are heard on CNN, it is expected that there will be a flow of videotapes and photographs that cover and explain the conflict. Most journalists are dispatched in a hurry and get in-country before the borders are closed. Others must make their way in by whatever means necessary. *DP* is part of the latter.

The large networks and news gathering organizations pay extraordinary amounts of money not only to send in news teams but also to charter airplanes, couriers and even military planes to get their dispatches out of the country. Satellite telephones and transmitters make it easy to send reports now, but the units are expensive and heavy to pack.

When Russia sent its troops into Grozny, there were plenty of journalists and reporters. As the situation became embarrassing, the Russians began to simply round up and send journalists out of the country. Previously, Dudayev had expelled all Russian reporters because of their inflammatory articles. When the Russian and Western press began to highlight the Russian incompetence and division, the Russians rounded up the Western press. Unlike major conflicts where the press are carefully clothed, fed, housed and "spun" by briefings, press releases and carefully prepared interviews, Chechnya was the opposite. Russian troops couldn't care less if they shot at the glint of a camera lens or a sniper's telescopic sight. Mortars, bombs and shells dropped by the Russians cared even less.

We wanted to see for ourselves, so we sent in a correspondent to try to understand the situation firsthand. The story of just what it takes to get into a war zone like Chechnya will give you some idea of the new face of reporting war.

We made our preliminary arrangements before leaving Istanbul with the "Caucasus Peoples Federation," a group that was supporting Dudayev's fight in Chechnya, or Chechenstan as it is locally known. The plan was to allow us to go in with a group of "volunteers," or mercenaries, via Baku in Azerbaijan through Dagestan and then on to Grozny. Although they could provide some forms of transportation to the border, from Hasalyurt we would have to walk for about three days through the mountains in the middle of winter to reach Grozny. Although we were being sent in under the protection of the Chechen forces, there was no guarantee who would be in charge once we arrived.

We set off the day before Christmas with minimal survival gear: our cameras, a stove, some tins of fish and warm clothing. We fly to Baku, in Azerbaijan, to meet the people who will take us into Grozny. The "friends" turn out to be members of the Lezgi Mafia, one of the toughest groups in Russia and the Transcaucasus region. The Lezgi number about 1.5 million and live in the north of Azerbaijan and in south and central Dagestan. Our goal is to fly 1800 km east to Baku and then travel 400 km north along the Caspian Sea through Dagestan and then west 50 km over the border into Grozny.

These entrepreneurial bandits have decided that since things are heating up (and as they don't know the difference between *DP* and NBC), they will need a $5000 transportation fee. Now normally when you make a business transaction in any country, you have some basic understanding of the value of money, and the intentions and general cost of a service. When you are dealing with the Mafia in Azerbaijan, however, there is no guarantee that you will not end up a frozen cadaver with a slit throat two miles out of Baku.

Seeing how we have a plan "B," we have nothing to lose by negotiating this fee down to a paltry $1000 which included transportation, food, lodging but no cable TV.

Plan "B" was the official Russian tour of Chechnya. Most Westerners are not aware of Moscow's new entrepreneurial spirit. Journalists who are accepted can arrange a $4000 junket into Chechnya from Moscow via military transport. We opt for the lower-priced, more adventurous ground operator version via the locals.

We make our deal over tea and cigarettes, and, once accepted, we are as good as kinfolk with these tough characters. Although we are kissing cousins, we also agree to pay our fee once we are over the border in Hasalyurt. The man who is to take us there tells us we will have company. He is bringing in 10 mercenaries and volunteers from Iran, Uzbekistan and Tadjikistan who will be joining us 10 km short of the Azerbaijan-Dagestan border. Oh, he mentions casually, a load of antitank missiles as well. We don't ask him how much money this one trip will clear but it is obvious that war is good for business in these parts.

One of his men drives us two hours north to Quba in a Lada, complete with reflective tinted windows. The Mafia may have money, but they sure don't have taste. We stay at an old Russian farmhouse surrounded by apple orchards as far as the eye can see. Now abandoned, it was a way station and safe house for the Lezgi Mafia. In the courtyard are two tractors with the antitank rockets. The men are packing oranges, apples, flour and other agrarian items to camouflage the clearly labeled crates.

We are awakened early the next morning and set off north toward Qusar, a town about 25 km short of the Dagestan border. We are now traveling in three groups. The first group consists of two Lezgi, who would travel ahead of us to meet with the local officials, grease the border guards, and ensure our safe passage into Dagestan. Behind us come the volunteers, now happy farmers bringing in foodstuffs. The border is officially closed, but the guards just stare dispassionately at us and never bother to even wave us down or check our passports. We thought the mirrored windows were bad taste; now we know their function. Inside Dagestan, we stay in the car until we reach an old Lenin Pioneer Camp, a relic of the Russian regime, where primary and high school kids learned the ways of the revolution. It is the Soviet version of our Boy Scout Camps.

That night we have a typical Azeri meal—smoked meat, and smoked fish, washed down with homemade vodka strong enough to remove paint. Tonight will be cold, but the fire from the vodka will warm us up.

After our feast, we set off down a small side road that leads to the official checkpoint at the border. The cart track is used by the local farmers and is too bumpy to allow large trucks. There is little reason for a 24-hour border patrol, and, by "coincidence," there is no border patrol that night. As we travel along the grey Caspian sea into Derbent, we learn some unsettling news. Moscow has replaced the local police and border guards with special security team members known as "Omon." This is indeed a bad "omen." Security is tight because one of Dudayev's assistants has made a visit to Turkey and asked for the Turks to send assistance to Chechnya via Azerbaijan. The sudden heavy presence of the Russian military is to cut off any aid coming to the embattled capital of Grozny.

We are told this by a Lezgi mafia customs official. The fellow who holds this oxymoronic post advises us that in order for us to continue through Dagestan, we will need to become citizens of the Dagestan Autonomous Region.

That night, a man from the local police force brings two blank passports and we become Dagestanis for $300 each. It is a busy night as we fill out forms, and complete the passports. Before dawn the next morning, it seems that our new status is to be rewarded. Our transport is a brand-new BMW bought (or stolen) in Germany. We leave our old passports behind as partial payment and to avoid being searched and arrested as spies. Dagestan is a war zone with a penalty of two years in jail for crossing the border illegally. The Russian soldiers are also empowered to detain and/or execute people whom they suspect as volunteers or spies.

I wonder who Sefail Musayev is, but I carry his passport thankfully. The fact that we cannot speak a word of Russian makes every border crossing a gut wrencher. The Russians are not in any mood for levity, but our Azeri driver/guide manages to chat and joke our way through a total of seven checkpoints. At each tense checkpoint my hair turns a little greyer, the lines on my face are etched deeper and I wonder what the hell I am doing here. When we reach the bustling city of Mohachkale (or Makhachkala), we finally can breathe. From here it is 170 km to the border of Chechnya. From this point on, our driver knows nothing of the conditions ahead.

We drive on in our beautiful new BMW, feeling like royalty, although we are the last people the Russians want in this area. We come to Kizlar, and our driver stops to talk with a Chechen contact family, who works as a link between the Chechen Mafia and the Lezgi. We ask about the Reuters journalists who are based in Hasalyurt. We have made an earlier deal to use their transmitter and satellite phone. The news is not good. The day before, the Russians severely bombed the Hasalyurt-Grozny road, knocking out a number of bridges. The journalists who were staying in the local sports stadium and using it as a base for their forays into Grozny were rounded up and sent back to Moscow.

After coming this far we have no way to send out our information and no one to take us across the border; all that lies ahead of us is a bombed-out wasteland.

After much discussion with the Chechen family, we learn there is one chance. If we can make it to Babayurt, another border town, we can try to contact a group of Chechen volunteers who are to cross the border soon. They mention that we will be safer in Chechnya, since the Russians are increasing their crackdown on foreigners and volunteers in Dagestan daily.

Kizlar is about 40 km north of Hasalyurt, and Babayurt is halfway in between. One of the refugees from Kizlar staying in the house offers to come with us to help us get into Chechnya and to ease our way past the checkpoints that await us. Our luck holds, because the Russians have concentrated their Omon special forces south of Hasalyurt and the checkpoints to the north are manned by local Dagestanis. We meet up with a group of 20–30 Chechen volunteers who are preparing to cross the border that night. We discuss the various ways into the country. Most agree that to try to walk over the mountains into Grozny is futile since the snow is now 4 to 5 meters deep. The 130-km trip will take at least a full week, with an excellent chance of being attacked by jets or helicopters during the day.

We decide to tag along with the heavily armed volunteers. We begin our trip in a convoy of cars and cross the empty border post. At around midnight, the drivers of the cars drop us off and return. We will continue on foot. We walk for six or seven hours, covering 20 km of frozen lowland impeded only by a slight snow cover. We let the main group of armed volunteers go on ahead of us. Our group was not armed, but if they meet up with the Russians, we are close enough to hear the sound of gunfire before we stumble into the same trap.

The cold is numbing, and we plod on through the night like zombies. The wind whips and slaps our faces making icicles on my mustache. The moon is our only light. After a while, we come upon a dirt track that leads to the village ahead. The wind not only brings cold and pain; it now brings the sound of heavy gunfire, alternately fading and building. Our temperatures begin to rise, as we go through the fields leading down to the village. Rockets and automatic weapons crack and thump in the crystal-clear night. As we crunch our way down to the village, the light of the dull blue sky begins to rise like a curtain at the start of a movie. The sound of the Russian helicopters increases from a muted drumroll to a thunderous chorus.

My cold hands reach for my frozen cameras in anticipation. This is the play for which we have come, the drama to which we have fought so hard for admission. Now on with the show.

—Sedat Aral

COLOMBIA

Un Favorito, Por Favor

Colombia is both a spectacular tropical vacation area and a war zone. Somewhere in the middle is the hard-edged business of drugs that keeps the rich, wealthy and the poor, destitute. I spent quite a bit of time on a tropical island breaking Americans out of jail, diving, and getting a tan. I also got to know the locals very well.

I had agreed to go out with the official's daughter. She was coming into San Andreas tomorrow from Cali for Holy Week. To decline the social request would not be a wise idea. I watched in amazement, as this distinguished gentleman was able to piss in the sink at the same time he was washing his hands. We were in his hotel suite, which served as his full-time home. He was a very high level government official on the island. Instead of wallpaper, he had cases of Mumm's stacked up from floor to ceiling, creating a pleasing but somewhat industrial pattern. His choice of music was limited to the one or two AM radio stations on the island—he used a state-of-the-art quadraphonic stereo system to blast out Julio Iglesias. Like most of his possessions, they were "gifts" or leftovers from customs inspections of travelers.

He explained how he makes his money. He has a group of three to five "beach boys" who sell coconut oil on the beach to tourists. Along with the golden fragrant oil in old beer bottles, they offer hash or marijuana to unsuspecting tourists. As the sun goes down, they turn in the money they've made and carefully point out each and every person who bought drugs that day. During the night, the doors of the surprised victims are crashed down and they're trotted off to jail at gunpoint. They then pay the judge, the lawyer, the DAS, the F2 and, of course, the Aduana dearly for their freedom. In fact, they even have to pay for meals while they are in jail. As he adjusted his evening clothes and carefully combed his hair, I thought he looked rather dashing for a thug.

—RYP

DJIBOUTI
Humanitarian Combat Warrior

The French Foreign Legion is probably the most romanticized military service in the world. Unlike the "legion" of adventure trekkers, climbers and rafters, some people view the military as their path to adventure and glory. Many readers of DP have either served or are curious about serving in this tough brutal corps. This letter from a DP reader gives unusual insight into this world.

I joined the French Foreign Legion at Fort de Nogent on June 17, 1982. I joined for all the stereotypical reasons that young men do. Bored and dissatisfied in the British Army, I had read Simon Murray's book, *Legionnaire*, and decided I wanted to be the best—an elite soldier. Most of all, I wanted to fight. To a certain extent, I achieved that goal. Actually, I went AWOL from the British Army to join the Legion. The first thing my father knew about it was when the M.P.s turned up at his house and started chasing my little brother down the road thinking he was me. (My father was a civil servant, so the whole incident was very embarrassing to him and he was really angry with me, to put it mildly.)

I spent seven months in Beirut in 1983 and two years in Djibouti from 1986–1988. What I didn't realize when I signed up for the first five years was that 99.5 percent of the time I would be bored shitless, and 0.25 percent of the time I would be looking for clean underpants. My experiences in the Legion included work as a parachutist, sniper instructor, cold weather commando, long range reconnaissance patrol, combat diver, amphibious assault, unarmed combat and military skier. I completed my tour of duty as an infantry corporal in charge of nine infantry Legionnaires.

Life in the Legion was like a clip from a recruitment film. Everything I did was regimented. We marched at 66 paces a minute, singing marching songs in French and German. I worked from reveille until almost lights out five days a week and again most of the day on Saturday. Sunday was my day off unless I had guard duty, exercise duty, a course to study or had managed to land in prison. (Speaking of prison, the platoon commander can have you sent to prison for seven days for poor humor and if you're not smiling when you come out, you'll get another 15 days for a permanent bad attitude).

I wasn't permitted to wear civilian clothes for the first five years unless I had a leave pass for 72 hours or more. (I learned you don't get those unless you've spent a tour of four months or more abroad.) My salary in the Legion ranged from UK$2500 to UK$18,000 depending on risk/country. Most of the guys end up spending their wages on knives, cameras, booze, drugs and whores.

Fights are common, not only between Legionnaires but also between Legionnaires and NCOs. So, it's very much a case of survival of the fittest. (Only recently have deaths on Legion bases begun to be investigated.) Rules are strictly enforced. It is not cool to drink a bottle of whisky, smoke an ounce of grass with your mates, then hit the town. It is definitely uncool to beat up a gendarme in Marseille, throw his sidearm in the water and then run away. If he catches up with you and you're arrested, it can take years before you're free.

Life in the Legion is simple, brutal, and seems surprisingly normal because of the indoctrination recruits undergo. The Legion is a politician's dream; the indoctrination is such that, unlike a normal army, where it might be glorious to fall in combat, many Legionnaires think they are already dead. I only began to see it as abnormal after I left.

I left the Legion after my two year tour of Djibouti, moved to England and married the Ethiopian bar girl I had lived with in Djibouti. I had met her at the Hotel Menelek when I was a corporal in the Legion. (Some psychoanalysts might say that I was keeping the Legion with me after I left.) I may have left the Legion physically, but mentally I was, for all intents and purposes, still a Legionnaire. I was tough, arrogant, abrasive, sexist and violent. The first civilian job I took was as a shelf stocker in a supermarket. There was little demand for snipers in Southeastern England. Because I was uncompromising and ruthlessly efficient, I swiftly became shift manager. Most people who knew me before would admit to a grudging respect...but in reality they were frightened by something they could never comprehend.

My marriage broke up and my desire to "get away" led me to Mogadishu in 1993 where I worked for the Save the Children Fund. I ended up doing aid work because I was so desperate to get away from my Ethiopian wife and I thought I could manage logistics better than most (in a war zone!). There are many opportunities for ex-military guys both in the U.N. and in N.G.O.s. For the first time, I started to appreciate people for what and who they are. But I was still a "cowboy" at heart, death and risk were not cognitive thoughts for me.

I met my wife Isabella when she was a nurse working for the Save the Children Fund in Mogadishu. She's a Kiwi and I traveled to New Zealand with her on Christmas Day in 1993. It wasn't until I was racing around Rwanda as team leader for an international rescue committee in 1994, six years after leaving the Legion, that I thought about being killed and realized I had too much to live for. I didn't want to get killed in Rwanda because my wife was four months pregnant. I had finally broken away from the Legion. I was lucky and met the right person. We now have a daughter and live in New Zealand. I love them both very much. They have given me the sense of belonging that I was searching for when I joined the Legion. I'm a very private sort of a guy (as you'd expect from an ex-sniper), I have no close friends other than my wife and daughter. Maybe someday I'll write a novel about my experiences... I'll call it "the Humanitarian Combat Warrior."

—**Martin Gilmore**

ERITREA
The Man Without a Gun

Jack Kramer covered a number of wars and his story of meeting the rebels is one of my favorites. It deals with the fascinating people, place and time that make revolutions so electrifying.

One evening, without prelude and so unexpectedly that for a minute I think he is joking, Kidane says, "Would you like to meet the freedom fighters in the mountains?" As if he is inviting me to dinner. "A squad could cross the border tomorrow night and be back in three days."

I say I'd really like to but unfortunately, I have this prior engagement....

Years later, considerable numbers of reporters, documentarians and writers are to go behind the lines with the Eritreans, not least the Australian novelist Thomas Kineally, who wrote *Schindler's List* and an emotional novel about Eritrea, *To Asmara*. But it will be years before that will happen, years in which the Eritreans will acquire not just tanks and heavy artillery, but much more importantly, jeeps in which to carry us frail vessels called journalists. Meantime, I have just arrived in this distant Sudanese town, barely aware there is a place called Eritrea, which in any case is most decidedly not my objective. Addis is my objective. If I am to go with these people at all, it can't just be across the border and back. Back in Kassala, I'd be in the same fix. It will have to be all the way across the territory to its capital, Asmara, from which I can then get to Addis on my own. Which is of course, a totally hypothetical notion: I am not about to disappear into some trackless hills with an off-the-wall band of African guerrillas.

Kassala is a backwater town on the Atbara River in the Sudan, a few dry miles from the Abyssinian frontier. By Kassala, the vegetation has begun to get thick. But the town is suffused with the atmosphere of the desert. The train station is out of town. I'd just dragged myself off the slow train from Haiya Junction, when suddenly a band of camel-mounted Bedj comes galloping at breakneck speed across the river and into the town.

In town, along with a clutch of Yoruba pilgrims bound for Mecca, I sleep on the floor of one of the outbuildings of the police post, a single-room building devoid of any appointment, save a few straw mats upon which duty officers sleep and pray. A single bald electric bulb burns constantly. Asleep in one corner is Yacoub, trustee and servant, a half-breed with a huge head, for which he was nicknamed, an Ethiopian, or at least, they tell me, in the pay of the Ethiopians. He is serving a sentence for bomb-tossing. "At whom?" I asked. "At the Eritreans," he later tells me. "At the Communists."

I am in no mood to understand. Eritrea is not my objective. My objective is Addis Ababa, and I have a headache: That goes with travel in these parts. It had been hard to get a visa for the Sudan. Americans were being turned down out of hand. Finally, I got a two-week overland permit. Now, it is virtually expired. In London, the Ethiopian embassy said I wouldn't need a visa for Ethiopia. They reminded me what an ally we had in Ethiopia; indeed, almost all the military aid we are sending to sub-Saharan Africa is going to the Emperor, commander of black Africa's largest standing army. "You're an American," they'd said, "a visa for Ethiopia is just a matter of picking one up at the border." Now I am at the border. My Sudanese visa is expiring. His Excellency's consul is hemming and hawing.

It is dangerous to cross here. "*Shiftas*," he says. "Bandits." But just to show what a good chap he is, he'll wire Addis.

It is Thursday. The next day, everything will be shut for the Muslim sabbath. I deal with the tension by pretending to create options should the answer come back as no.

I meet an Indian, a *Hendi*, in Arabic. Does he know the Eritreans? No, he says, over instant coffee at his radio shop, but will I photograph his infant daughter? We bicycle through Kassala's *suk* to his house on some suburban mud flats. I wait in the sitting room, as his mother prepares Japanese Kool-Aid and his wife prepares the baby. The sitting room is dominated by a single ornament: a blinking neon 'Sankyo' sign. As I wait, I see a young Bedj approach the yard with a wooden bowl of fresh milk. At the door, he glances about nervously, almost, it seems, like a wolf in a kennel, sets the bowl down, and hurries off without a word. The Hendi's wife appears with the infant. The child's face has been powdered almost geisha-white, her lips and cheeks are rouged and her eyes are made up like the eyes of houris in ancient illuminations from the Sind. I take the photos, drink the Kool-Aid, the Hendi says thank you, and, as I am leaving, he says that although he does not know the Eritreans, he does know Hassan mi Jack, and Hassan mi Jack knows the Eritreans.

Hassan mi Jack rents and repairs bicycles, refrigerators and Waring blenders. On the wall of his storefront office, which is also his repair shop, there are two pictures: one of Mao as a

young scholar in Kiangsi, another of a female Chinese guerrilla about to pitch a grenade. The man is dark, imposing,
heavy, gregarious. On his head, he wears a fake leopard turban.

"My name is Hassan mi Jack," he says. "They call me Jack
Palance, the Man Without a Gun. Only I have a gun." And
he pulls a.38 revolver from the top drawer of his desk.

Do I want to meet the Eritreans? I will meet the Eritreans.
Unfortunately, he cannot be there to make the introductions,
but if I take a table in the central gardens at about 9:30 in the
evening, they will approach.

The central gardens of Kassala are an overgrown, ragged
place, lit at night by lurid yellow neon bulbs, buzzing loudly
with the electric hum and whine of nocturnal insects. The
great Egyptian diva, Um Kalsoum, hoarse with static, moans
soulfully over two loudspeakers. Small, circular metal tables
are scattered about. A little stand serves fruit juices and tea. I
come early and sit alone with a hot glass of tea. At 9:30
promptly, a young man in a crisp white shirt and black trousers approaches. I stand, we shake hands.

"I am Kidane Kiflu," he says in a clear but exotic English,
the sort of English you hear from those who seldom hear our
difficult language spoken but are especially intelligent and
study hard, the English of a bright but provincial Japanese
schoolboy. "I am of the Eritrean Liberation Front." Years later, when I learned he'd become more than something of a
figure, it wasn't surprising.

We talk of this and that for most of that evening and most
of several following evenings. He speaks of how Italian influence is heavier in Eritrea than it is in the rest of Ethiopia; his
native province has been an Italian colony since the grab for
Africa in the 19th century; the Italians hadn't marched into

Ethiopia proper until the eve of World War II. On the question of independence, he offers the party line. He asks to see what I'd written.

During these days, the Eritrean insurgency is dominated by Muslim Bedouin like those camel-mounted Bedj I'd just seen galloping into Kassala. Kidane Kiflu is a Copt from the densely populated highlands. His native language is Tigrinya, but he also speaks the Amharic of Ethiopia's rulers in Addis Ababa, and well enough to have been accepted at the University in Addis on a scholarship. Like a fellow Copt and native speaker of Tigrinya, Meles Zenawi, who would become the president of Ethiopia, he'd dropped out to join the revolution. But Zenawi, the man who will lead all of Ethiopia in the nineties, is a native of Tigre province just south of Eritrea, and dropped out to fight for the overthrow of the government. Kidane was a native of Eritrea, and, for the sake of a distinct and independent Eritrea, this Tigrinya-speaking Copt had made common cause with Eritrea's Muslim tribes.

Six of us leave Kassala at dusk, squeezed with a driver and all our gear in an old Peugeot taxi that takes off straight out over the desert. There are three scouts—Ismail, Ibrahim and Ali—and two cadres—Abdullah and Abara. We all wear cheap muslin robes over khaki uniforms, the robes to be discarded when we cross the border. The robes of the scouts also cover AK-47s, what they call Kalatchnikovs.

The cadre Abdullah is slight, just seventeen, a quiet zealot. Abara is a heavy, 30-year-old Copt, a former schoolmaster, who seems to be leaving the meager comforts of Kassala with great reluctance. Neither carries a weapon, save a single suicide hand grenade apiece.

Soon enough, the old Peugeot can go no further and we get out and begin walking toward the barren mountains of the border. We walk well into the night. Eventually the sound of domestic animals (agitated at our approach, braying mules, bleating goats, the unloved yapping dogs of Islamic countries) indicates a Bedouin settlement ahead. The Bedouin feed us and we sleep in their huts. For several hours in the morning, we wait for someone to come with a camel, but he never comes. At 5 a.m., we leave the settlement and climb further into the foothills, until finally we come to a deep wadi. Here, we camp, still waiting for the camel. We wait all that day and all the next, changing camps only once, rough muslin robes still over our uniforms.

Abdullah, the young Muslim cadre, digs into the sand of the wadi for water, but finds none. Our supply, kept in goat hides and tasting of goat hide, is running low. He and Abara try to reassure me. They keep repeating the instructions I'd received from Kidane: If anybody asks me who I am, I'm to reply simply that I was a student: "*Ana talib.*"

I fall asleep in the heat, hallucinate a little, and wake-up disoriented, a face in my face asking, who are you?

"*Ana talib.*"

"Who are you!"

"*Ana talib.*"

The camel never comes. Finally, at dusk on the third day, we begin climbing on foot. It is hard. We have to rush. "Hurry," they keep saying. We have to get to the border before dawn. When at last we get to the border, it is just dawn. My feet are swollen. Just over the crest of the last mountain of the border chain, Ibrahim takes out his binoculars and scans the great flat Eritrean plain spread beneath us. At first, it looks greener than the Sudan behind us. It is studded with green acacia trees. In the dawn light, it even looks cool. The dew is heavy. But on second glance, you can see how flattened the acacia trees are, as if bent to the desert wind. Their branches are stiff and thorny. They are almost miniature trees growing close to the ground, and I am to discover beneath them more thorns, barbed ones, that will pierce our shoes and stick to our legs as we walk, so that periodically we'll have to stop and pick them out. And beyond the plain, faint but evident even in the half-light of dawn, you can see another chain. And there will be another, they told me, and another....

It takes a day and a half to reach the second chain; still we'd met no one. The whole trip is to take seven days. Four and a half days have passed. We'd barely penetrated Eritrea. The evening of the fifth day, the scout Ibrahim comes running back, gesturing, "*Yacoub. Wahid sanaf b'il Abu Shanab.*"

Yacoub is what he calls me; *wahid sanaf* is one squad. Soon enough, from just over a rise at the horizon, there they are— seven men, widely dispersed, at the extremities, uniformed riflemen with Enfields, just left of center a man with a Bren gun, and slightly to the rear, a native leading a camel.

Neither group quickens pace, though we can see each other long before we meet. In our group, only Ibrahim, the joker, is vibrant, the rest betray no emotion, though surely they are glad finally to have made contact. Nor does any sign come from the advancing squad, no shouts, no waves. When we are within talking distance, Abara, the older cadre, says, "*Salaam alaiykum,*" "Peace be with you" to which the leader of the advancing squad (older than the rest, middle-aged, moustached, a.45 strapped to his hip, a camel crop in his hand) says, "*Alaiykum salaam*" "With you be peace." When finally they reach each other, they embrace in a long and formalistic ritual, and then we all do the same with each member of the squad, in the same long and formalistic ritual we are to repeat across the breadth of Eritrea, a ritual characteristic of all the Horn and Arabia and, to a lesser extent, Arab and Islamic cities, asking questions about the well-being of mothers, fathers, brothers, sisters, uncles, aunts and cousins, all of whom we will hear are well (whether they are or not). And our mothers, fathers, brothers, sisters? Well indeed, we say. And theirs? Well indeed. And again, they ask of ours. And again, we ask of theirs.

Little emotion is shown, but our collective sentiment is close to true joy. It is evening. We build a fire and rest for the night, drinking rancid but wonderful water from whole, untanned hides of goats.

The next morning we set out for the camp of Abu Shanab, this time with a camel to share. As we move, the scouts fan out and come back with reports: Many people, they say, have heard that a white man is coming. I can't imagine where in this barren country "many people" might be, and the notion of a man uniquely white rings as archaic as being called Mr. Jack by Abdullah and Abara. But the next morning, two native runners catch up with us to find out if it is true. Abdullah tells me we will soon be in the camp of Abu Shanab, and the day after that, just before we reach the camp, we pass through a Bedouin settlement, fenced by thornbush against unseen predators: jackal, wild dog, leopard. From atop the camel, I can just barely make out the forms of black-robed women as they peer out at us from the shadows of the doorways of their huts.

There are many more natives at the camp than uniformed guerrillas and many camels. Some of the natives wear crude muslin robes, but others are dressed like those wild Bedj back in the Sudan, Kipling's fuzzy-wuzzies, with elaborate gold, orange and turquoise robes with leather girdles, leather-sheathed sabres, knives and elaborately saddled camels. All wear their hair in those great fuzzy-wuzzy dos, all carry stout staves. The guerrillas wear uniforms like us, khaki shorts, khaki shirts. All mingle together, in assemblies under trees.

Abu Shanab is a big man with a sergeant-major moustache and a sergeant-major's booming voice. The natives argue loudly among themselves, and one has to be led from the meeting by a guerrilla sergeant-at-arms. At this, a nine- or ten-year-old boy in guerrilla uniform and carrying a small Italian carbine, jumps to his feet and begins shouting, apparently in defense of the native. Abu Shanab waves for him to be quiet, but he goes on. Abu Shanab waves again, and the same guerilla sergeant-at-arms drags the young boy—screaming and in tears—from the assembly. The assembly, which has been laughing lightly, laughs aloud and goes back to its dispute.

The boy, it turns out, is Abu Shanab's recalcitrant son, sent to the field with his father by a mother who can't handle him.

The next day we leave Abu Shanab's camp with a fresh camel and fresh scouts, but things do not go well. We all get sick, and all around us is sickness and death. The twentieth day out of Kassala, thirteen days past schedule, it begins to seem we are traveling in broad circles. Abdullah is offended by the question. Abara rubs his feet and brushes his hair and says something about a battle somewhere, something about helicopters. It is hot.

####

There are many Ethiopians who honestly believe Eritrea is part of Ethiopia and Americans who see Haile Selassie as a heroic figure who was right to want Eritrea.

There were many knowledgeable Americans who saw the war here as the stuff of devious Levantine politics, clandestine factions, sinister games of cell versus cell. It was hard to argue with all that went on. In one nearly self-defeating episode of internecine killing, the original Eritrean Liberation Front, heavily Muslim, Arab-financed, was subsumed by the breakaway Eritrean People's Liberation Front, led primarily by Tigrinya-speaking Copts like Kidane—in fact, by Tigrinya-speaking Copts inspired by Kidane.

To Americans knowledgeable of all this, I was hopelessly naive. Exasperated, one once looked at me and asked, "Do you really think what you've got here is Emiliano Zapata and his boys?"

I didn't have anything to say, so he filled the awkward silence: "Of course, that's reducing it to the absurd, but do you really think…"

In fact, I hadn't taken it as a reduction to the absurd at all. Zapata and his boys were exactly how I saw them and never mind the Levantine moments.

On the evening of that twentieth day, as our latest complement of scouts (at each guerrilla encampment, a new set would take over) genuflects deeply in the evening prayer (a white spot of sand on their dark foreheads as they rise), it becomes suddenly and frighteningly clear: We have been traveling in circles. We are supposed to be traveling northeast, almost precisely in the direction of Mecca. But if the direction we are traveling is truly northeast, then Mecca will have to be due south, for the guerrillas are facing due south from the direction they have told me is northeast.

Abdullah, the zealot, himself suffering disease, refusing comfort, pushing himself, says nothing. Abara admits it. "Just trust us," he says.

Somewhere out there, something vague is happening, and then something not so vague, a battle we don't even hear, and then its backlash, forever and unexpectedly raking past us. We travel almost entirely by night.

One evening, they tell me a runner has brought orders for them to leave me. They introduce me to Hassan, an Arabic-speaking young cadre, who will take me to the other side of the town of Keren. Down the slope, by two wounded guerrillas, a female guerrilla, the only one I'd ever seen with them, is helping to pack and saddle a mule. They ask me to give them all my tape, all my 35mm film, all my notes. It is supposedly for my protection, and again they put me through the drill: If I am picked up and they ask me who I am, what am I to say?

"*Ana talib*, I'm a student."

"Just trust us," they say. But they don't watch closely, and it is possible to wrap one roll of 35 mm in a sock and to stick the sock in a hip pocket. Leaving the bivouac with Hassan, I turn in the saddle to wave good-bye. The pressure of the 35 mm cartridge in my hip pocket spikes any tendency toward excessive sentiment.

From then on, says Hassan, we will move exclusively by night. Hassan is a different sort of cadre than Abdullah and Abara. He speaks English hardly at all, only Tigre, a Sematic language close to Tigrinya but more characteristic of Eritrea's Muslims, and Arabic, long the *lingua franca* here, and that is how we use it. He is quiet, confident, and with the scouts (there are now three), much more the combat commander. And yet, for all that, he carries no weapon, only that single hand grenade.

The first morning out, Hassan leads the way up a short pass to an escarpment high above a valley. The valley is vast and much different from the valleys behind. The countryside is green, and I can see farms plotted out to a far horizon. From the hell behind, it looks like some fairyland ahead. The descent into the valley is very nearly precipitous. The mule is surefooted, but often I have to dismount as the trail winds down along ledges that keep disappearing into the face of the cliff.

At the bottom, we are in high grass country. We stop briefly by a village. The village structures are more permanent here. A delegation comes out, there is some nervous negotiation, and one of the village men comes along with us as a guide. He leads us at a quick pace to a wadi with high grass growing on either side, so that I cannot be seen, even atop the mule. We proceed single file down the wadi, one man behind me, Hassan just in front, the others in front of him, the point man way ahead. We move about half an hour, when suddenly shots crackle in the air. Hassan spins, waving me back, shouting "Ethiopi! Ethiopi!" Blood leaves my head; I wheel about on my mule and gallop back up the wadi. Then, just as suddenly, there are more shouts. "*Agif! Agif!*" ("Stop. Stop!") I pull up my mule and look back. Hassan, kneeling, is looking back as well. The shots have stopped. There are still shouts from back down the wadi. It turns out that it is not Ethiopians at all, but another guerrilla squad that has mistaken us for Ethiopians as we have them, and opened fire. We have been approaching each other at the junction of two wadis. As I reach the junction, I see our point man genuflecting deeply in prayer. Each time he rises, I can see that white patch of sand on his dark forehead.

The night is cold. At the next village, there are more nervous negotiations and finally a new guide. As we are about to leave, the new guide refuses and we have to wait for another.

At last he comes, there are some hurried whispers in the dark, and we take off so quickly that there is no time to explain, myself atop the mule, galloping up the wadi, while (to my total astonishment) the others run along on foot beside me, keeping right up. As I gallop, the black, thorny branches whip and cut my face. We are moving fast, too fast, it seems to me, for even these tough men to last. There is no actual panic, but the heavy breathing of the running men, and of my galloping mule, and the rushing slap of plastic sandals on the sand of the wadi strike a distinct note of hysteria held in hard check.

The branches whipping out from the embankment of the wadi get thicker, the shadows ever more black. There is no moon, hardly any sky to be seen above the suddenly dense vegetation in this near-desert country. Eventually, it crowds in so close that there is barely room to move single file, and at last we are forced to slow down. Just as I think the vegetation can get no thicker, we suddenly break into a large clearing which turns out to be the soggy bed of the Anseba River.

"Halhal," Hassan whispers, "Halhal min Anseba." It is all he needed to say, for he knows that I have learned well enough of Halhal, an Ethiopian combat base, and the name of a major battle that had been fought during the worst of the miseries with Abdullah and Abara, and aside from disease and infection, the reason for those miseries. As we move through country, the Ethiopian Second Division is scouring to find the guerrillas who have attacked Halhal. Though it is the dry season, in the middle of the bed the river still runs, black and deep.

Twice we follow promontories that seem to lead to the other side, wading up to our chests. It is cold, dark. Both times we have to turn back. The water rushes about my feet, as I ride the mule toward the other side. The guide, the guerrillas and Hassan cut in front of me, cross and scout up the river. Just over halfway, the mule suddenly begins sinking into the sandy bottom. She panics and throws me into the river. I am up and after her, but her panic is compounded as she struggles to pull herself free and sinks ever more deeply into the sucking bottom. I am into it myself nearly to my ankles, the water about my waist. She is down to her rear haunches. The others are in front of me, out of sight. I pull at the mule's saddle. Her eyes bulge. She heaves against the sucking sand. She seems to be coming out of it. In the cold I begin to sweat, and to sweat more. I feel somewhere near panic myself, but look at that panicked, stupid mule, eyes bulging, inviting disaster even as she is slowly coming free and think I can't be that stupid. In the midst of our mutual sweat and pulling, this mountain-nimble animal lurches free with an awkward heave and stumble. Afoot, I drag her up the Anseba, toward the men, remembering Hassan's whispered, "Halhal min Anseba…" and find relief from the fear and tension in anger: "The idiots!" I fume silently at my betters. All that noise. Then I discovered the reason for their slight commotion in the dark. They have discovered an orange grove and are delightedly picking oranges. Oranges! The first fresh thing I will have had in 21 days, a steady diet of sour milk and gruel finally broken. Sweating, soaking wet, shivering in the cold, we suck on oranges one after another.

Leaving Anseba and its little jungle, we begin once again to climb. Unlike Abdullah and Abara, they are able to tell me what is happening. Now, at last, we are due north of the town of Keren. We'd begun southwest of it. The plan was to circle the town, ending up southeast of it. We couldn't move directly from the point southwest to the point southeast, because the turf in between is securely in the hands of reinforced Ethiopian brigades, as is the town. A trip that might have taken a few minutes by car, a few hours by foot, is taking three or four days. Fatigue hits hard at three in the morning. Once again, we are very high up. Just before dawn one of the scouts pulls on my sleeve and bids me look back. I look back, twisting in the saddle. Beneath us, I can see, quite clearly, the lights of enemy-held Keren, the first electric light I will have seen in 21 days. Dawn is just breaking as we collapse, still soaked, on a cold mountain hillside.

The next day is pleasant. It is warm. We spend all day just lying about the hills, a lot like the foothills around San Francisco. We joke, eat some more Anseba oranges. A goat is brought up to us from one of the villages below, and we slaughter it. One of the guerrillas slings his Kalatchnikov over the branch of a tree, and, straight-faced, I pretend to reprimand him for something every recruit in every decent army is disciplined not to do; if we are surprised, he will have to stand up to get it. I never imagined myself their superior, but I'd put on their uniform and should have been. He takes me seriously. Hassan chews him out. They'd all been trained not to do that, he says and he tells me of his training in Syria, how fortunate he is to have been sent there, how much he'd learned. For example, he says, he'd never before known that 80 percent of the U.S. population is Jewish and that the war in Vietnam was being fought to make money for Jewish millionaires. "And I know it's true," he says. "I've seen pictures of their houses."

In the late afternoon, a headman, a Copt, comes up from one of the villages. We talk, eat another meal, and he offers me his daughter in marriage if I settle in his village.

In the evening, I go down to the village to prepare for the night's march. I'd taken off my uniform. I am to leave Hassan and his squad, the last of the guerrillas. From then on, the headman will lead me. From then on, Hassan reminds me, I can tell no one who I am or where I'd been. "Who are you?" he smiles.

"*Ana talib.* I'm a student."

The squad follows me down. All day we'd been joking. Now they are silent.

Near the edge of the village, the headman saddles my new mule. It is a nasty beast. It bucks and kicks as he rides it, but finally it settles down. He gets off, I get on, and again it begins to buck and kick. Finally, it settles down and I am about to ride around a hut when Hassan stops me.

"Not yet," he says. "The men are preparing."

I get down off the mule. Hassan looks around the corner of the hut. "OK. Now." I follow him around.

The squad is standing at attention, their ragged uniforms squared away to the best of all possible efforts. Hassan comes to position before them. He calls them to present-arms, and they bring their rifles up in snappy British manual. Hassan executes an about face and hand-salutes. Not knowing quite how to respond, awkwardly, I return his salute. He calls the men to port-arms. I shake his hand and thank him, and we embrace as we had in the desert. With each of the men I do the same. The headman come forward with the mule, I mount and we leave. Just once, I twist in the wooden saddle to wave back; it is a different wave than it had been a few days before, with that 35mm cartridge in my pocket. It is dusk. They are the last guerrillas I am to see.

As night comes, time begins alternately to rush at me and slow down to excruciatingly long hours. I lose all sense of it. He moves relentlessly, this old headman. We move upward through narrow corridors, dark cathedrals of rock that rise forever, echoing every pebble drop. I am barely able to stay awake. I keep slipping from the saddle, waking in rude starts. It is cold, silken webs spread from tree to tree, brushing across my face, and I am constantly hallucinating—old friends wait for me, perched in trees just ahead; old loves lie dead on the boulders beneath me; jackals bark accusations, howl of my guilt; Ethiopians lie in wait. We move on, slipping over rocks, through unseen thorned branches that whip at our faces, down gullies, over boulders, up narrow rock defiles that bruise our ribs as we smash against them. Up and up, again to high mountains. Finally, we stumble into a village. Dogs are yapping. The headman leads me to a hut and calls out by the thorn fence that surrounds the hut. Two adolescent boys come out. The headman speaks with them, and we enter the mud hut, warming ourselves at a small coal fire. The headman is exhausted. He speaks briefly with the boys, and then suddenly there is a fight. The headman springs at one of them and begins beating him with his fists. The second boy steps in, and we settle back down by the fire. I am confused, but without the strength to meet my confusion. I just want to sleep. For the first time, I notice how much this second boy looks like Kidane Kiflu.

In gentle textbook English, he asks me who I am, why I had come.

"I'm a student," I mumble, "*Ana talib.*"

"No," he said. "I know who you are. I know why you come. You come for freedom."

The headman disappears. Just before dawn this boy with the face of Kidane Kiflu wakes me up, leads me down to the Asmara road and says good-bye. I stick my thumb out. Within forty minutes I am atop a semi loaded with tractor tires. An easy hour after that, I am in Asmara—high, cool and Italian, where congenial Neapolitans prepare cappuccino with the latest machines.

True to their word, the Eritreans return all my tape, notes, film. They haven't even bothered to develop the film. Kidane sent the package, and with it a letter in long hand, in the same exotic English: "Allow me please to convey to you my heart-felt greetings. I hope you have had an enjoyable and not ag-onizing experience...due to the terranian nature of Eritrea and due to circumstances. I hope to write to you of the latest developments. I saw your article on a Lebanese Newspaper and our people here are startled by your presentation. Please convey Greetings to all members of your Family."

I have said that in the years after I met him in Kassala, Kidane Kiflu became something of a figure. I've also said that Eritrea never commanded much attention in the U.S. Kidane Kiflu became well known in the small world of the Eritreans, and I only learned of his prominence in the course of dry re-search.

Poring over a propaganda tract mimeographed on pink paper in which the Eritrean People's Liberation Front at-tempted to explain why it had been forced to move against the Muslim leadership of the Eritrean Liberation Front, I came at last to the middle of the last paragraph of the thir-teenth page:

"...they placed six members in prison and subjected them to harsh treatment. Further, right in the heart of Kassala they murdered the two revolutionary fighters, comrades Kidane Kiflu and Welday Gidey, who for many years had energetical-ly worked to redirect the course of the struggle. They were under the impression that if they killed these valiant and insightful leaders, the rest could hardly accomplish anything. The dead bodies were placed in sacks and put on a taxi to be transported to a trash dump called Hafera. On the way, however, as if to plead their case to the world-public, the corpses of the two martyrs fell out in the middle of the street."

—**Jack Kramer**

ETHIOPIA
Sharifa's Story

The revolution in Eritrea was the first country created by Africans from an African country. What was more impressive was the role of women in fighting for their new homeland. The suffrage of women was not given to them by men it was fought for with blood, sweat and tears.

The first time I heard of Sharifa, I wondered if she were real. Her tale was so perfect. She couldn't be. She had to be.

Then I heard the story again, and then again. Three sources—real story. And then months later, I heard it yet again. The ring of myth was beginning to attend Sharifa. Sometimes her name wasn't even Sharifa, and, with each telling, her beauty became more storied. As if the women of Abyssinnia are not beautiful enough as is, and as if her story would be any the less were she not beautiful.

Regardless, a story with a life of its own is a reality in its own right, and this one is Eritrea, through and through.

When I was there, way back in 1968, she must have been about three. Twelve years later, she was her father's pride, about 15, with an ability to maintain her modesty and flash her eyes at the same time, dressed always in the gauzy folds of white and brilliant color—turquoise, yellow, orange—colors characteristic of Muslim women's dress in this part of the world. Tattoos graced her forehead; she was laden always with hand-hammered jewelry, some of it washed in gold, some of it 14 karat.

Her father, a widower, was not a vastly wealthy man, but he was a merchant in a part of the world that is anciently mercantile and where women have been walking banks, wearing much of the family's wealth as jewelry. Of course, it's a man's world. Sons, especially first sons, are what count. But Sharifa's big brother had frustrated, even humiliated, their father. He'd rejected his family responsibilities, his inheritance, had run off to fight a war that was clearly unwinnable.

At least, he had Sharifa. Second only to a father's pride in his eldest son was his pride in a beautiful, marriageable daughter, bedecked in jewels that spoke of family status, of a father's accomplishment, of security.

Unmarried daughters may have been seen as burdens for some; for Sharifa's father, she represented security even more than her jewels. She stood for home and family, as much as impetuous young sons stood for the insecurity that was everywhere. Sharifa was a daughter of substance, exhibiting with schooled perfection the well-known modesty of Muslim women in public, exhibiting just as clearly (at least for her father) the less well known power a strong woman can wield within the family. His male world, after all, was itself largely one of competing, bargaining, feuding families. Fathers put themselves at the center of those families, but in each one, it is a woman who is the essential element.

Sharifa was an astute questioner of the details of her father's all-male palavers, having an active mind focused always on the family; she had in effect replaced her brother as her father's point of pride.

It was a scene full of timeless qualities, set in a part of the world that often seems timeless. The proud, well-to-do, but vulnerable merchant father, the almost predictably rebellious son, the female as an anchor in a sea of troubles.

The one element that isn't timeless, of course, is the specifics of the prodigal son's defection. There's nothing timeless about Soviet tanks.

Of course, he put it all in what he called "revolutionist" terms...which don't quite stand the test of time. The reader would recognize it for the propaganda it was and, likewise, my callow gullibility for what it was. In fact, it's probably best to leave the arguable details of their war with Ethiopia to the *Oxford Companion to World Politics*, whose entry on the subject was written by an Ethiopian scholar:

> *With its defeat in World War II, Italy relinquished its legal right to its colonies to...France, the United Kingdom, the United States and the Soviet Union [to] dispose of...by agreement, failing which they would submit the matter to the UN General Assembly. Libya's and Somalia's cases were determined without much ado at the UN; Eritrea proved to be difficult, principally because of Emperor Haile Selassie's interest in acquiring it, and U.S. strategic and geopolitical interest in the Red Sea region. The convergence of these two interests and the dominant U.S. position sealed the fate of Eritrean self-determination.*

> *Instead of gaining independence, as demanded by the majority of its inhabitants, Eritrea was joined with Ethiopia in a lopsided federation...imposed by a U.S.-engineered resolution. Eritrean protests were ignored by the UN, which bore responsibility for the integrity of the federation. Finally, emboldened by the impunity*

with which he had violated the UN arrangement, Emperor Haile Selassie abolished the federation in 1962....

####

I've never seen a massacre, and with luck I'll never see one. In Vietnam, Eritrea, the western Sahara, Iran, Lebanon and the southern Sudan, I've seen mute evidence, heard stories, but I'm reluctant to repeat them. What can I really know of them? Talk is cheap. Suffice it to say that sometime near the end of the seventies, when Sharifa was 15 and her father's pride, her village suffered a massacre.

We don't know who they lost. We just know that while her father kept functioning, he apparently went days unable to talk. He must at some point have felt rage as well as grief, but when he did speak, he saw the war no differently. It was foolishness. This was Ethiopia. Even counting Eritrea's Christians, they were at best 3 million barely armed men, women and children against the tanks and bombers of a nation of 58 million.

And beautiful Sharifa? She witnessed her father's grief, but showed none, and then one day her father came home and she was gone. Where? "We're not sure," her sisters said. "She left most of her jewelry."

"Where?" her father repeated.

"To join the revolution."

In a rage, he gathered up two men and three camels and galloped into country he'd never dared enter and found her at a training camp, about to be inducted. He insisted she return. She refused. He raged that this was no fit enterprise for a woman; it was indecent. He grabbed her. She pulled back. He called her a whore. He said she was no longer any daughter of his. He demanded her remaining jewels. She ripped them off and threw them at him. For the past 15 years, they had spent every day of their lives together. They were not to see each other again for another 15 years.

####

By the time young Sharifa reached the field at the end of the seventies, a lot had happened. The Muslim-led Eritrean Liberation Front I found in Kassala had become the Eritrean People's Liberation Front. After barely surviving a spate of internecine bloodletting, it was now run primarily by Tigrinya-speaking revolutionaries like Kidane, but with Muslim recruits like Sharifa joining, as she would put it, "by the tens."

In the year after Haile Selassie was deposed, the Front had virtually won the war, with its troops occupying major towns and even entering the capital. Again it had suffered brutal losses, as the Soviets and Cubans intervened massively for the Dergue. Then came hunger, as the Ethiopians pursued a scorched-earth policy, which international aid agencies, in need of Ethiopian approval to move relief supplies, felt constrained to portray as "drought." Then came famine, as the Ethiopians used food as a weapon, refusing to let relief through to Eritrea.

But they survived, and now they were rebuilding, yet again, but this time they were building something more.

No longer heavily Muslim, the Front no longer had the appeal it once did for Arab backers, but it still had some. Meantime, the force it was fighting was fat with Soviet hardware, which meant that after most engagements, more Soviet hardware was carefully inventoried in the bush warehouses of the Eritrean Peoples Liberation Front.

The likes of Kidane Kiflu are now credited with enormous organizational and logistic talent. To Ethiopian pilots flying

Northrup F5s, MiGs and Antonov bombers, the ground below looked barren, deserted by a population on the run. When I was with them, it was indeed barren. But this was Sharifa's time. Laboriously hidden from view in country with virtually none of Vietnam's notorious jungle cover were machine shops, munitions factories, motor works and fuel depots. There were truck yards for tractor-trailers and tanker trucks, whose drivers made routine nightly runs cross-country, off the road, over hostile turf, as well as hidden warehouses of stolen materiel, artfully inventoried for efficient access. In addition, there were hospitals in caves, staffed by young Eritrean surgeons and internists trained largely in the U.S. and Italy. Hospitals complete with operating theaters, intensive care wards, maternity wards, infectious disease wards, rehabilitation wards in which amputees were forever busy making artificial limbs, processing paperwork, issuing orders.

But more than all that, in a part of the world long maligned for its bloodymindedness, home of the baboon, the hyena, the cutthroat clan bandit, and after a trying contest that had pitted Muslim Eritrean against Christian Eritrean, they were forging some wildly diverse people into a unified nation.

Right through the war, Western intelligence experts who were convinced that Eritrea's Copts wanted to be part of Coptic Ethiopia and that its Muslims wanted to be part of the Sudan, simply refused to believe what was happening, and they couldn't be blamed. Here, indeed, was a people ready to die for their God, their tribe, their clan, their family, maybe even for the ancient Empire of Ethiopia. But for Eritrea? What was Eritrea besides a short-lived Italian colony, populated by dozens of tribes anciently antagonistic to each other, with virtually no national or religious coherence?

In fact, tiny Eritrea is so diverse that it may be more representative of the Horn of Africa than any other country. In the vastness of the Somali steppe and along the Somali coast, virtually everyone is Somali, save a few Bantu who are farmers...and, for that matter, can be found farming along the Red Sea coast of Arabia. The Sudan, of course, is richly diverse, and in the south has a large population of blue-black Nilotes, many of whom have given up their river gods for Christianity. But the Sudan's diversity is spread over yawning territories, and it is an indelibly Muslim state. Likewise, Ethiopia has many Muslims, but is an indelibly Christian place. Eritrea has all the variety of these much larger places, even a few Nilotes who worship river gods, and it sits perched between the Horn's Muslim and Christian worlds.

This makes for an interesting place to write about, but it does not make for a nation; some argue it makes for everything a nation is not.

Go tell it to the Eritreans.

They made Sharifa a forward observer for a mortar crew. It was a shock. She thought maybe she'd be a nurse. She didn't complain.

In all my time in Eritrea, nearly a month from west to east, I saw just one female guerrilla. But nearly a dozen years had passed since then, and Sharifa wasn't unique. There were thousands like her.

Part of the reason was the vision of leaders like Kidane Kiflu, who had made the revolution. Another reason was the men—the rank-and-file troops, the brothers, uncles, cousins, fathers of these young women—men who would ordinarily never tolerate such disgrace to their women, but now had a special reason not to protest.

They were dead.

This is not the United States, where every year feminists break new ground, but women still do not serve in combat. This is a part of the world where women are confined not just by ancient religious stricture, Christian and Muslim, but are often circumcised, which means considerably more for a young bride than a young boy; it means that her clitoris is cut off. It's a part of the world where it is not rare for a woman to be infibulated, which means her vaginal cleft is sewn tight— pleasure for her man, excruciating pain for her.

When Sharifa joined the Front, the Ethiopian Army was a quarter million strong. There were at best 90,000 Eritreans wearing the uniform of the Front, and so many men had died that almost 30,000 of those troops were young women like Sharifa.

Were most spared combat? Every guerrilla is a combat guerrilla. Every square foot of Eritrea was contested. She must have been stunned: all around her, women, pious young Muslim women, sweating with men, amputating limbs, loading trucks, loading shells into the breeches of heavy artillery, locking and loading in combat.

She was wounded, recovered in an underground hospital, was wounded again, married a guerrilla named Osman, the commander of a squadron of captured Soviet tanks, gave birth to a daughter in the same underground hospital, got a letter from her brother on another front, got a letter that her brother was dead.

Did her father know? She did not even try to write. The "field" was another world. For most of the guerrillas, there could be no communication with that world back in the villages. These boys and girls did not march off to war. They simply slipped away. In the hearts of their parents, each was given a funeral, and she knew that her father was no different.

You do not send a child off to serve the duration of a 30-year guerrilla war and expect him to return; few did. After the war did finally end, there was story after story of elderly mothers and fathers suffering heart attacks when unannounced, their "long-dead" child showed up at the door. Sharifa knew that she was as much in the world of the dead as her brother.

Still, there were victories. Eritreans in tanks meant a war with front lines, trenches. Liberated zones. She dug trenches and helped administer liberated zones, and here she could see more clearly how the men were responding. There was no shame. They called their young women in uniform "our backbone."

But yet there was an undercurrent. She had lost her long beautiful hair, gone off to war, and everywhere, the men respected her, but it seemed much like the respect they paid the infirm who had gone off to war and lost a leg. In the villages, the beautiful young girls in their robes and jewelry looked up with awe at these young women with cropped hair. In this world where girls began losing their marriageability at 19, these young women were delaying marriage to serve. Some like Sharifa would marry guerrillas. More often the men with whom she fought would marry the pretty young things with long hair. Now and then, a guerrilla married to a female guerrilla would divorce her for the "genuine article." In one village, there was a father very proud of his short-haired daughter in uniform, but he would not let her near his other daughters.

The 3 million souls of Eritrea never enjoyed the support of a great, or even second-rank power. Ethiopia, a nation of 58 million, had the support first of the U.S. and then of the Soviet Union. As the Soviet Union imploded, the largest standing army in sub-Saharan Africa began to weave like a punch-drunk fighter.

Methodically, the Eritreans closed in. Again, Sharifa was wounded. Again, she was in a hospital in a cave, but this time her husband Osman was able to visit. It was spring, 1991. A huge Ethiopian garrison held both Asmara and its U.S.-built airbase, out of which the Ethiopian Air Force was now flying constant bombing runs. An Eritrean force swung around to the south of Asmara and cut the garrison off, virtually inviting the Ethiopians to commit yet more troops to relieve their men in Asmara.

The Ethiopians accepted the invitation. The full force of the Ethiopian Army—heavy artillery, self-propelled guns, troops in armored personnel carriers, tank brigades deployed on either side of the Asmara Road—rolled north, supported by Ethiopian fighter-bombers flying out of both Addis and Asmara.

Osman's squadron of captured, jealously maintained Soviet tanks was called to join the battle.

In May 1991, Ethiopian fighter-bombers out of Asmara and Addis hit the Eritrean force with air-to-ground missiles and napalm. The tanks closed in. Inside Asmara, the Ethiopian force deployed to break out and link up with the relief force. It was not to be. When it was finished, more than a battle was over. A 31-year war had come to an end.

The Ethiopian Army was in the midst of a panicked retreat from which it would never recover. Eritrea was free. Osman was dead. Sharifa went home.

There was no way she could call ahead. Outside of Asmara, Eritrea still doesn't have much in the way of phone service. She could only show up, the prodigal daughter, old and tired, with short hair, a daughter and no husband. She told herself she had nothing to be ashamed of. If she was still disowned, so be it.

He was stunned, of course. He didn't say a thing. But as it began to get dark, he moved his belongings out of his bedroom and into the mud courtyard in the back. He said the house was hers. She was the head of the family now. "I was wrong," he said.

—Jack Kramer

A Run For the Border: Northwestern Ethiopia

Getting into war zones can be one of the most heart-stopping events in a DP'ers life. In this case the Sudanese representatives of the SPLA assured Roddy that he would have no problem getting in to cover the fighting between the SPLA and the north. Luckily another DP contributor, Jim Hooper got in through the south and returned unscathed. Roddy however was made a guest of the Ethiopian army for a while.

From the air Assossa looks like a dismal and singularly uninteresting town, but typically African with its corrugated iron rooftops reflecting the sun's glare. The flight from Addis Ababa, the Ethiopian capital, has taken almost two and a half hours and is about to deposit me on the border with Sudan— where I am heading to join the Sudanese People's Liberation Army (SPLA) on their latest spring offensive against the Islamic government of Khartoum.

For the previous week in Addis Ababa I engaged in a series of meetings with the local representative of the SPLA to work out a series of rendezvous points along the border. Theoretically, providing I can slip past the Ethiopian army on the border, my crossing is all arranged. I will be meeting SPLA guerrillas at one of three places on the other side of the border. There is only one border, temporarily closed, to cross.

On landing, Assossa is as depressing on the ground as it looked from the air. There are no taxis, nor any other type of transport, a soldier informs me while eyeing me curiously. It is an inauspicious start. Plans A and B have automatically flown out the window. Only Plan C is left. I mull it over as I check into a hotel, only distracted momentarily when the reception takes one look at me and immediately doubles the price on the grounds that I am a foreigner. It is, I muse, a pity I can't give him something nice in return...like forged money which, with a bit of luck, would see him in prison for a few years (preferably after I am long gone). But then we can't have everything. And, aside from the lack of electricity and running water, the hotel is actually quite nice.

Sitting on the bed I pull out a military map of the border area and with a Silva compass begin to work out the bearings. Plan C is a night march across the border, which is roughly 25 km as the crow flies. I plan on being able to leave the town at 3 a.m. This would give me four hours until I have to find a spot where I can rest for the day before completing my march across the border the following night. In the meantime I wander around town: first to find out if there are any buses going to Addis the following morning. There is one at 7 a.m. and I'll have to pay on the bus, a helpful official at the rundown bus station informs me. I say I'll probably be on it unless I decide to fly or manage to hitch a lift, which is the fiction I maintain to anyone who asks how long I'll be in town, in the hope that nobody will miss me in the morning. If they do I can only hope that no one wants to take any responsibility for my disappearance.

For the remainder of the day I wander around town looking for the best place to leave in the morning and checking
for any military observation posts in the near vicinity of the
town. But despite the large number of soldiers who, for Africa at least, look at least semicompetent—never a good sign,
there appears to be nothing, except most of the local population, that will hinder my progress. I troop back to the hotel
to wait for darkness. Awakened by a knock on the door, I find
the receptionist wanting my passport for the benefit of one of
the local boys in blue. I refuse to surrender it and say he's already taken all my details.

A couple of hours later he returns and is more insistent. My
passport, he promises, will be returned in a couple of hours.
He swears on everything he can think of and like a fool I believe him.

My passport, when it eventually arrives the following
morning, is accompanied by five rather scruffy individuals in
military uniforms. One of them speaks understandable English and wants to ask me some questions. He tells me to
pack my bags and come with them. Feeling somewhat resigned, I comply, and we all pile into a Russian-made military
jeep. Heading out of town, we take the road that leads north
to the Sudanese border and the town of Kurmuk, which had
been my destination. I am momentarily cheerful at the prospect of getting closer to my destination, even if the chances of
reaching it are rapidly receding. We pull off the road a few
miles out of town into a military camp. As we drive through I
notice nine 105 mm field guns and hundreds of boxes of
shells—fairly normal stuff for a military camp on the border.

Coming to a stop we climb out and I am taken to a room
that obviously serves as someone's sleeping quarters. I make
myself comfortable on the mattress while the translator ex-

plains that they simply want to ask a few questions. The interpreter sits next to me while the trio sitting on ammunition boxes opposite do their best to imitate the Spanish Inquisition. Thankfully it's a poor imitation. Notes are taken on a scrap of paper—only after a pen that works can be found. For half an hour the questions come, anything but thick and fast. The most important questions inquire about my family tree. After giving my name I am asked for my father's name. I give it. Then comes the turn of my grandfather. "He's dead," I say. The interpreter's English breaks down a little here and he passes on "hesdead," as my grandfather's name. "No, he is dead," I repeat. English is obviously not the translator's strongest point, as he now thinks I am correcting his pronunciation and repeats "hesdead" more clearly for the benefit of the three wise men opposite. "Listen you fucking moron, he's dead OK!" I repeat while drawing a finger across my throat. They want to know his name anyway and with a sigh of exasperation, I give it.

After much muttering it's time to pile into the jeep for another cruise around town. This time, however, it appears that they are looking for a more senior officer to deal with my case. He is found, eventually, in a local bar playing cards. He takes one look at me and declares that my presence, so close to the border, is illegal. I try to counter this by arguing, quite truthfully, that no one told me it was illegal and that if it was, why did the official state airlines, Ethiopian Airways, sell me a ticket. An infallible line of argument, I think.

He dosen't see my point of view.

After he issues a rapid string of instructions in Amharic to my escort, I soon find myself en route back to the military camp. I ask what's happening... "You'll be staying a while until your case is resolved," the interpreter informs me. Er, and how long will that be, I casually ask. "Maybe a month," comes the reply. How about a quick telephone call? "No, you're an illegal." Cigarettes? "OK." At least I've got cigarettes: the outlook could be worse.

Arriving back at the base the three wise men, whom I guess to be from military intelligence, a misnomer though it may be, scuttle into a building leaving me in the hands of a succession of different guards, some of whom speak English. I manage to bribe one to make a telephone call to a journalist I know in Addis Ababa. The second I palm the twenty dollars into his hand, (a good two weeks wages), he launches into a denunciation of the dishonesty of the Ethiopian army—no doubt in an attempt to make me confident I can rely upon his absolute integrity and reliability. I suddenly feel that I have almost certainly wasted my money. He is, as we Shakespeare scholars say, protesting a tad too much. With the return of the Three Wise Men I am driven to another part of the camp and installed in a small room with a bed in the corner. Taking out my penknife I carve a '1' into the wall and lie down on the bed.

Allowed to sit outside the following day I pass the hours listening to my walkman and watching the humdrum of the daily camp life. The camp has no perimeter fencing and to stave off utter boredom I make fictional escape plans. The few soldiers who try and talk to me are promptly told to get lost by my personal guard sitting ten yards away with an AK-47 in his lap.

The food the guard brings me is a disaster. I wake up at around 2 a.m. in the sure knowledge that I have about 30 seconds to get to the toilet before disaster strikes. Being locked up, I bang on the door to attract the guard's attention. There is no reply. In desperation I force open the wooden window shutters and poke my head through the window, peer into the darkness and try to scan the buildings around me for any sign of my guard. But he has obviously gone temporarily AWOL. It is, of course, a gross dereliction of duty—but I'm not complaining. As cautiously as I can, I climb out the window before sprinting to the toilet. It's overcast and moonless. No doubt if I was Rambo or Jean Claude van Damme, this would be the moment where I steal the jeep, race out of the camp throwing grenades—which would be handily available—at the few sentries who try to stop me and hightail it to the border and further adventures. But I'm not Rambo, there probably aren't any keys in the jeep, and quite frankly my concerns are more immediate. The toilet would be repulsive to a rat, but in my distressed state, I'm not a rat.

Back at my quarters I light a candle and smoke a cigarette. The light attracts the guard who should have been on duty, and within seconds there's a soldier shoving his face through the window almost shouting in Amharic. I understand the tone, if not the content, and he obviously wants to know what I think I'm doing dressed in the middle of the night, looking as if I am about to escape. Running anywhere (with the possible exception of the toilet) is the last thing on my mind—as I explain to the other soldiers when they promptly turn up at the sound of my guard's raised voice.

After three days my interpreter finally reappears with the Three Wise Men to inform me that my case is being "considered" and to take away a fairly standard map, which they find in my belongings. I have a mental image of a bare room somewhere with a telephone that doesn't work and a variety of officials scratching their heads, drinking tea and wondering what to do about me. There have been no more questions since my initial, somewhat half-hearted, interrogation.

Now, though, the restrictions around me seem to have been lifted, and my cell is the center of attraction with soldiers stopping to ask me what I am doing in the camp and offering me cigarettes. My guard has been changed and my new guard, Abdul, is young and talkative. At 21 he has been in the army since age 16 and somehow speaks better English than any of his superiors. "Don't worry," he reassures me, "You have absolutely nothing to worry about, we are brothers." Nice though this is to hear, I can't quite see on what evidence he is able to base this optimistic judgment; and as for being brothers, well...he still has the AK-47, however kind he is. He does, however, let me exercise: and for five minutes in the morning and evening I am allowed to stretch my legs and jog the 20 yards or so between the barracks where I am being held, before being most cordially invited to resume my seat.

On the fourth day I get my answer while enjoying a late nap—there isn't much else to do. The Three Wise Men and an assortment of commanders crowd into my room, with smiles and grins all-around and inform me that I'm about to be released. After a hasty shave I'm driven to the grass runway and left to wait for the plane.

—**Roddy Scott**

INDIA

Kashmir Sweat

Three groups of Western tourists were kidnapped by muja-hadin in Kashmir, India. One was beheaded and the rest disap-peared. I decided to travel to Kashmir to understand what was going on and came back with a lesson in faith—faith in eventu-al freedom, victory and peace. There is a reward for any infor-mation leading to the retrieval of the hostages. You can check the latest at www.hostagesin kashmir.com.

Some say the blonde-haired, suntanned head of Hans Christian Ostro was balanced between his legs for effect while others say the head was found 40 meters away. Some say that the words "Al-Faran" were carved with a knife on his back, while others say they were on his chest. All agree that the Norwegian tourist was beheaded while still alive. This is not what Kashmir claims happens to its tourists. And the crude method of death mentioned above is supposed to be reserved for those in Third World countries where human behavior is still in a primitive, barbaric state—not for Westerners who are simply visiting what has been called among the most "beauti-ful and historic parts of Asia." But the truth is, even in Kash-mir, hostages are grabbed and prisoners exchanged.

News of trouble piled up quickly at first: One American escapes, a Norwegian is killed, the others are sick, and rescue attempts fail. There are conflicting reports of shootouts, executions, sightings and burials. And then silence. The families search desperately in vain. The world's best intelligence groups search in vain. Over half a million Indian troops search in vain. Then, as dramatically as the story appears, it disappears. Not surprising since the Westerners were about one percent of the 548 people kidnapped in Kashmir in that same year. Over 2000 people have been kidnapped in Kashmir since 1990, less than half of them survived the ordeal. Something evil is happening in northwestern India.

Kashmir is a tourist destination and it is a war zone. A quarter of a million Indian soldiers, long-range artillery duels, grenade and mine attacks have resulted in a death toll that climbs like a rocket heading into space. So far there have been more than 20,000 people killed with a burn rate of about 50 deaths a week. I decided there is only one way to find out what is going on in Northwest India—I put Kashmir on my list of places to visit.

My first stop, Delhi. You drive into town from the airport and then begin an inescapable spin into the city center. The British built Delhi in the shape of a wheel, with the hub being a group of colonial white three-story buildings that beam today in the bland splendor of a faded linen suit. Today, New Delhi is a sprawling city built more like a sewer with a central drain. Foreign tourists arriving from the airport serve as Delhi's main source of hard cash, therefore, compliant cab drivers funnel new arrivals to "official tourist offices" even in the wee hours of the morning.

It's 5:30 a.m., the air is still cool and thick—the best time of the day. But already the dirt and smoke hang low over the trees and people hurry about dressed in clean clothes. Soon the heat and dust will descend upon this bustling country and India will fade to quivering pastels.

Four hundred rupees gets me into town in an aging black Ambassador taxi. A 50's anachronism (still made in India), the Ambassador is a genetic mixture of Austin A-55, Morris Minor and bad Indian craftsmanship. (This Third World luxury on wheels can be yours for $US8500.) The early morning is also when the street cleaners poke supine men sprawled along the streets and gutters to see if they are dead or just hung over. One man is carted off, dead.

The cities of India consist of overflowing rivers of people running between buildings like an unstoppable torrent. Walking, crawling, riding, or running they are surprisingly quite efficient, forming huge mobile masses that rarely collide. Even the animals display a sense of order, so to speak, as the macaques in narrow alleys are creative enough to run along the tangled electrical wiring overhead and somnambulant cows sit calmly on traffic medians surrounded by oceans of smoke-belching vehicles.

Much of India is not dangerous. It is a refreshingly energetic, polite and industrious country. Some visitors may be mildly amused by the Indian habit of adopting the worst elements from various cultures whether they be 50's cars and motorcycles from the British, 70's weapons from the Russians, home decor from China, or 60's musicals from the Americans. American culture is transcendent here. India's Hollywood, or rather "Bollywood," now cranks out musicals that are reminiscent of "West Side Story," only it sounds like the songs are performed by Alvin and the Chipmunks on speed. You can't help but wonder if the youth of India, faced with carrying on centuries of complex culture and religions, just said "Fuck it, let's watch MTV."

Ticket to Ride

I take my driver up on his offer and visit not one but a dozen "tourist" offices. I walk in and find calm, friendly people behind the smudged dark glass of the counter windows of the air-conditioned office. Wherever I want to go, the answer is always: "No problem, sir. When would you like to go?"

I then inquire about kidnapping, murders, a rather large insurgency and the upcoming election with its resultant mayhem. Their smiles get wider, "No problem, sir. When would you like to go?"

They recommend the "Golden Triangle tour," a three-day excursion that takes travelers to Agra for the Taj Mahal, Jaipur and then back to Delhi. Having experienced the three-day journey previously, flanked by apocalyptic bus and car crashes (about one every 10–20 km), I wonder if this is actually more dangerous than going to Kashmir.

At one office, a Kashmiri man asks me darkly what I know about the hostages. He closes his office door as he sends the errand boy out for tea. We engage in a serious discussion about what is happening in Srinagar. We keep the conversation light but I sense he knows my purpose. I decide that I will return here to buy my tickets.

The next order of business is to wander around Delhi, engage in small talk, and hopefully get some bits of advice on Kashmir. Indians speak of Kashmir in the same manner and tone as a father would when discussing an unruly child. One man says "India has been patient and polite, but soon there will be a war—a 30-minute war, and this time we won't hand Pakistan back to the Muslims." Tough talk, but a good betting man's position since Pakistan has been thumped in wars over Kashmir three times before in 1948, 1965 and 1971.

The Valley of War

Kashmir is just one of India's ethnic, tribal, religious and financial conflicts. Kashmiris are independent, nonpolitical people living in a proverbial garden of Eden. When Britain divided India, the local mughals who ruled predominately Muslim Kashmir threw their lot in with Hindu India. Confronted by the idea of a Muslim majority being pledged to India, Pakistan and a large number of Kashmiris voiced disapproval and the problems started. Pakistan is not the gateway to Kashmir, nor do India's tourists want to vacation in a foreign, Muslim country. Kashmir was the most visited region in India until the late 80's and the gateway to the region has always been through Delhi and the South. Today it is not a war of Kashmiris vs. Indians. Any Kashmiri cab driver in New York will tell you that they would rather be pushing a hack rather than being press-ganged and forced to fight India. Kashmir is a war that Pakistan and India want, not the Kashmiris.

The tug-of-war for Kashmir is understandable. It's not some desolate Afghan desert or steamy uncharted jungle, rather a major tourist area immersed with history. Some people believe it to be the Bible's Promised Land, the place where Moses wandered to and was buried; one of the places where Jesus spent his youth and where he ultimately returned and died. There are many such legends about Kashmir and what's more, it is a beautiful, fragrant land inhabited by kind, handsome, creative and generous people. It is a land once blessed with peace, but when you hear a MiG-21 scream through the valleys, you realize that Kashmir is also a war zone.

Today, the border between Pakistan and India is an ill-defined series of armed border camps featuring daily firefights on scenic glaciers and artillery duels with cannons that can lob shells more than 20 miles. The Line of Control was determined in 1972, after the last war, and continues to be contested daily. Skirmishes are common and the resulting deaths are never featured in any newspapers There is also an active insurgency within Kashmir instigated and supported by Pakistan under the direction of its secret police, the ISI—the same folks that were the middlemen between the *mujahedin* in Afghanistan and the CIA back in the 80's.

On any given week, there are more than a quarter of a million Indian soldiers stationed in this tiny valley and in the mountains that surround it. Pipe-shaped MiG-21's fly hourly sorties as they thunder and echo through the valley. Every corner and crossroad is protected by soldiers hidden inside sandbagged, wire-fenced fortifications.There is no place where you cannot see at least 20 to 50 soldiers at any one time. Inside and outside the major cities and towns there are firefights, dozens of mine or grenade attacks, the odd village burning and massive sweeps for *mujahedin* every day. When asked about these specifics the tourist folks say that Kashmir is a great place to do a little trekking among fields of fragrant saffron and deodar. Yes, they admit, there are problems but nothing to worry about.

Before embarking on my date with fragrant saffron and deodar, I decide to play tourist and see what our officials have to say. I call the U.S. Embassy in Delhi to ask for advice on traveling to Kashmir. A bumbling, apologetic staffer offers a stern warning but cannot provide details, after all, they have a MIA somewhere in the cedar forests. Then I'm connected to an unnamed embassy liaison who sounds like an airline reservation recording. He tells me they are advising against all travel to Kashmir particularly because of the election. I ask for specifics. He has none. I ask him where he gets his information. He gets it from the press. Has he been there? No. I ask him where the hostages are and if they are dead or alive. He doesn't know. When I ask about the whereabouts of the Delta Force team, the German GS-9 and British SAS teams sent to Kashmir to help in the hostage recovery effort, the staffer finally shows a little emotion. " I can't tell you that," he barks. I get the same warning and lack of hard info from the Canadian embassy as well. It may be chilling to note that some of the kidnap victims also made calls before traveling to Kashmir, but they were told no problem. Well, now there is a problem, but no one seems to want to tell me what it is.

No one blinks when I buy a ticket from Delhi to Srinagar. I change a few crisp US$100 bills into a dirty brick of rupees. The two-inch wad is bundled with industrial-sized staples. I am given the secret on peeling the money: twist back and forth and don't worry about the rust spots or gaping holes where the bills were stapled. At 35.8 rupees to the dollar, that means I must carry bricks to pay for large items.

Kashmir is jammed up tight against the Hindu Kush, a name that appropriately translates to "Killer of Hindus." This region is also squeezed in by Pakistan, China and India. From the air Kashmir does look like Shangri La — a completely self-sufficient, isolated garden of Eden with no real connection to any of its neighbors.

I am intrigued by the irregular curved patches made by the stepped and irrigated yellow rice fields. Medieval European-style houses with steep, pitched tin roofs create jumbled intersections with no straight roads. Each village is softened by a ring of golden sycamore trees with leaves turning gold. In this medieval jumble of well-worn brick homes there is a sense of the English countryside.

Snow-capped peaks frame the rice fields and orchards that grow in the cool mountain temperatures and clean air. It is this scenery and mountain air that has attracted visitors from the hot arid flatlands to the south. Oddly, it doesn't look like a war from 30,000 feet. As we land, the hard scream of the engines warns me that reality awaits down below. We are landing at a speed that would be more appropriate for take-off—a technique similar to carrier flights where maximum air speed is needed in case of abort or evasion.

The plane slams down in Srinagar, and I notice rows of bunkers on each side of the runway as we whiz past. Russian-made MiG-21's and large camouflage transport planes stand ready to take off. The thrust reversers and hard brakes push against the seats and the belts. As I disembark, there are 20 soldiers ringing our plane, guns at the ready. My fellow travelers, who I thought were businessmen or returning locals, turn out to be journalists here to cover the election. A handful of anemic looking hippies in their early 20's look curiously out of place. It seems they are trying to recapture the love and drugs that brought thousands of their parents here in the early 70's before the Russians invaded Afghanistan and before *jihad*, or holy war, was in the news.

My plan is to stay at Adhoo's, a well known hotel for journalists and then head into the countryside. My cabdriver has other ideas. He extols the beauty of houseboats, the joys of trekking and the ecstasy that awaits me in the trout streams high up in the mountains. Because he has a polite and unnerving habit of looking directly at me from the front seat when he drives, I say that's nice, but for now please shut up, turn around and drive.

The convoluted and crowed road into town is overseen by a massive military presence. My newfound guide advises me sotto voce when to not take pictures by saying "military" as we approach each sandbagged bunker. I make him very nervous by taking pictures of the checkpoints as well as the scenic spots. The blast marks and nervous state of patrolling soldiers indicate that when my guide speaks of the various attacks that have occurred here, it is not a history lesson but something immediate and real.

Hundreds of skinny, mustached soldiers with ill-fitting uniforms stand guard every 50 meters as we enter Srinagar. Each corner is controlled by a 20' x 20' bunker crudely built of sandbags and covered with plastic mesh to deflect hand grenades. From within these bunkers peer the white eyes of dark skinned, helmeted soldiers with just the tips of their machine guns protruding.

Each intersection is clogged with soldiers on guard and roving groups of Jammu Kashmir Police outside the bunkers directing the chaotic traffic. They work in groups of four with short sticks and whistles. They argue, cajole, yell and threaten to keep things moving. They never quite agree on their diverse directions to each motorist as they wave their two-foot sticks and bang on the hoods of the cars. Meanwhile the jumbled traffic completely ignores them. As we sit stuck in traffic at the battle-worn traffic circles, my guide continues to rattle off a list of recent attacks at each bunker. I can visualize how one grenade thrown at the bunker would roll down into the stalled traffic and shred dozens of innocent bystanders. Any machine gun fire from the slit bunkers would add to the death toll. For now I am just stuck in traffic with about five-to-eight soldiers banging and yelling under the watchful eye of very nervous troops.

The journalists have missed the traffic jam and have beat me to the hotel. Much to my chagrin, there are no vacant rooms. All the other hotels in town are occupied by the military. What to do? Well, the houseboat doesn't sound too bad now. My driver seems quite pleased since he happens to have a cousin who owns a houseboat.

The British began the custom of residing in houseboats because they could not own land. The ornately carved boats became de rigueur in the 70's for marijuana-smoking tourists who could indulge themselves in the local weed safe in isolation from the police on land. Dal Lake is lined by empty houseboats, all 980 with romantic or foreign sounding names.

The houseboats of Srinagar are long, gently curved rectangular barges with a porch at the entrance and bedrooms toward the back. There is also a large sitting room, dining room and extra bedrooms. Most are ornately carved and fashioned out of the fragrant cedar that grows in the mountains.

There is nothing wrong with staying on a houseboat on Lake Dal but I didn't want to be a sitting duck. After I visit the boat, it seems to be a smarter place to be than the frequently attacked hotels with their great iron gates and barbed wire. The lake makes the gunfire and shouting echo at night, making it seem more like an amusement park complete with fireworks rather than a fully-active war zone.

The owner of a particularly fine houseboat next door to the one I choose to stay at tells me it took eight people working for five years to create his 20' x 80' masterpiece. It curves gently upwards at each end and is built of fragrant deodar, a local pine that comes from the mountains. As I talk to my neighbor, it becomes evident that the investment of so much money during a time where there are no tourists was not the wisest thing. But he was never in it to make any money to re-coup his investment. All he has is pride in the beautiful crafts-manship. Someday when the tourists return, he will have enough money to furnish it. As I get in a shikara or small canoe to visit his house, my host, who is returning from the opposite shore, assumes that I am jumping ship for his neigh-bor's boat and screams, "Wait, wait, I am coming, I am com-ing!"

It's not too profitable to lose track of your tourists around here.

I decide to go for a walk in the old town as the sun sets over the deep blue mountains. The owner of my houseboat, ner-vous about my visiting his neighbor, offers to come along. Or rather insists.

I like the cool crisp colonial feel of Srinagar. The solidly built British style mansions that overlook the lake give the city the feel of being in an upscale resort, which of course it once was. These homes are now occupied by Kashmiris who sell carpets, rice and wool.

Along the narrow streets are shops where carvers, weavers and craftsmen create the intricate handicrafts and goods the area is known for. The Kashmiris are excellent craftsmen and the long winters and lack of professional jobs give them plen-ty of time to create meticulously ornate carpets, paper maché, and needlework. Most of them work by the golden glow of a single fly-specked light bulb. Almost all families in the towns work the looms or carve during the winter to earn money. Their goods are usually sold by local co-ops which once pro-vided an important supplement to the summer tourism in-come. Now there is no summer tourism income and India does not allow wholesale exportation of these goods. Therefore, tourists must come to India to buy these goods, but the problem is, there are no tourists.

As if to add drama to my bucolic stroll, in front of me, a large brown eagle swoops down and repeatedly attacks a chicken who is walking mindlessly down the street. The eagle flies down the narrow lanes, claws spread and repeatedly attacks the terrified bird. The chicken finally runs under the house and the eagle calmly waits on a telephone pole for its prey to reemerge. An omen or a warning?

There is little evidence of the nightly tension here as the sun sets. True, the walls and streets are decorated with green scrawls of graffiti—"JK-LF" for Jammu Kashmir-Liberation Front or "AZ-JK" for Azad Jammu Kashmir. But children play, women cook and men smoke as if it is just another day. When I mention to my guide, Ahmad, that I have seen this graffiti in Pakistan, he is surprised that I know what this means. I explain to him that a few months ago, I was on the other side of the border where the Harkut and other groups are very visible with big offices complete with neon signs. When I say the word "liberation" for the second time he uncharacteristicly says "That is all bullshit."

I ask him what he means.

"They do not want liberation, they are just using us," he answers.

This is the first indication that my guide has opinions about what is going on.

Although both the people of Srinagar and their dwellings have suffered from the war, the buildings have fared better. The old town bears the damage from bombs, fire and bullets. In the blue dusk and warm light from the shops, I feel as if I am in a medieval village complete with rambling lanes and quaint cottages.

I stop to talk to the locals who introduce some of their friends as freedom fighters. A joke or a test? They are testing my sympathies. There have been three years of war in this town. Threatened by *mujahedin* and by the Indian military, there is no safe political or moral ground for these people—survival is foremost. I notice the soldiers on patrol are now wearing bulletproof vests and helmets instead of their crisp uniforms.

My guide, who is Muslim, asks me if I like Muslims. I say yes. He asks me what I think of the *taliban*, whom I visited a few months earlier in Afghanistan. He asks in the same manner someone would ask you about a football team. He is uncomfortable with the image Muslims have in this Hindu-dominated region. It is portrayed as Muslim against Hindu, but in reality it is the Muslim Kashmiris who are dying.

He apologizes , then asks me if he can take me to a carpet shop; he gets a three percent commission and I don't have to buy, just look and have some tea. Inside the carpet shop, there is a Japanese businessman intent on negotiating down the price of the carpets. I listen to the pitch, examine the merchandise and learn that a carpet costs US$5000–US$8000 here. A large sized carpet with fine knots takes two years to make and is made by hand with each fiber hand knotted and tightened. The photo album of satisfied customers is a popular sales tool here. The pictures all date back to the late 80's. The Kashmiris will weave any design you would like these days. They need the money.

Walking back to the houseboat in the dark I find myself in the middle of a night patrol; 12 men are spaced 20 meters apart (in case of grenade or mine attack), carrying sub machine guns at the ready. There is no curfew tonight, but anyone out on the streets at 8:30 at night better have a good reason. The night is when the *mujahedin* attack and the soldiers make it clear from the looks they give me that they don't like my presence.

The Next Day

Only five people were killed yesterday. But today is a special day. The new government will be sworn in and the *mujahedin* have called for a general strike. This means shops must be closed, no one is to work and truck drivers and cab drivers are to stay home. Along the road there are soldiers every 20–50 feet. There is no civilian traffic allowed, only armored military vehicles. Naturally, this is the day I have chosen to take a drive in the country.

Ahmad greets me by saying, "Please hurry, our cab driver is afraid." Hyperventilating would be a better term. The driver says hello and flashes me a pained smile. He rattles off his warnings: the ministers are being sworn in today; the *mujahedin* will strike; the roads are closed; there is a general strike. He asks in a pleading tone if we can skip the Tomb of Yusaf, a tomb that is said by some to be the tomb of Christ. It is right next to the mosque and things are buzzing right now. I tell him that today I will go to Gulmarg, a popular trekking area on the unofficial Pakistani /Kashmiri border. We are going on a holiday jaunt to the front lines.

To protect us, the driver has created a homemade "PRESS" sign, and with the characteristic Kashmiri artistic flair, has used three different colors of ink in an intricate design. I ask him why he just doesn't put a bullseye on the passenger door. He smiles that pained smile again.

As we drive out of the city and toward the mountains, my guide points to certain spots and intersections. All that can be seen are bunkers with blast marks from previous attacks. Pointing out recent grenade attacks instead of scenic wonders seems to be the standard patter of cab drivers. We pass through the town of Gumpti. Ahmad says "We are afraid of this place." I ask him if there is a way to tell the *mujahedin* from the local people. He says, "The fighters are taller, like Afghans, and, like Afghans, they love to fight."

We pass through yellow rice fields on roads bordered by poplars and sycamores turning gold in the autumn weather. The blue snow-covered mountains in the distance are clean and pure against the trees and fields. The only reminder that we are in a hot zone is the constant presence of passing armored troop carriers, road patrols along the roads and various checkpoints.

My driver and my guide continually scan the roadside for anything unusual. To break the suspense, I decide to talk about cars. I am fascinated by our antique 50's Austin-like HM Ambassador, a car that is still made in India. I ask Ahmad what the HM means. He nervously says Hizbul *mujahedin*. I point to the "HM" sign on the dash, and he corrects himself, "Oh that, Hindustan Motors."

The guide and the driver chat nervously. Someone has too much interest in our passage. Ahmad warns, "That man was watching us." They both look over their shoulders to see if it was a curious local or a *mujahedin* writing down the license number for summary retribution. It's amazing how much driving gets done here even though the driver is looking over his shoulder instead of out the front windshield.

The scenery of the countryside is spectacular so I have to get some photos. I get out and walk through the rice paddies, now dry and mature. Men and women from the villages squat on their haunches, and using a small sickle, they snick off handfuls of rice stalks that are left to dry in the sun. Later the stalks will be threshed over a rock or wooden bench. The warm sun on my back, the crunch of the sickles and the bee-hive shaped mounds of rice stalks make for a very bucolic set-ting.

Wrapped up in photographing this rural scene, I unknow-ingly step right into a concealed machine gun nest and almost trip over the barrel of a .50 caliber gun. The two camouflaged soldiers are polite, but urgently direct me away from their post.

Getting back into the car I begin to wonder just how much I think I see and how much I don't see. We enter a village called Magam, about halfway to Gulmarg. Just before we reach Magam we pull off the road to let a convoy of dark col-ored troop trucks and armored personnel carriers rush by at high speed. Just behind the roof of each truck is a machine gunner squinting grimly behind large ski goggles.

There is something going on up ahead.

As we clatter towards Magam, the scene becomes less pas-toral and more ominous. The soldiers we are seeing are not the anemic recruits we saw back in Srinagar. The cropped mustaches, tight bandannas and well-oiled weapons...they've come from where the fighting is.

We arrive in Magam shortly after the main excitement — a shootout, followed by a military sweep and then another fight to the death by *mujahedin* holed up in the basement of a house. The soldiers are busy questioning the locals and searching homes. They don't seem to pay much attention to me.

There is an odd, evocative scene amongst the chaos. It's hard to tell if the crowds are looking at us, watching the sol-diers or under arrest. I don't quite know who is who. Who is *mujahedin* and who is villager? Who is under arrest and who is informer? Who is spy and who is an innocent bystander?

The people that don't fit in this scene are the Hindu and Ghurka soldiers who look nervous and twitchy.

Off in the distance another tableau is laid out. I watch a squad of soldiers coming in from patrol through the rice fields. They do not stick to paths between the paddies and are nervously making their way to the village. I remember seeing this scene on television back home a long time ago, except the setting was Southern Vietnam. This is India's Vietnam. The foe is within and without.

There are hundreds of soldiers now, lining the villagers up and checking papers. Some just stand around while others search. The soldiers are friendly and I hand out Mr. DP stickers that feature our laughing skull mascot. Soon the Indian Army officers come over for stickers. I ask them about the hostages. With some conviction they say the hostages were here but now they are gone. They say the hostages are south in Jammu. They won't come up this high this winter.

We continue our trip to the front lines. Our taxi clatters up the mountain toward the border. As we sign in at the military checkpoint guarded by Ghurkas I notice in the logbook that two Taiwanese tourists have passed through here the day before. A few miles later the road disappears. It has been taken away by a landslide. There are horsemen, or pony wallahs, waiting here. The horses formerly carried tourists around the hills, but the horsemen say they have been sitting where the road is washed out for ten days without seeing tourists. The Taiwanese never made it this far so they must have turned back at the checkpoint or given up when they saw the road was washed out.

Gulmarg is the site of an 18-hole golf course (the world's highest) and a rather impressive ski lift built by a Swiss company surrounded by rustic chalets. Now the hotels are empty and falling apart, the ski lift is in pieces. The golf course is kept well cropped by grazing goats and today there is one family sitting peacefully on an abandoned putting green enjoying the scenery.

I hire small mountain ponies to take us up to the vale of Khilanmarg and then the mountain of Apharwat.

My anemic horse, Peter, keeps tripping over my legs, which I have to hold up to keep from dragging on the ground. My pony wallah says that Peter is small because he had little to eat when growing up. I offer to switch and carry Peter up the mountain and the horseman laughs.

We ride through Gulmarg and up into the mountains. I ask Ahmad if there are *mujahedin* here. He says occasionally the guides see groups of 20–40 armed men in the forest, but it is best to turn in the opposite direction. Has anybody seen the hostages here? No, but there is a rumor that they were spotted walking towards Jammu in the Kishtawar area. Kishtawar is beyond the southeasternmost point of Kashmir and we are on its northerwesternmost point. There have been many sightings and rumors of sightings of the hostages, but this one makes sense, as it is impossible to survive high in the mountains. Even the shepherds go down in the winter.

The October sun is warm, but the temperature in the shade is ten degrees cooler. At these altitudes it gets bitterly cold at night. The only shelter are seasonal herders' huts and abandoned villages. Up here there is no food, no communications, no transportation other than by foot or pony. The kidnappers would have to rely upon villagers for food, clothing and concealment. But there are no villagers here. People will later ask me if I was afraid of being kidnapped. The answer is no because, quite frankly, the thought does not enter your mind when you are surrounded by the solitude and beauty of the mountains.

In the valleys below, the snow covers some areas. There is no undergrowth and the grass has been trimmed by grazing animals. Despite sporadic snow cover, we can travel unimpeded in any direction in the valley. The downside is that there is no natural cover, no place to hide. We can spot shepherds two to three miles away. The air is so clear that we can see the 8000-meter high Nanga Parbat (The Naked Mountain) off in the distance. Ten miles away we can see soldiers on patrol are visible in the form of tiny bobbing dots. Kashmir would be a very difficult place to travel through undetected.

If I thought I could come here and learn all there is to know about the hostage situation without any probing, I would have been very disappointed. And, as I expected, the locals are hesitant to discuss anything; the military has no idea where they are, and at the same time they say they know where they are.

The rumors I am chasing down seem to be ill-founded. In truth I didn't come here to find the hostages—it would take great conceit to assume that I can learn something that the relatives, FBI, CIA, SAS, GS-9 and other intelligence and military special operations groups have not—but rather to understand the lay of the land and background of the conflict in Kashmir. The five abducted Westerners are not the first hostages to be taken here and they will not be the last. Sometimes knowledge requires studying the obvious and circumstantial. More importantly, I am trying to understand how every traveler's nightmare occurred in the hopes that others will not have to enter the same dark underworld.

I want to see how close we can get to the border. The horses cannot walk in the steep, deep snow, so we climb until the snow drifts becomes too high. It is cold now and I am not dressed for alpine exploration. A military camp looms on the summit above. My guide says going further is ill-advised. "From this point two things will happen, either we will be shot at by the military or we will freeze to death." Realizing that the Pakistani military is not looking for overnight patrons and that we have 4–5 hours to return, I turn back.

Back down below the snow line we rest by a natural spring next to the destroyed ski lift. Two MiGs streak over us, sending those now familiar thundering echoes through the mountain valley. By now passing MiG's serve as a reminder to look at my watch. It must be tea time.

As we descend we chat with some shepherds who are laying in winter feed for their animals. A small calf bleats. The shepherd says it has been born too late and will not make it through the winter. They will kill it and head down in a week or so. Have they seen anything? The old shepherd's tan and weathered face tells me he has not lived this long by chatting about such things to strangers. He just smiles and poses for pictures with his daughter.

Driving down the winding mountain road, we are waved off the road by soldiers. From up the hill comes a convoy of Indian Army trucks. In the middle of the convoy is a Mahindra jeep with big red letters spelling out COMMANDING OFFICER complete with stars at each end. Inside is a portly, campaign bar decorated man and his driver. Not the secretive choice of transportation in a war zone. On the way back through Magam, troops are still mopping up. The villagers still stand passively watching them and then at us. I notice a group of young, well-muscled soldiers wearing black bandannas around their heads and carrying short assault weapons. They also wear special ops gear and soft-soled shoes. The war has come here.

That night back at my houseboat, I talk to an 80-year-old who was once a travel guide in the 30's and 40's, who casually puffs away on his "hubbly bubbly" as the British used to call hookahs, and reflects on the state of his country. He speaks in the same archaic form of colonial British. He talked of how his country used to be "damned cheap" and how "he was a jolly chap" in his youth. He remembers walking 14 miles to school. He recounts the joy of tourists when he showed them his country and how much he loves fly fishing, hiking and camping. But with the war, not to mention his bad legs and old age, all that is over. But it is still his country. This is a statement that the *mujahedin* and Indian army cannot make yet.

He has lived through the three wars with Pakistan but the past year has been the worst in his life. He says he wishes he could trade eyes with me so that I could see what he has seen. He doesn't speak the horrors and I do not ask him to. He points to his silver hair and to his heart and blames the deteriorating condition of both on the war. He says things are getting better now. He hears through the grapevine that there are now about 100–400 tourists a week and he hopes the new government will work out the problems. The prime minister is a good man, he says. But I don't think he cares anymore who runs the country.

Changing the subject, I ask him about the tomb of Yusaf and his eyes light up. "You know about this?" he asks excitedly.

I tell him what I have read and heard: Jesus' Hebrew name is Yazu. That Jesus wandered as far as India in his youth between the ages of 12 and 25 and returned to his beloved Kashmir after his staged crucifixion is a belief shared by many. He was also rumored to have traveled back to England with Joseph or even walked across the New World. According to local legend, Jesus was known as Saint Yuz Asaf, a man who performed miracles and preached in the first century A.D.

Some Kashmiris believe that their valley is the true promised land and some believe they are descended from one of the lost tribes of Israel. It sounded like the usual Chariot of the Gods stuff but worth exploring.

I ask him what he knows about the tomb. He says the tomb contains the body of Yusaf.

"He is your prophet and he is our prophet. Yusaf is all around us," he says.

I ask him when Yusaf was buried there.

"Four thousand years ago, before there was history," the old man says.

Who is Yusaf?

"Yusaf is everywhere, everything. When you breathe in and out that is Yusaf. Everything around you is Yusaf."

So much for accurate historical recall.

Not knowing quite where to go with this outburst of religious enthusiasm, I ask if the man in the tomb is Jesus Christ? He says quite frankly that he doesn't know.

As I go to bed my guide says, "Make sure you make yourself very clean tomorrow." He even tells me how to wipe the dust off my hiking boots. "We must be very clean for Yusaf tomorrow."

The next day we head for the Tomb of Yusaf. It is in a very nondescript building near the famous wooden mosque of Srinagar. The mosque was originally built in 1385 and has been burned and rebuilt five times since. Constructed with wood shingles and 300 cedar trunks the mosque retains its medieval look and also seems to retain its inflammatory character as the mullahs whip up hatred against the Indian army. The mosque is the flashpoint for most demonstrations and resultant violence in Srinagar.

All traffic is prohibited from entering this area, but we cajole the police into letting us pass. Large blue APCs with turret gunners roar up and down the street around the mosque. People gather to make their prayers at the mosque. My guide prays and kisses the ornaments as we enter.

Inside is a glass container and within that is a faded, dusty, shroud-covered tomb. A cement block inset with a pair of unauthentic looking footprints sit nearby. Otherwise there is nothing. Outside are demonstrations and troops. Inside, my guide is praying quietly. Is this the tomb of Christ? Does it matter? Is there a reason why he has chosen this beautiful but troubled land? Why would a prophet be in a Muslim country run by Hindus surrounded by Buddhists? I wonder if he or anyone can hear my guide's Muslim prayers. Like the hostages, this is an enigma whose need for a solution is overshadowed by the harsh reality of survival. But my trip to this tomb taught me that it is important to understand that the Kashmiris can accept these enigmas without facts or resolution. I think I have found my answer. The hostages are here and they are not here. Kashmir is a war zone and it is a tourist haven. It is whatever it must be for people to survive.

Things are heating up outside and my guide says it is time for me to leave. I think he is concerned I will miss my flight until he points to the angry crowds outside. I realize the quiet tomb has made me forget where I am. I head for the airport.

We go through five identical in-depth searches on our way to the airport. Every single item from film cannisters to food bars is opened. My batteries are taken out of every single battery powered device I have and are confiscated. A box of matches is taken and stuck in a soldier's pocket. He shrugs as if to say better in his pocket than in the trash. My guide is pressed against the fence by the crush of people. He asks me to think about him at Christmas and send his family something. He says Kashmir is dying. I thank him and wonder why he has chosen a Christian holiday to ask for something for his Muslim family.

The airport is packed with soldiers. I sit next to a Sikh army captain just back from the front. He says the war is fairly routine now. "They fire 500 rounds; we fire 1000 rounds back." There are casualties on both sides. I tell him of my trip into the mountains and he looks at me rather incredulously. When I give him the details he nods his head gently.

"The west is very dangerous," he says. "You never know who your enemy is. Is he *mujahedin* or Kashmiri or both?"

I ask him about the hostages and pull out a map. He pushes the map back in my hand and says, "Please, do not show me anything. I am not supposed to talk to you."

I realize that we are being watched by a number of officers in the waiting lounge. I ask him about the hostages and if the rumors that they were recaptured and held on an Indian military base are true. "That is silly" he says.

I ask him if the army knew where the hostages were.

"Don't you think that if we knew where they were, we would go in and get them?" he asked insulted.

I ask if they really did kill the leader of Al-Faran and if the hostages were wounded in the resultant fire fight.

"That is something I cannot talk about."

He gives me some tips. The spring is the most dangerous time, when the snow melts and the terrorists (as he calls them) can move freely without leaving tracks. The winter is much safer and there are fewer attacks. The militants like to use big road mines that they set off under the troop trucks. He has been here a year and a half and is tired of the fear and killing. He pulls out the army campaign ribbons he has for Kashmir and then quickly tucks them away.

He tells me he is bringing back dead soldiers to their families in India. His job is to explain to the bereaved families what must be done, the paperwork, how to file for benefits and how to conduct the funerals of their children. He is not too emotional about his job since he brings out a lot of dead soldiers. One thing he is happy about is the Army accepting his resignation. He plans to emigrate to Toronto to set up a trucking company with his brother. He says he is in love with Canada. But there are problems there. His brother has been forced to cut his hair and abandon his turban because of all the locals calling him "Paki." He is afraid that he too will have to cut his hair and beard. "Paki" is an odd insult to a Sikh from India fighting a war with Muslim Pakistanis in Kashmir.

On the other side of me is a young Canadian couple returning from backpacking through India. They were told it would be safe, something utterly believable for them because "there sure is a lot of security." I tell them that 45 people died this week and that the man on the other side of me is paying excess baggage fines on stiffs. They laugh, thinking I am kidding. I notice they clutch a well-worn Lonely Planet guide to India. They said they had heard that there was a war here but that it is much better now. They are right; there is officially no war here. The government even bans books that reveal the disputed border between Kashmir and Pakistan instead of the official version. And in a way my touristic friends were right. They went hiking, had a good time and are heading home tanned and happy. They are surprised to hear there were some other tourists who came here for the same thing but never even made it to the hiking part, let alone the airport.

Back in Delhi, I have dinner at the home of a Kashmiri who has moved his business from Srinagar to Delhi. During my initial fact-finding stay in Delhi he was fascinated by my desire to seek out what is really going on, and wanted to talk to me when I got back. He has a curious habit of calling me "My Dear" or "Dear," but I'm not dissuaded since I am getting accustomed to their humorous use of the colonial British tongue. I meet him at his house to have dinner with his family.

He owns three houseboats and a small hotel in Srinagar. Many families have handed down tourist businesses since the 1930's. He wishes I could have met his father since he loved to fish and hike. He also has a fondness for the mountains, something that every Kashmiri seems to take great pride in. He is essentially a refugee, albeit better off than most, from the war. He says the fighting is between Pakistani *mujahedin* and the Indian army. He doesn't believe Kashmiris have taken up the fight. "Why would you risk your family and your little ones?" he asks. "If Kashmiris were to fight, it would be for independence, not to be part of India or Pakistan. It is not worth dying for India or Pakistan."

When I ask him about the hostages, he gives me the same reply virtually every other Kashmiri had given me, "What do you know about the hostages?"

I tell him that I think the Al-Faran have gone back to Pakistan and that the hostages have either been moved south or are dead by now. One thing is for sure: the hostages are the last thing the Kashmiris have to worry about. He agrees, as if to help me understand that the hostage situation is not the work of Kashmiris. "The Kashmiris only have two enemies; India and Pakistan," he says. "We do not know why India needs or wants Kashmir, or why Pakistan needs or wants Kashmir."

The hostages have become a riddle, an enigma and a mystery. And like religion, the weather and the future, it is something Kashmiris are very comfortable accepting.

"We are not a fierce warring tribe, but a people who love our cool mountains and who exist by showing others our beautiful country," my host says. " We just want our own way of life and not be forced to live in the heat and squalor of Delhi. Why do we sweat in this heat when we could be in our beloved mountains with our families? "

But for now the Kashmiris sweat.

Back in America, I talk to James Bowman, the campaign director in England. He is sure that the hostages are still alive. It helps that Terry Waite, former envoy for the Anglican Church, and once a hostage himself, is involved. The families return regularly to put a fire under the government and check with their own group of Kashmiri investigators. They have met with the prime minister of India and have begged him to warn tourists of the dangers in Kashmir. He won't. But he encouraged the relatives to do what they can to warn off other unsuspecting tourists. As for the two-year-old question: "Are they dead or are they still alive," the families firmly believe they are alive. Some journalists and governments say they were executed on Dec 13 or 15 last year. No one has proof and no one has produced a hard bit of evidence other than the eyewitness testimony of villagers who say they have seen the hostages.

Kashmir is a dangerous place. And for the hostages it will forever change their view of Westerners being able to ignore minor politics in search of adventure or relaxation. Westerners are an ideal negotiating tool and once they lose that status their existence becomes a liability. The long confinement of other hostages like Terry Waite and Terry Anderson have shown that time may be on their side. For now the families work, wait and wonder.

For now they sweat.

—**RYP**

IRAN
Hijacked

In 1980 Coskun was a 23-year-old neophyte war correspondent. He went to Iran to cover the beginning of the war with Iraq. His film of the war was confiscated by the Iranians and he returned to Paris empty-handed. He then flew to Iraq, to cover the other side with a quick stopover in the Turkish city of Dyabikar to cover the Turkish military maneuvers. He was in for a surprise when he caught the plane from Ankara to Dyabikar.

Our Turkish Airlines *Boeing 727* takes off as scheduled around 5:30 p.m. for its 35-minute-long flight. But one hour later we still have not landed. The other passengers and I start feeling uneasy. I wonder if the wheels of the plane are blocked. Suddenly, the voice of the pilot breaks through the tension: "Ladies and gentlemen, we might be obliged to land in Diyarbakir. Otherwise, we will head toward Iran. I now give the microphone to a Muslim brother." Instantly, the entire plane knows we have been hijacked.

Yilmaz Yalciner, the leader of the hijackers, carries on with his statement, given in the most imperative intonation:

"Islam takes over the plane. Long live the Divine Ayatollah Ruhollah Khomeini…. *Shariat*, the unique sure way to bring happiness to the entire human race, is the name of our mission. We are changing the route of this plane so as to go to

Tehran, the cradle of the Islamic Revolution. Then, my three Muslim brothers and I will proceed to Afghanistan, where we will fight alongside the brothers who are leading the jihad [Holy War] against the Russian atheists. For this reason, I am now going to pass around the hat. Whatever you give, make sure to give with your heart."

The passengers, in a state of shock after this announcement, search their pockets for some money. The collection begins. The passengers, afraid of the reprisals, give as much as they can to the militant who is passing a bag. Yilmaz Yalciner counts the money and gets back to the microphone: "Eighty-nine Turkish Lira [US$100]," he says, "it's really too little for people like you, but thanks anyway. Don't forget that we are going to fight with this money against the atheist Soviets."

For the passengers, the unbearable wait starts.

Nobody moves anymore; there is little to talk about, and everyone knows the gravity of the situation. All of us are probably thinking the same thing—fanatics are unpredictable. All we can do is wait anxiously for their next move.

Once more, the voice of the hijacker breaks the heavy silence: "All women onboard must cover their hair—it is a rule of Islam. And Islam only constrains you to do good things." The 28 female passengers quickly cover their hair with whatever is available, including the white cotton cloth of the headrests of their seats. Some women, short of anything looking like a *chador*, shroud themselves under their husband's jackets.

Being a photojournalist first and a terrified passenger second, I pull out my camera and start taking photos. I am more concerned about running out of film since I do not know how long the ordeal will last. I find myself elated that I am at the center of what will be an international story, but scared out of my wits that the usual *laissez passer* accorded to the press will not be observed by the Muslim fanatics. The hijackers seem just as terrified as the passengers but apparently find comfort in carrying out this simpleminded and dangerous act.

At first, I photograph the passengers clandestinely, but this is not the story. Then I have an idea. I inform my friend Osman, a radio journalist, sitting next to me about my intentions to talk to the hijackers and ask their permission to take photos of the whole event. He quickly dismisses the idea as insane and advises me to adopt a low profile instead, so as not to attract their attention.

My hunch is that the hijackers are Iranian. I figure that if I show them the recent stamps in my passport and some of the recent Iranian photos I have with me they might allow me to document the hijacking. I head toward the first-class compartment where three of the militants have gathered, and tell them I am a journalist and ask permission to take photos. One of them, Omer Yorulmaz (I learned his name later), calmly tells me to wait and he will check with the leader in the cockpit. In the meantime, I go back to my seat to get my cameras. He comes out and tells me I can enter. I am elated.

As I quickly take photos of the crowded cockpit, I notice the contrast between the tense but efficient crew, and the theatrical laughter of the hijacker (Yilmaz Yalciner) as he holds a gun close to the right temple of someone sitting behind the pilot. I am even more elated with the fact that this is the first time a hijacking has ever been photographed in the air.

Suddenly, Yalciner commands me to stop. I realize his smile is a natural schoolboy's reaction to the camera and not indicative of the tension in the cockpit. Ignoring me, he resumes his negotiations with the pilot. I am being watched carefully by another hijacker. The pilot, Ilhan Akdeniz, is trying to convince Yalciner once and for all: "It is impossible," he says, "to violate Iran's airspace. There is a war going on! They are going to shoot us down with missiles! They won't want to know whether we've been hijacked."

Yalciner's answer surprises everyone, "Don't worry, the Muslim world knows me very well. Khomeini knows me too. Stop worrying—we'll make it to Tehran.

The pilot explains there would not be enough fuel. He asks if the plane can land in Dyabakir to refuel. The hijackers, convinced, agree. That issue resolved, the lead hijacker seems to relax and resume his casual demeanor.

He turns toward me and tells me abruptly, "I am not a mean terrorist. I am a good terrorist. So you're a journalist? "So am I, and the three brothers, too," he explains. "You can take more pictures of me, you know, but I must admit, I don't know how to pose," he adds before bursting out laughing.

They are all working for a banned publication called *Shari-at*. Hence, the name of the "mission" they are undertaking. They are religious terrorists belonging to the "Akincilar group" (independent Sunni Muslims linked with the National Salvation Party).

I resume taking pictures of the scene, and of the passengers. The passengers still have no idea what fate has in store for them. These hijackers appear unusually calm. They are obviously fanatics to the point of candidness; they seem to be absolutely confident that they are going to get to Tehran. But I can feel their tension. I lie to them pretending I understand their motivation and want to provide them oodles of publicity. They are quite willing to talk. I ask them how they managed to smuggle their guns onto the Boeing in spite of the tight security control. Yalciner pulls out a book, which he opens to show me that it had been hollowed to make room for a pistol. He laughs heartily about the clever trick he has played on the security guards. Another shows me an attaché case filled with Turkish lires so that they can survive in their new country, Iran. It is hard to tell whether I am in the presence of childish stupidity or enormous confidence.

We make small talk until the plane lands at Diyarbakir. The passengers don't know what city or country they are landing in. Most passengers know that bad things start to happen once hijacked planes touch down.

I become self-conscious realizing that I am the only one who does not seem afraid. The passengers look at me with hatred and fear. Am I a hijacker? The confusion makes them suspicious. I find myself in a no man's land, between the passengers and the terrorists. Because of my decision to document this criminal act, the terrorists have made me part of their drama. By not intervening against the hijackers, I have become a coconspirator in the minds of the passengers. The camera has given me a special passport.

The hijackers also treat the cowering passengers differently. The burning light in the hijackers' eyes looks nothing but ominous.

We wait on the ground. The stewardesses attend to the people quietly and efficiently. The air in the plane is hot and stale. There is no more water or food. The plane feels like a tomb or a submarine that had sunk to the bottom of the ocean. Outside our plastic windows the ground crews, the vehicles and the world seem a thousand miles away. Time is irrelevant.

It is not hard to figure out what is going through the minds of the 148 people aboard. The hijackers are also getting tense, and I sense it is time to stop taking pictures.

It is now 8:30 p.m. We have only been on the plane for three hours but no one aboard would forget this day. Given the time for reflection, I remember why I am going to Diyarbakir in the first place. I realize that the hijackers have made a fatal mistake: They have landed in the center of a major military base and smack in the middle of preparations for showy military maneuvers. I was supposed to cover the strength and power of the Turkish Army. I was about to be center stage. To make matters worse, the Turkish and European press are there in full force. Faced with the tedious coverage of a nonevent, they were delighted to be at the scene of a hijacking. The worst part is that the new hard-liner president of Turkey himself, Kevan Evren, is at the airport and has taken charge of the event. He declares, "No concessions."

The negotiations between the hijackers and the Airport Authority are going on with no apparent progress. The hijackers make a concession—they will free the women and the children. But it really doesn't matter what they agree to, since their fate is being decided for them in the smoke-filled meeting rooms inside the airport.

At 10 p.m., 19 *Celik Kuvvet* (Steel Force) commandos take off from Ankara and Adana. Their planes land at Diyarbakir at 11 p.m. At midnight the airport is blacked out and the plane is by itself on the tarmac. The fear aboard is palpable.

It is now Tuesday. We have lived another day. At 1 a.m., electronic listening devices are installed on the body of the plane to locate the hijackers. Four more hours are necessary to prepare the rescue operation. Inside the grounded plane, the passengers are aware of, and can see, nothing.

At 5 a.m., the commandos split into two groups. One group silently cuts open the rear door, while the front group creates a minor diversion near the cockpit. The commandos burst through the back of the plane, yelling, "Lie down everybody," followed by a shoot-out. The sound of the firefight in the small enclosed space is deafening.

The passenger I photographed in the cockpit is wounded and later dies in the hospital. I duck under my seat, afraid that my camera might be mistaken for a gun. I regret not taking pictures, but realistically I know I would be killed instantly.

Crowded below the seat, I have just enough time to hide some film in my underwear and to give some rolls to Osman, the radio journalist sitting next to me. The three surviving hijackers surrender quite easily as if all was in good fun.

The passengers are asked to lie down on the tarmac and later we will be driven to army barracks. I am pointed out by some of the passengers as one of the hijackers. In fact, the news wire reports include me in the list of hijackers arrested in the assault. I am taken into custody for interrogation.

After some minutes, most of the passengers are freed and brought to the barracks. Five passengers and I are kept behind. The three hijackers are taken away in a truck. Then the police throw the six of us in a second truck, which follows the first one. My cameras have been confiscated. I still feel confident that the whole situation will soon be clarified.

There are six of us crammed into the same jail cell. We are tired, dirty and thirsty from the 12-hour ordeal. Two engineers, one Italian and two Turkish customs officers who usually control the passports on board, Osman, the radio journalist, and myself are detained. The police suspect the customs officers of complicity. They want to confirm the identities of the foreign engineers. Osman is detained because he is a journalist, and I, because I am a suspected terrorist. The hijackers are put in another cell not far from ours.

My interrogation is a lot tougher than I anticipated. I am bullied by the policemen when they discover that I work for SIPA Press (SIPA means donkey in Turkish). When I tell them that I was born in Siirt, they realize that I am a Kurd. They find my story hard to believe—that I would simply ask permission to take photos because it is my job. They do not believe I am only a journalist, and I am sent back to my cell. During the entire night, we can't sleep very much, as we are disturbed by the comings and goings of our jailkeepers accompanying the hijackers to their interrogations. We can hear a lot of their yells. We are very uneasy about all this. We can also hear the news on a radio set. I gather that everybody believes I am the fifth terrorist and I therefore should not expect any mercy.

The next day, Osman is freed and I have time to give him some more film to take to SIPA. I am left alone in the cell. Later on, the terrorists and I are sent to another jail well known as a torture center for prisoners captured by the military.

Luckily, this time my interrogation is shorter. I am told I will be released because they checked my identity and they understand I have told the truth. It seems also that some people (journalists and politicians) have vouched for me. Never underestimate the usefulness of political contacts.

I am very surprised and elated when I am finally released. I rush back to SIPA's headquarters in Istanbul, just in time to learn that only a handful of my photos have been published in Turkey as well as around the world. Most of them had been lost due to Osman's mishandling of the developing process. But there were more rolls of film that I had hidden under the aircraft seats that had still not been recovered.

—**Coskun Aral**

IRAQ
Things Go Better With Coke

Although Kurdistan is not an official country, it is treated as one by the CIA. The United States used the large Kurdish area north of Iraq to train terrorists, assassins and spies to help harass and bring down Saddam's regime. The CIA is neither as smart nor as wiley as the Kurds or Saddam. The three main Kurdish groups (PKK, PUK, KDP) do not see eye to eye nor do they have similar agendas. When the son of KDP's Barzanis formed an unholy alliance with Saddam Hussien things changed very quickly in the north. Within days the PUK was ousted, over a hundred CIA trainees were executed and the American agents had to hotfoot it over the border to Turkey.

"Welcome to Iraqi Kurdistan," says the sign. Immediately below the words a picture of the legendary Kurdish leader, Mullah Mustafa Barzani, beams reassuringly—as if to discourage any negative thoughts that you might have upon entering one of the world's more troubled regions. But if journalists and aid workers are welcomed with open arms in Kurdistan, most of the local population have a somewhat different perspective on their *de facto* Kurdish state. Six years of autonomous Kurdish rule in northern Iraq have left many not so much with a vague desire to leave, but a desperate urge to get out any way they can. But then, as a general rule of thumb, wherever the press pack heads en masse can only spell bad news for the local populance. If it's not a natural disaster, it's famine and war that have journalists flocking to such places, like so may bees around a honey pot. In the case of northern Iraq it's generally war—Kurd versus Kurd, although the specter of massive food shortages occasionally raises its ugly head, and, of course, from time to time Saddam Hussein makes an appearance for good measure—just to keep the international community on its toes.

Just one month prior to my arrival, Saddam had made a rare appearance—to the joy of the international media circus—and had helped the faction headed by Massoud Barzani to oust the rival faction of Jalal Talabani from the region. Even by Byzantine and Macheavellian standards of Kurdish politics, this was cynicism in the extreme. You could almost be forgiven for forgetting that Saddam has spent most of his spare time lobbing chemical weapons at Kurdish villages in northern Iraq—no doubt maintaining that it was all to do with population control, which is such a worry in so many parts of the Third World. Well, it was certainly population control, no error, to the tune of somewhere in the region of 250,000 Kurds. (It was otherwise called genocide.)

From the northern Iraqi town of Zakho I set out for the self-declared capital of Kudistan, Erbil. For $15, I manage to procure a taxi for the five hour journey, although after six years of sanctions, most cars are little more than battered old wrecks—rusty, unpainted and more importantly barely able to go more 20 kph. I'm drinking the local equivalent to whisky and watching the news on television when a message is thrust into my hands. "Urgent Appeal" the paper is titled. I read on with growing interest:

"It is for three days that our country and people are subjugated to the most aggressive foreign invasion in the border areas adjacent to Iran in the Governorate of Sulymanya.

"Iran is carrying out this attack with the cooperation of Jalal Talabani. We call upon all the countries throughout the world to help our people against this barbaric invasion."

It is signed, "Massoud Barzani." The next morning I dash straight for the local public relations office to see what's happening and to ask to go to the front line. Eventually, though, I hitch a lift with other newly arrived hacks. All is relatively calm, a group of peshmerga inform us. Clustered around a Toyota pick-up with a 12mm Dshk loaded on the back, they fire off a brief burst somewhere in the vague direction of the other side. We take advantage of the "calm" to pay a visit to the rival faction—but not before someone produces a white T-shirt to tie to the car's aerial.

As we cruise through no-man's land, it is not long before we see tiny figures on the distant mountain tops, and as we pull round a bend, the first checkpoint becomes visible. Slowing to a stop, a curious group of peshmerga gather around us to find out who we are. "Sahafya," or press, we say in our best Arabic. We are waved on with due decorum.

Koi Sanjaq, our first port of call, would hardly qualify for a town in the west. Its dusty alleyways and two main roads resemble a large village, but it is a typical Kurdish town with the inevitable street stalls selling everything from the tasteless locally made Aspen cigarettes, at about 15 dinars (50 cents) a packet, to ammunition webs. It is also the birthplace of Jalal Talabani. Today, however, it is crowded with Talabani's victorious militia, who have just retaken the town. The streets are jammed with hundreds of peshmerga, wearing green ribbons around their foreheads, and with Kalashnikov assault rifles slung over their shoulders. Children are shouting excitedly and waving green flags at the passing vehicles full of fighters.

We are led to the local headquarters where we meet the commander. He is none other than Kossrat Rassul, the former prime minister of Kurdistan (from happier and calmer days). He is dressed in traditional Kurdish clothing which is adorned only with a pistol at his hip. "It is," he says with a mischievous smile, "good to be a peshmerga again...politics was so boring." We ask if it will be possible to interview Mr.Talabani, and he promises to arrange it. There is, we notice, a rather substantial quantity of brand new assault rifles. Where, we muse, have these come from? "We bought them from the market," says Mr.Rassul, with an enigmatic grin, making the origins of these new weapons as clear as mud. He is not lying, (surely he wouldn't deceive the press?) and is doubtless referring to the Iranian market. We mutter sardonically *sotto voce* amongst ourselves. Otherwise, though, we have carte blanche to go where we like.

But first we are packed into Toyota Landcruisers, one for us and two for our "escort," to be driven to Jalal Talabani's mountainous camp of Zahle on the Iranian border. The drive is like a Camel Trophy race as we cruise up the massive mountainous peaks and along hairpin bends that make me shudder just looking down into the ravines far below. "So are we in Iraq or Iran?" I ask our driver. "Half-half," he replies, laughing. Talabani, when we eventually reach him, is hospitality itself as we are invited into his tent for a roast kabob supper. His manner only changes when we do the formal interview and he venomously denounces his rival, Massoud Barzani, as traitor to the Kurdish people for inviting Saddam into the region.

We head back immediately. We have to get our film back to our respective agencies as fast as possible, returning to Koi Sanjaq in the early hours without breaking down. The journey through the high mountain passes that make up Kurdistan is broken only when we stop for the periodic roadblocks. Manned by Kurdish militia, locally called peshmerga, they dress in the traditional costume: baggy trousers, waistcoats, cumberbunds, ammunition webs and AK-47s. The roads, in places, are littered with ammunition casings and the occasional burned out car or tank. From time to time I ask the driver to pull over in a village to buy a can of the universally available Coca-Cola. Sanctions there may be, but it seems that alongside weapons, Coke will always get through wherever you are. Before Erbil, however, I stop at the mountainous town of Salahudin, home to Massoud Barzani and the HQ of the Kurdistan Democratic Party. The region is in one of its sporadic peaceful lulls. I have my doubts, however, as to how long it will last.

Twenty-four hours is the answer. It is my first night in Salahudin. I am drinking *arak* and spending an unpleasant few hours in the local hotel Grotsville. But at dawn we manage to persuade a taxi driver to take us across the front line. This time, however, we are not so lucky. Our taxi driver is plainly barking mad: he drives towards the first check point as if it is the final lap of the Grand Prix. And we pay the price: the peshmerga at the check point open up on us with their AKs, although the first indication I have of this is the sight of bullets ricocheting off the tarmac around us—the sound came later. It is time for cool, calm, collected thought and fluent clear use of the local language, so I scream "Stop" as loudly as I can, as if the driver wasn't sitting right next to me, but miles away. But the bullets, to my relief, are wide, merely warning shots, and once we establish our bona fides at the check point we are waved through. No harm done, except to nerves.

It is only on arrival in the self-declared 'capital' of Iraqi Kurdistan, Erbil, that we learn that fierce fighting is taking place near the town of Dhokan. We dump our film and are almost immediately on the road again. An hour's journey and we are mingling with long columns of peshmerga marching haphazardly down the road; others are trooping up into the mountains, from where there is already the chatter of heavy machine guns. On the roadside there are two open-topped jeeps with small katusha rockets mounted on the back. Beside the jeeps the operators are peering through binoculars and range finders, muttering like mad professors. The depression of a remote control switch sends a red streak into the sky amidst eardrum shattering noise. As I watch the white mushrooms sprout on the opposite side of the valley I am foolish enough to be mildly pleased not to be on the receiving end. But, as usual, the other side are not to be outdone. A minor tit for tat ensues, the slight hiccup being that we are on the receiving end of accurate field artillery, a trifle more powerful than the katushas.

Before long the constant whistle and then scream of the shells begins to reap a grim harvest. It's the human equivalent of nine pin bowling, as the wounded are rushed off the battlefield; I decide prudence is the better part of valor. Unfortunately so do most of the fighters, and the jeep I am trying to climb into is full. But if the fighters think that retreat is an option their commanders have other ideas and promptly order them all to dismount. Even not being able to understand Kurdish the gist is clear enough: "stay and fight, it's what you're paid to do," is obviously the rather unwelcome message they are getting.

The situation soon begins to degenerate into something resembling a black comedy. From my new vantage point—a safe(ish) distance from the shelling—I watch as one group of fighters start setting up roadblocks to prevent their colleagues from retreating. But soon the men at the roadblocks are outnumbered and outgunned by those retreating. I am transfixed with admiration at the speedy way they change tack and let their colleagues through.

On my walk back to my taxi I meet a commander. He has no doubt as to what the problem is, "It is all the fault of the British government," he declares. "I see," seems to be the best response to this rather outlandish statement. "Yes," he continues, "the British, for their own perfidious reasons—old imperialist habits die hard—are supporting the other side." I promise to take the issue up with John Major, in the unlikely event of ever meeting him, before I head back for an evening's drinking at the hotel to prepare myself for the next day.

—**Roddy Scott**

LEBANON
Living with Death

The war in Lebanon was similar to Bosnia. A complicated brutal war with outsiders helping to fan the flames and eventually put them out. During this period Lebanon descended from a modern affluent Mediterranean tourist spot to hell on earth. Coskun covered this war for six years and narrowly avoided descending into the madness himself.

For more than 15 years, the war in Lebanon was the compulsory and compulsive topic of headlines and television news throughout the world—a hopeless quagmire of death and destruction. A place where we could never figure out who was killing who or why.

With its 17 different religious communities and an obsolete political system, Lebanon was, and still is, the ideal battlefield for warlords who have wanted control of this ancient region. Lebanon also became the best place for marketing and testing weaponry coming from all corners of the planet.

The war began in Ayn er-Remmane (a suburb east of Beirut), on April 13, 1975, with a massacre: During the inauguration of a church, by the leader of the Katayeb party, four people were shot dead from an unidentified car. The retaliation was immediate. A few hours later, in the same place, Christian militants machine-gunned a coach transporting

Palestinians from the camp of Sabra to the one at Tall ez-Za-
tar. Twenty-seven people died in this coach and three more in
the crowd. The answer was prompt: One hundred Christians
were killed the very next day. Massacres and revenge had become a common feature of this war.

Unlike the wars that make good movies or backdrops for
spy novels, Lebanon was not black and white, good and bad.
Lebanon was and still is a nest of wars. It is a civil war between several of the 17 religious communities. It is a national
war in which Lebanese fight Palestinians, Lebanese (or at
least some of them) fight against Syrians, Lebanese (or the
majority of them) fight against Israelis. It is a religious war
between Christians—the majority group when the state was
created in 1920. It is a war of sects between Sunnites and Shiites, the latter of whom constituted the majority, and within
the Shiite community, between Amal, pro-Syrian, and
Hezbollah, pro-Iranian. It is a war between militias of all factions, but more particularly, from the Christian group. It is a
social war pitching the poor (Christians and Muslims) against
the rich (Christians and Muslims).

What made this new medieval hierarchy so bizarre was that a few months prior, Lebanon was called the Switzerland of the East. With an affluent population of just under 3 million in 1975, it was a comfortable, tolerant, harmonious and beautiful place, and was an important seaport, banking center and holiday resort.

The war in Lebanon was my "home" for many years. I became acquainted with a lot of different people, learned about their difficulties, saw many of them wounded or dead. I saw history firsthand. The new war of terror was fraught with booby-trapped vehicles, suicide commandos, kidnappings, and so on. I would like to think that in later years, people will look at my photos, examine the faces of the people who fought this war, and try to understand why humans can do these things. I flew in and out, depending on the level of activity at the time. Like drifting in and out of a bad dream, there are certain incidents that capture the war in Lebanon and will explain the unique people, places and activities that have shaped this turbulent region.

1980—Poppies and Missiles

The history of Lebanon is best left to scholars and philosophers, since, like the rest of the Middle East, it is like a mass of knots that once untied, bears no resemblance to the original structure. When I first came to Lebanon, the war had been raging for five years. Eager to earn my spurs as a war correspondent, I went to visit the Druses, an ancient heretic sect born in Egypt around the year A.D. 986, and later classified as Muslim. I was there on a short assignment to take photos of SAM-106 missiles being secretly deployed in the Bekáa Valley by the Syrians who (at that time) backed and actually controlled the Druses. Along the road, I saw hashish plantations that kept the militiamen loyal and well paid. Drugs were an important source of income for all the militiamen controlled by the Syrians.

It is not surprising that in a war-torn country with a dismembered economy, the people try to make the quickest profits possible. The missiles were there all right, amidst the hashish fields.

1982—A View to a Kill

I flew into Cyprus (the Greek side) from Paris because the airport in Lebanon was closed. We then waited for two days before taking a cargo boat transporting wood to the Lebanese port of Jounieh. The Israelis had crossed their common frontier with Lebanon and were moving forward toward West Beirut. Their ultimate target was to be the headquarters of the Feddayins of the Palestinian Liberation Organization (PLO), led by the ever elusive Yasir Arafat, and other Palestinian groups. Around the same time, the Israeli Air Force launched heavy bombing raids using American-made fighters and Israeli-made *Kfirs*.

It is hot and sunny out, but the black smoke has turned everything to grey. From time to time, I can hear small explosions accompanied by bursts of flames.

The journalists are all staying at the Hotel Commodore off Hamra Street. This is where the journalists usually gather to watch the war. Today, I have decided to set up my observation from the terrace of the Hotel Carlton, a cheaper place but affording an equally cinematic vista of Beirut under the bombs. The Carlton Hotel is situated in the residential quarter of West Beirut in Raoucheh, by the coast. I spend time with an Algerian journalist named Sadri. The streets below are empty. Everybody is seeking refuge underground. For the first time in my life, I am watching the heavy bombing of a modern city. We stare in amazement at the jets hurling down dangerously close to the ground (100 to 200 meters). At the same time, warships launch their shells from the Mediterranean Sea, shooting missiles of 150- to 240mm caliber. The noise and destruction are overwhelming—30,000 people die during those terrible days, most of them civilians buried in the rubble of collapsing and burning buildings. I am struck by the Israelis deliberately killing innocent people—people who are not attacking them, but who are easy to kill. I do not know whether to be angry or appalled.

We decide to climb down from our "watchtower," on the 13th story's terrace, to take pictures of the destruction. There are two armed men ahead of us. Suddenly, the two of them turn toward Sadri and myself, abruptly asking us to hand over our cameras. I think at first they are going to take all the cameras, but I soon understand that they only want mine because I have got the latest Nikons whereas Sadri has only old Leicas. Our two aggressors then shoot around our feet and start shouting at us to freeze. Then they frantically run away, holding our cameras tightly in their hands. A young Palestinian man, wearing a *keffieh* and a sash, who has been watching from a nearby balcony, comes down to the street and asks us for details, then starts making a call on his walkie-talkie. Soon men in jeeps and military vehicles arrive on the scene. They ask us, "Where did the thieves run?" After indicating the way, I am told that direction leads to the headquarters of the Panarab party, the Mourabitoun, which follows Nasser's ideology.

The bombing is still going on, but the Palestinians seem to ignore it; they surround the Mourabitoun building, and one of them, using a megaphone, requests the cameras as well as the surrender of the thieves. Their answer does not come in words but in bullets. The Palestinians reply in kind. During the shoot-out we take cover under a car. The car explodes from a grenade thrown by a Mourabitoun, and we are dragged out by a Palestinian fighter. The shoot-out lasts about 30 minutes. Finally, the men inside the building send out our cameras. The cost for their return has been three men killed and 10 people wounded.

1982—Through a Glass Darkly

I knew a young man, a Christian Maronite, during those turbulent days in Lebanon. He had told me about his education at the Sorbonne (he spoke perfect French) and revealed his refined taste for arts and culture. He was involved in a shoot-out against another faction, and I was there to cover the event, confident in my friend's desire to protect me from harm. But under fire, the blood lust comes. He becomes another person, shouting, firing, demonstrating his joy at killing people. In the massacre that ensues, it is obvious that he is deriving great pleasure at cutting off the heads and ears of his victims. He even tries to kill me, after having declared his friendship the very day before, when he sees me taking pictures of what he is doing.

####

I had planned to go to Khalde, near the front, with my friend Reza, an Iranian photographer working, like me, for SIPA, a photo agency. We decide to leave in the very early morning and on foot, since nobody wants to take the risk of driving us there due to the intense gunfire. We want to see for ourselves how far the Israelis have advanced and to take some pictures.

Khalde is a small town facing the Mediterranean Sea about 10 kilometers away from Beirut and about eight kilometers from Baabda, the inland town where the Lebanese presidential palace stands. The Israelis had been progressing very quickly over the past few days, using the coastal highway across Israel and Lebanon. Baabda is about to fall, and soon afterwards so will Beirut.

We walk in the rising heat toward the white smoke in the distance and listen to the sound of the gunnery; we are also aware of the brisk clattering noise made by the bursts of machine guns and the isolated shots of automatic weapons. We come across two soldiers walking slowly in the heat. One is helping the other, who is obviously terminally wounded. They do not utter a word as we pass them and do not even acknowledge our presence when I take their picture.

Nothing unusual perhaps, but enough to force us to breathe a little faster and to feel a little edgy.

The tension and mounting fear get to us, and Reza stops and says he will not go any further because it is too trying to do anything in such adverse conditions.

For some reason, I decide to carry on alone, and there I am walking and getting tired when I see a group of people near a petrol station. It is on the front. I am stopped by one of them who is carrying a Kalashnikov. He asks who I am, listening carefully to my answer. Then he tells me that he and his friends belong to the SAIKA, a pro-Syrian organization fighting against the Israelis. As soon as he understands I am Turkish and I speak a little Arabic, he befriends me, telling me his name, Saleh, and offering me some tea and sandwiches.

We all sit around an improvised table made from an oil drum. I take some pictures of him. One photo is still my favorite, a portrait in classic warrior pose; he's ready to shoot on sight, looking through the hole left by a shell in the inner wall of an abandoned house. All the while, the bombardment is going on around us.

Then it happens: First a giant flash of white light, followed by a shock... around me everything seems to be rocking, and I lose consciousness for a minute.... When I wake-up again, I can see nothing but dust. I think that it must have been the explosion of a shell. Everything is so silent that I think I have lost my sense of hearing.

The dust settles and I realize that I am surrounded by the pieces of hacked bodies. I panic. The next thing I remember is that I can hear again; people are shouting and running in every direction. Around me nothing is the same anymore: tables upturned, glass broken, dust, rubble...blood, torn limbs...and so on. I look at myself frantically. I have been lucky. I am complete, without even a bruise, but I am trembling. Then I see them: Saleh's eyes, wide open, transfixed, staring at me. The explosion had instantly killed most of the people who were drinking tea around us. Only Saleh, the Syrians and I have been spared.

All of a sudden, a man comes to the scene from the burning petrol station, brandishing his Kalashnikov. He starts yelling that I am a spy, responsible for the bombings, and that I ought to die. He shoots in my direction. For a second, I am petrified. Saleh understands the danger faster than I, and he shouts at me to run away to a safer place. Thanks to his intervention, I realize that my life is at stake and I start running away as fast as I can, leaving the burning petrol station behind me.

Nobody has followed me. I shut myself in a bath cabin. And I cry and cry and cry....

I stay in the bath cabin for a few hours, till the end of the bombardment. In the evening, I go out and walk back to Beirut. I am still in a state of shock when I meet a fellow photographer, Patrick Chauvel, who works for Sygma.

As I tell him my story, I realize that in the panic, I have left all my cameras behind near the petrol station. Chauvel cheers me up and tells me not to worry. His words cannot calm me, since I realize that without my cameras I am just an idiot wandering through a war zone.

The next morning, I start asking everybody how I can go back to Khalde to fetch my cameras.

I find an Italian nurse working, like Saleh, for the SAIKA organization. She drives me in her ambulance to look for the leaders of the SAIKA. We find them just as the bombardment is resuming.

We go inside a grocery store to feel the illusory but comforting presence of a ceiling above our heads. The gunnery is intense. We have nothing to do but wait anxiously. I feel useless without my cameras. Suddenly, as if answering my silent prayers, one of the combatants comes smiling like a politician, proudly handing me a video camera. I explain to him that it is not mine since I only work with still cameras; he says I can have that one as a replacement. I agree to take it anyway to prevent an argument. I can tell by the stickers that it belongs to the CBC (Canadian Broadcasting Company) who are staying at the same hotel as I am.

Back at the hotel, I return the videocamera to the Canadian television crew who had lost it the day before.

I feel anguished not to be able to take pictures. Luckily, Robin Moyer, a *Time* correspondent, lets me borrow one of his cameras.

Two days later, the Italian nurse comes to tell me that my cameras have been found among the corpses of Palestinians in the morgue of Sabra in West Beirut. One of my cameras is broken, but the other one is still usable. I am happy to retrieve them but sad to do so on corpses. I cannot help thinking that a piece of these people is inside my bashed cameras, along with their joy when they took pictures of each other with my cameras and how their happiness had been halted so stupidly and so suddenly.

####

SIPA covers only half of my expenses while I am in Lebanon. To stay one night in Beirut costs as much as US$400 in a big hotel, so I decide to stay in a hotel inside a refugee camp opposite the Hotel Commodore. The other journalists can afford to be driven around in armored vehicles and stay in the Commodore. A Palestinian named Mahmud has become my driver, and he provides me with all sorts of information and help.

####

I take an interesting shot, in East Beirut, of a woman carrying a child in her arms running away from the explosions. She is surrounded by soldiers carrying machine guns who seem to protect her amidst cars and rubble and smoke. One can see how the people had to move from house to house during the bombing in order to avoid getting killed. This picture has been taken with a broken camera (that's why it is blurry) because of the bombings.

The other journalists cannot go out of their hotel. I manage to snap this shot and others, because I am close to the action. But it is impossible to send my film out because of the siege. The American television crews organize "shippings," but the print journalists who want to use this system have to pay $10,000 per package. I only have $100, but my friend Reza proposes to put my film with his own in an envelope to be given to the American newspapermen.

I am most surprised when I get a telegram of congratulations a few days later. The pictures had reached Paris via New York, and I am told that one of my pictures had been chosen to become the cover of *Time* magazine, *Paris Match, VSD* (French) and other magazines around the world.

####

Being a war correspondent, I can say that I was there when it happened. My photos are silent witnesses to war. Most people see these scenes on TV during their evening meal, are very moved for a short while, and then flip the channel to something else. But a magazine photo can haunt you for a long time.

####

I am in a street not far from the Hotel Commodore, the general headquarters for the Red Cross, when a booby-trapped car explodes. Usually journalists arrive with the police and the military too late to capture anything but the confusion and wet blood.

For once, I am there right on time and I have the reflexes to take photos during the panic scene which follows the ex-

plosion. Everybody is running, desperately looking for shelter
or just to get away.

I notice a young man start running who is wearing only a
white singlet and carrying his pajama-clad son. He is followed
by his wife. He is holding a silver pistol in his right hand. I
start taking pictures of the three, rapidly running along with
them as they rush in my direction. I am quite excited with my
eye glued to the viewfinder, and so the pictures will come out
a little blurry. I see him leveling his pistol at me, taking aim
and shooting, but I don't connect his actions with reality.
And he keeps shooting as he runs by me. All around me, everyone is screaming and yelling. The explosion has blown out
all the windowpanes around us, and the noise of the glass
crunching and shattering under the feet of the passersby adds
to the cacophony. Then the sirens take over, first those of the
ambulances, very quickly and on the spot, as usual in Beirut,
then those of the vehicles of the civil protection.

After the scene has calmed down I walk back to my hotel,
and it is only then, in the lobby, that I realize what had happened. The hotel attendants and the clients are all watching
me with a look half disgusted, half concerned. I looked at my
clothes, trying to understand what is wrong; then I put my
hand on my head. When I remove my hand, I see that it is
smeared with blood. The man's bullet had grazed my scalp.

1985—The Show Must Go On

In Beirut, a massacre always follows another massacre. The
chain is impeccable and implacable. This time, it is the Druzes who are responsible for the deaths of some 300 Christian
combatants of the Kataeb party and of the Lebanese forces.
The Druzes have lived for centuries in the mountains of the
Shuf and been considered to be ferocious warriors. Their

leader is Wallid Jumblatt (the son of Kamal Jumblatt, founder of the PSP, Progressive Socialist Party).

The Druzes have just finished a merciless battle in the mountains overlooking Beirut, in the southeast of the city, which they won against the Phalangists. Once their victory was assured, they immediately perpetrated a massacre in order to avenge another massacre perpetrated against them (so they claim) by the Christian Phalangists.

I go to Bhamdoun, about 20 kilometers southeast of Beirut with two other journalists to visit Wallid Jumblatt and see the situation. The two other journalists are Samy Ketz of the AFP (*Agence France Presse*, French Press Agency) and David Hirst of the *Guardian*. We have been blindfolded to prevent us from seeing the exact location of the headquarters.

We meet with Wallid Jumblatt; then we go to see firsthand the extent of the damage inflicted upon Bhamdoun and its defenders. Although we are forbidden from taking pictures, we are not blindfolded and I am able to take some photos with an autofocus camera. I count approximately 300 dead. Most of them had been killed, after having been captured, hanged with electrical wires, and dragged through the streets, where they were abandoned like trash. It is hard to understand how killing, and killing cruelly can be such a joyful activity.

I am able to photograph the gaiety of the Muslim combatants after they have massacred their enemies. Some of them had discovered some mannequins in a shop and amused themselves with one of these, transporting it to the street in front of me, and then hanging it with a cable. A placard was attached under its strangled neck on which they hastily wrote the name: Amin Gemaye (the Christian president of Lebanon). One of the Muslim militia kisses a dummy dressed in a grey flannel three-piece suit. The whole scene is surrealistic. They do it because they are aware I am recording their actions. It is not much different from what soccer supporters do after a match or what happens during a carnival. The camera is a tease.

####

The Muslim militiamen of the AMAL movement had asked some photojournalists to accompany them. The sky, usually bright blue, is evenly grey-white, very shiny, and quite disturbing for the eyes—not very good for pictures either. The militants want us to come to the vicinity of an ancient well situated 10 kilometers north of Sidon. It's in a region that was recently under the control of the Lebanese forces and has fallen into the hands of the Shiites of the AMAL movement and the Druses of Wallid Jumblatt's PSP. They had just made a horrible discovery.

Hunters had signaled to the militiamen the presence of corpses in the bottom of an ancient well. The militiamen had to go down wearing gas masks. When we arrive, they show us the decomposed bodies of Muslim militants killed a year before on a beach near Sidon during a massacre by the Christians.

Later, I learn that there is some doubt about the identity of the corpses I had photographed near Sidon. Some people claim that they are not Shiite Muslims but perhaps even Christians. A small voice awakens in my head:

Like a bullet, I pride myself on my lack of alignment or cause, but I am becoming a tool for killers, a weapon to be used by whomever wants to create damage.

####

Some time later, I take a photo-souvenir of a very special sort. It is in Jieh, a Christian village set along the road to Sidon. This village has been besieged by Wallid Jumblatt forces. They eventually managed to break the resistance of the villagers, and on their victory, they allowed the photographers to take pictures of their rejoicing. They look like the famous hunters of the safari days in the African savanna, proudly posing with one foot on the slaughtered lion. The difference is that the lion has been replaced this time by an unlucky and very dead enemy soldier.

The men are proudly posing, lifting their weapons high above their heads in a victory gesture, while stepping joyfully on the corpse of their enemy, as if they were walking on a carpet.

Without this picture, the world might seem saner, cleaner and fairer, but now that this picture is recorded, people will know how low humanity can sink.

####

Weapons and soldiers. That's what the war is about, no? I have taken countless shots of both. It is always a surprise for me to see how the soldier identifies himself with his weapon. Everybody knows that there is something sensual about holding a weapon. In the case of men holding a gun or a machine gun, it also has something to do with male pride. I have never encountered a soldier who refused to be photographed, and in every case the rifle or gun is raised upward like an erection.

In Lebanon, stereotypes are falling apart. There is a clash of cultures and images. In past wars, soldiers were like football players. One red, one green. One good, one bad. Here, everyone is evil, everyone is righteous. There is no regular army to speak of. The militiamen are usually dressed in a hodgepodge of half-civilian, half-military clothing. They choose

freely the fashion they want to follow after their favorite my-
thology, revealing an incredible mixture of Western and Ori-
ental influences. Some of these men wear big cowboy hats, or
T-shirts with the picture of Ayatollah Ruhollah Khomeini on
them, or hairbands and ammunition bands crossed on their
chest like Mexican revolutionaries in Zapata's time.

All the world's a stage and we are just actors upon it.

These past days, I have accompanied the Druses militia
close to the demarcation line in the Shuf mountains in southeast Beirut. They are fighting against the Christian Phalangists, using Soviet-built tanks that they received from their
Syrian allies. With these weapons, the fight will be fierce and
not likely to last very long. I manage to get close to what is
happening. I always have to remember that I only have a still
camera, not a movie camera. I have to take shots with conti-
nuity, so as to make my "story" understandable. Sometimes I
wish I could just watch and direct what is happening to tell
the story. I am allowed 36 pictures for each camera I carry;
then I must reload.

I try to capture the essential moments even though I have
no idea of the outcome of each battle. The dust flying, the
oblique light of the sun contrasting with the silhouettes of
the soldiers, the sudden movement of a tank, the bursting of
a shell, the assault of the infantry, the last moments of a soldier brought on a stretcher to an ambulance. I am able to
take these pictures because I follow the militiamen everywhere instead of staying in a downtown hotel with the rest of
the journalists.

*I am becoming biased because I am learning too
much.*

1986—I Am the Piano Player

Snipers get their kicks shooting at isolated and unarmed people. Many snipers are mercenaries hiding out in apartments on top of buildings.

I meet a sniper today, a Frenchman, who uses a rifle specially designed for his line of work, made in the U.S.A. He would shoot people, then play the piano, mostly Mozart, then resume his watch, waiting for the next target to come along. He killed children or old ladies without remorse or hesitation. Dozens of deaths have been attributed to him, but he has never expressed the slightest regret because, as he explained to me, he was on the demarcation line, the line that separates Beirut into two parts, East and West, and it was not to be crossed. Therefore, he had every right to do what he did.

Special rifles are available for conscientious snipers. For example, the American M-16 with a field glass and the Soviet-made Brejnev. I took many pictures of people trying to pass the demarcation line; very few of them made it.

My advice concerning snipers is to never be number three. The first one across the street has a 90 percent chance, the second has a 50 percent chance, but the third has no chance at all, because the sniper has had ample time to adjust his aim and tracking.

I am beginning to remember rules that should never be needed.

The main contradiction of a war is its perpetual vacillating between lawlessness and obeyance to strict and strange rules. To kill at random whatever comes in front of your rifle does not mean there are no situations where some sort of rules are followed. In the past, for example, the soldiers were not supposed to go about killing each other during certain periods of the day, at night, and on Sundays.

In Beirut, there is an unwritten tradition, somewhat bizarre, probably inherited from the Middle Ages, and respected by all parties: Shoot from 5 a.m. till 8 a.m., then stop for breakfast, and resume shooting up to lunch time, stop again for lunch and a siesta, and resume shooting until sundown.

1986

The influence of Muslim fundamentalism is felt more and more in Lebanon. It comes from Iran whose leaders have always said they wanted to export their Islamic Revolution to all the Arab countries first and then to the rest of the world. As Islam is the second most important religion in Lebanon, it was normal that the new ideology would provoke a tremor in the diverse Muslim communities. Things would have been complicated enough that way, but the Iranians infiltrated the country and trained the people to the new ideas so that many turned to Iran as a model to follow. A movement was born that was soon going to be well known throughout the world for the expediency of its methods and for its extremism. This movement is the Hezbollah, the Party of God.

The Shiites have been influenced by the Khomeini-like AMAL militia. I have taken many photos that show the extent of the personality cult to which the famous Ayatollah is subjected in the various Muslim communities and factions.

Fanaticism is an indispensable feature of many wars, especially those fought for religious reasons. Everybody remembers the kamikaze of the Second World War who gladly gave their lives for their Emperor-God. The same thing happened in Iran during its eight-year-long war against Iraq, and in Lebanon. Sana, the young Palestinian girl who blew herself up in the explosion of a truck she had loaded with explosives, was a modern kamikaze. She took the time to explain her gesture to journalists (including myself) and had taped a message that was distributed to the press after the success of the operation.

####

Looting and robbing became very commonplace in Lebanon. People actually went shopping with a weapon.

I come across the body of an old man who has been murdered for the plastic bags full of goods he had just bought in Beirut.

I can imagine him, just moments before, walking peacefully under the bright blue sky, feeling the warm sun on his back and the heat bouncing off the hot road. The shining light is difficult to bear, so he lowers his head. Suddenly, everything seems to blur, the world around him stops, the light diminishes, and a pain digs into his belly. He has dropped his bags; blood is gushing out of his bowels. He dies wondering what he has done to deserve such an ending....

Why am I taking a picture of this?

####

I have heard that the young Lebanese militants have taken up Russian roulette as a badge of courage. I introduce myself to a group of militants averaging 19 years of age. I gain their trust slowly, and I eventually ask them how they feel about the war and how they cope with anxiety, fear of death, and the like. I also talk to them about my own fear of death; then I switch from this topic to war being a big lottery, and what do they think of games, gambling, etc. At last, I am able to ask them about Russian roulette, saying only that I have been told it is common practice for the militants but that I have never seen proof.

They remain mute for a while; then one of them nods in a silent acquiescence. He explains to me that almost all the militants, whatever the party, play this game, that he himself has played it often and that it is quite an enthralling experience, quite addictive in fact. I then ask him to permit me to photograph them during a game, but they quickly reply that it is not possible because all this is done clandestinely and that if their chiefs hear about it they will be punished. I eventually manage to photograph them, but due to my subjects' suspicion of being jinxed I am barred from taking pictures of the real game of death.

The table is set with a white tablecloth. The bets have already been taken. The game is for money and for the thrill. The rules of the game are simple and well known. Everybody bets on the chances of the shooter surviving and the game starts. The game must be played with a six-shot revolver, usually a small Smith & Wesson or Colt Detective. One bullet is loaded into the chamber, and the cylinder is spun around. Without looking, the player must hold the pistol to his temple and pull the trigger.

If he survives, the gun is passed, the barrel spun and the trigger pulled again.

The game can stop at any time or start anew. In Lebanon, some men have taken to playing this game alone.

This nihilistic game is perfect for Lebanon, where life is worth little and drugs and death provide the entertainment. In the beginning of the war, they were content with smoking hashish or marijuana to pass the time. Now it is cocaine and heroin. Death is the ultimate high.

The young bearded man has put a gun on his right temple. He is now facing his possible imminent death. The others watch him in awe. For a brief moment, he is a superior being, a true hero; in a second he might become a true zero....Like a powerful drug, every drop of adrenaline surges to his brain, he pulls the trigger slowly, his testicles tighten, and then...click. Today he is lucky—after all, it was but a mock game.

Two days after having posed for these photos, he tried his luck once more, with a loaded pistol this time (the very one in my pictures), and died. There was no click.

How can young men kill themselves for no reason? Russians invented this game when they were bored on the battlefield. These photos were taken 10 years after the beginning of the war. These young men have known nothing but war, death and violence during the crucial years of their adolescence.

I have heard that sound before. Click is the sound my shutter makes when I push the button. With that click comes the same rush of adrenaline, the feeling of omnipotence. As long as I click that shutter, I am immortal, free from death, separated from the horror on the other side of my lens. But someday I will not hear the click.

The incident happened during Terry Waite's press conference at the Hotel Commodore, the headquarters for the French press. An Anglican minister from England, Waite had come to Beirut to help find a solution to free the hostages and ended up kidnapped and remaining as a hostage for more than three years himself.

A car with three passengers inside is the target of a shoot-out probably just aimed at scaring Terry Waite. When the car stops in the middle of the street, I realize that the driver has been hit by a bullet. I rush to help the driver, forgetting about taking pictures, and try pulling him out. An American journalist (working for *U.S. News*) comes to our rescue, but we both arrive too late. The driver of the car is dead.

Later on, the driver is considered a hero by the militiamen and other witnesses of the simple violent event. The shooting is filmed by the cameramen who have come for the press conference and is shown around the world by the TV networks.

Just another death, no pictures, another nameless victim.

####

I am traveling in and out of the main Palestinian camps of Beirut, Sabra and Chatila and Borj el Barajneh. They are all situated in the south of Beirut, not far from the City of Sports. The war is more violent than ever. The leader of Shiite militia AMAL, Nabih Berri, who is also the minister of state for South Lebanon and who proclaimed himself minister of national resistance to fight against the Israelis, receives his orders from Syria and has the camps attacked.

The AMAL and the Lebanese forces militiamen can be organized like search-and-destroy teams and go from one house to the other to accomplish their task, or they surround a quarter and wait patiently for the end, cutting all the roads and blockading the supply of food and water. The people inside are starving, and some have already died of hunger and thirst. Those who are daring enough to get out are killed instantly by the militiamen standing outside.

The women and the children are, of course, suffering more than the men, because they cannot fight and must wait anxiously for the outcome of all this. They already know by instinct that the worst is always guaranteed. I also try to record their suffering for their history. Sometimes the women come to me, begging me to stop this nightmare, as if I can do something about it. My so-called "neutral position" makes everybody believe I can be a go-between.

Some Palestinians manage to sneak out of the camps, but the militiamen are waiting outside, and whenever they have a doubt about the identity of one person or another, they apply what is known around here as the "tomato test." It consists of asking the person caught to pronounce the Arabic word for "tomato." A Palestinian will denounce himself immediately by pronouncing this word as *panadora* instead of *ponadora*, which is the way the other Arabs pronounce it around here. Once a Palestinian is found, he is usually taken aside and executed. Hundreds of people have already died that way, or another, since the reawakening of intercommunal feuds.

####

Today, I follow and photograph a child who has probably become half-crazy because of the bombings. He is hanging around in the camp of Sabra, wearing only his underwear and a pair of grotesque pink slippers, far too big for him. As soon as he sees me, he starts behaving like a clown, dancing, chanting, making faces amidst the rubble and the ruins of the camp. I take many pictures of him, because he seems to me the epitome of what has happened to the people here. Being very young, he represents the future of this world without a future. His hopeless behavior reminds us of the hopeless world that humankind is proposing for the young generation of this country who were born with the war. Next to him is a young man wearing a funny straw hat, his face covered by a yellow handkerchief like a bandit set out to attack the stagecoach in the western movies, but this one has given it a personal touch—he has poked three holes in his mask in order to breathe and see. This young man was following the kid; he is probably his brother or a relative. I found the contrast between the two very weird.

####

I did something unusual, even for me, a few days ago. Something which has left a bitter taste in my mouth. Photojournalists are sometimes like vultures hovering above and around those who are going to die or who have already met their demise, in the vulgar expectation of a spectacular shot.

The light is bright as usual in this "blessed" country, but the sky is uniformly white. I go to a Palestinian camp near Sidon during a heavy attack. The camp has been bombed nonstop for many days. The shells keep exploding around us, damaging only the walls of the houses, until one, guided by I don't know which force, bursts out very close to a group of people. A child happens to be there....badly injured in the chest and belly, he dies almost immediately.

I then see his father, a man in his late twenties, coming to his side, in a very dignified way. He covers the frail dead body, still dripping blood, with a white sheet in the false hope to stop the draining and to resuscitate his son.

He quickly understands that the task is beyond his limited powers and he lifts his child in his arms, unaware of his weight, and directs his steps toward the cemetery. I decide to follow him. We are alone. No one else has come. I am taking photos all the while. I will never forget the gaze in his eyes.

In a universal gesture of love, devotion and pity, he is looking for the proper place to bury his child.

There are still human feelings in Lebanon. I am thankful I still have mine.

—Coskun Aral

LIBERIA
Theme Park of the Macabre

West Africa has never been known for stabilty, amenities or civilization. It is why both England and America created pretend countries for ex-slaves in an attempt to erase all the evils done by slavery. It didn't work. There is dark bloodlust that erupts and drags the people down with it. This blood lust is made bizarre by the Liberians love of American culture, slang and identity. In other words Liberians look to America as the mother country.

Getting into Monrovia is cheap, getting out is not. The Russian Hind ferried journalists into the war zone at no charge (we find out later that it costs $5000 to get 11 people out). When we arrive we find out that the new economy is driven by journalists, $12 for french fries, $4 for a beer or a half a gallon of water. We take a ride with the U.S. Marines who are evacuating terrified expats and civilians. Considering that we are being dropped into a confused fire fight, we find it funny that they explain how our life jacket works and give us ear plugs to avoid hearing loss.

The Sea Knights fly in a group of three, it seems to be over-kill against the freaked out kids with broken rifles and sticks below. Shots are fired up at us from the ground. The Marines respond with devastating firepower from all three helicopters. The choppers land in the huge compound in the U.S. Embassy. We sign a release form absolving the Americans from any blame. A strange formality after watching the machine guns blast away at the fighters on the ground. This is a land with no laws, no higher court and nobody to protect us. It is truly the law of the jungle. As the throbbing Sea Knights lift off we are keenly aware that there is no way out know. We have arrived in Hell without a return ticket.

The size of the compound is roughly ten football fields and there are about 2000 Liberians camped out. At one end is the loot market. Here everything from escargot to computers are for sale. All the material has been looted and there is a definite shortage of buyers.

We stay at a Lebanese run hotel. It is supposedly safe here because the two Lebanese brothers (who fought with the Falangists in Lebanon) pay off the warring groups. It has the curious distinction of being used by the factions as the marker for the end of the fighting since it is about 200 meters from the well-protected U.S. embassy. It costs $200 a night but they fulfill the two main needs of all combat journalists: a satellite phone and a bar.

The fighting rages on at night but it is quiet in the morning. We walk out and meet with Roosevelt's group, the Krahns. It looks like a nursery school, children as young as 6 or 7 are among the fighters. I guess it's not much different than playing G.I. Joe except this is the real thing and you get killed when you lose instead of crying to your mother. The morning is the time when the soldiers scrounge for food and booze, clean their weapons and play a little football. They also smoke weed which grows wild here. As the drugs and alcohol take over, the insults will begin and the fighting will begin.

We decide to see what the government forces are up to. It's a long walk, since there are few private cars and only scrounged gas. To use a silly but appropriate cliche, it is hot as hell.

The fighters like journalists. They think they will be famous if we take their picture. In fact many will do things they would not normally do because they think they might be on the cover of *Time*. Beheadings and mutilations are offered but refused. It is almost a design your own atrocity place for the "bang-bang" folks.

The situation is understandably confused. Roosevelt's troops control the suburbs and Taylor's troops control the center. It is important to keep in mind that Taylor's forces are not thrilled with the idea of journalists documenting their activities. The peacekeepers called ECOMOG are rarely keeping the peace. For now Taylor's forces have rockets and mortars and usually win any pitched battle. The battles start with a charge. One side (usually Roosevelt's) will break and run, drawing Taylor's troops deeper into the suburbs and unfamiliar areas. Then the Roosevelt troops will circle around and attack the attackers from behind and the sides. The government troops will break and run to the safety of their lines. Along the way a few people are left dead or dying. The dead ones are the lucky ones since now the blood lust and adrenaline take over and the atrocities begin. The fighters invite us to watch what will happen. We put our cameras away.

We go to visit the hospital. All they have is prayer. There is about one doctor for 10,000 people here. As we leave the hospital we bump into a tough group of Roosevelt's men. These fighters have been trained and carry AK-47s. They are surrounded by children who carry anything that even looks like a gun. They wear bizarre items like wigs and life jackets that they say protect them from the bullets. They are here for the thrill, the smell of blood and the exhilaration of escaping death. They dance, sing songs, yell insults and wiggle their private parts at the opposing side to incite a battle. One kid fires his rifle in time to the music playing on his Walkman. It is common to see a small child beat an older person senseless with his rifle just for fun. The leaders give the children drugs making them even more savage.

The one place that no one trifles with is the U.S. Embassy. Snipers shoot to kill and they don't miss. Marines with machine guns have no qualms about wiping out any foolhardy warriors who shoot at them. The dead are like a macabre theme park. Each side uses a totem or fetish to show their territory. Monrovia is decorated with severed heads put on tables as warnings, children with deep knife wounds and bloated corpses. I get some other journalists to help me drag an old man who is wounded in the face by shrapnel to the hospital. It seems to be a trivial symbol of decency in this godforsaken place. We know that he will not make it, but we feel better for helping him.

Running low on money and getting weary of the brutality, we buy places on one of the Hind helicopters back to Freetown in Sierra Leone. There is a huge fuel tank and a large Coca Cola sign inside the worn Russian helicopter. Like the end of a bad nihilistic science fiction movie we are leaving a social experiment gone badly wrong and can't wait for the lights to come up and the darkness to end.

—**Coskun Aral**

My First War Zone

*Anthony Morland was another DP'er who wandered into
Monrovia during the war. He was there at the same time as
Coskun and provides a sense of perspective between the two.*

At least the dogs had a good time of it. From the balcony
of the Mamba Point Hotel I could see a small pack of mon-
grels, perhaps half a dozen, gathered on a beach where huge
Atlantic rollers crashed incessantly, ignorant of the mayhem
that had brought these shores to international headlines.
Food had become very scarce so I was surprised to see the
dogs gorging themselves, tails wagging contentedly. Most
people could hardly afford the inflated cost of feeding themselves, so it seemed unlikely anyone would think of the welfare of animals.

They hadn't. A convenient telescope revealed the largest
and fiercest of the dogs chewing on something I couldn't
quite make out. A slight adjustment brought into focus five
swollen brown figures, then an arm, then my first ever human
corpse.

"Welcome to Monrovia," said a war-junkie photographer, handing me a beer.

####

I arrived in the Liberian capital in early May, three weeks after the city exploded into an orgy of factional clashes and violent looting. U.S. Marines were still evacuating American citizens and other "friendly nationals," a massive operation that promoted this hitherto neglected corner of West Africa to the number one media event across the globe.

Back in April, ashen-faced evacuees landing in Freetown—the capital of neighboring Sierra Leone—had spoken of being robbed in their homes at gunpoint, often by children carrying automatic weapons as tall as themselves. Hundreds of fighters, many making their first visit to the capital after battling in the bush since civil war broke out in December 1989, roamed the streets of Monrovia, exhilarated by the freedom to help themselves with impunity. Little of the cash generated by Liberia's rich resources of diamonds, timber, and scrap metal had gone much further than the faction leaders during the war. Pay day for the foot soldiers had arrived at last.

The West African peacekeeping force, known as ECOMOG, sent to Liberia in 1990, and in charge of security in the "safe haven" of Monrovia, seemed powerless to prevent either the looting or the battles raging downtown. Some witnesses saw ECOMOG troops joining in the pillage.

The first journalists to land at the U.S. embassy, courtesy of the Marine Corps, were greeted by an exasperated Ambassador William Milam.

"What the hell do you want to come here for? Everyone else is trying to leave!"

####

Liberian civilians certainly were not having a good time of it. The million residents of a capital whose population had doubled since the start of the war because of its "safe haven" status did not get much airtime on the networks. A few thousand, however, were granted their fifteen minutes of fame by virtue of being crushed for ten days into a leaky, rusting Nigerian freighter with little food or water, let alone sanitary facilities, as Liberia's West African neighbors, one after the other, refused to let it dock.

Did the hundreds of paid-up wanna-be Bulk Challenge passengers left behind in Monrovia's port feel lucky to have been spared such a nightmare odyssey? No. Living in freight containers neatly arranged in rows on the port's football pitch, sometimes more than a dozen to a container, their unanimous sentiment was: "We've had enough. We want to leave now."

####

If Monrovia was a mess before the spring clashes—with no power lines, little running water and that tired look of a city in dire need of several thousand gallons of fresh paint—by the time the fighters had made their mark, with rockets, bullets, spray paint and a burglar's disregard for the personally sacred, downtown areas of the capital became uninhabitable. Most of the time the city was deserted by all except a few uniformed and armed peacekeepers and Lebanese traders busy welding closed the steel shutters of their supermarkets and electrical goods stores. Occasionally, when calm broke out, civilians would venture out in search of water, food, and lost relatives. Sticking close to the side of buildings, they would snake in single file only to scatter in seconds when gunfire erupted.

The streets were strewn with a bewildering variety of refuse. Rubble from shelled houses, rotting corpses, ragged clothes, passports (boxes of unused ones had been stolen from the foreign ministry) and other documents. I could hardly take a step without sending shell casings clattering or treading on somebody's cherished collection of family photographs, rejected as worthless by the looters—who, incidentally, emerged from the ranks of all of the factions. Jimmy, for example, a 27-year-old Libero-Lebanese, was at home when the frontline moved past his house. Ethnic Krahn fighters swarmed in, put one gun to his head, another to his belly and told him: "We're gonna steal everything and then we're gonna kill you." They were halfway done with the first part of their promise when the frontline changed again and the Krahns swarmed back out to do battle, giving Jimmy a chance to flee to the building next door...the Mamba Point Hotel. From the balcony, Jimmy had a clear view of so-called government forces (in reality fighters loyal to Charles Taylor and Alhaji Kromah, but what's important is they were fighting the Krahns) taking over from where the others had left off. By the time they were through, Jimmy's house looked like it had been derelict for years.

The only vehicles that moved were ECOMOG's armored personnel carriers, looted aid agency 4x4's, and windowless and often doorless jalopies, spilling over with heavily armed youths, their factional allegiance displayed in messy graffiti. One group had installed an antiaircraft gun in the well of a stolen pickup truck.

When fighting broke out in early April, thousands of civilians fled the city center for makeshift camps for the displaced, such as the Greystone compound, a 27-acre site once housing just seven U.S. diplomats and their families. It quickly became the temporary home to 20,000 Monrovians. As if the threat of cholera and other diseases were not enough, Greystone's residents had to put up with a daily diet of gunfire and explosions as factions battled just outside the compound's walls. Stray bullets ended their trajectories in tragedy on several occasions.

At least the kids with the guns had a good time of it, even when doing their utmost to kill each other. Perhaps it was fortunate that this was an activity carried out with staggering incompetence. Most of those involved in direct combat were very young teenagers already veterans of a war that by 1993 had claimed the lives of 150,000, mainly civilian, Liberians. Only commanders were beyond their twenties. They had adopted a bizarre variety of *noms de guerre*. Among the "senior officers" I met were Generals No Mother No Father, Housebreaker, Fuck Me Quick and Butt Naked.

Those without guns, a good half, made do with what they could find to justify sticking with the gang. Waterpistols, broomsticks, garden rakes, rolling pins, air filters, Coke bottles and powerless power drills were among the makeshift weapons at hand. Those with guns often had no idea of how to use them. On the first day I dared to leave the relative safety of the hotel, I found myself chatting with a group of fighters. Suddenly there was a loud explosion and a blast of hot air rushed up my leg. I looked down to see a small crater in the tarmac and the teenaged gunmen next to me looking sheepishly guilty. He had fired his rifle accidentally, almost with tragic consequences for my left foot. The gun's magazine, like many in the city, was held together by adhesive tape printed with the logo of the aid agency Save the Children Fund.

Much of the fighting itself was also chaotic, a tragic parody of cowboys and Indians, cops and robbers—with real bullets. From our ringside seats on the hotel balcony we watched battles conducted with Kalashnikovs held high above the heads of the young warriors, who screamed obscenities in Liberian English at their enemies. A favorite war-cry was "Yo ma pussy-oh," a genital insult also daubed on many of Monrovia's walls.

It was not uncommon to see boys of nine or ten on the frontlines, the bravest or most brainwashed of them all. Looking into the eyes of these boys, self-assured arrogant eyes, long-robbed of anything resembling childhood innocence, was a chilling experience. One morning such a child got into an argument with a comrade fighter some ten years his senior. They shouted at each other at the gates of the Mamba Point Hotel, neither willing to back down in front of the rest of the gang. The older boy calmly removed a rifle from his shoulder, passed it to a friend and squared up to the child, whose nose reached no higher than the gunman's chest. Undaunted by the other's size, the child continued to remonstrate and the argument grew more heated. The child then fished in the pocket of his shorts and pulled out a hand-grenade, held it to the face of his adversary, fingering the pin. I was no more than a couple of yards away.

"Shut up, man, or I'll pull it! I tell you man, you don't shut up I'll fucking pull the pin!"

Despite my presence and my appeals to wait until I had made myself scarce, I believe that pin would have been pulled had the gang's leader not intervened.

####

Ray Benedict, a lanky, befreckled twentysomething (he was unsure of his age) with implausibly ginger hair, was not a typical Liberian fighter in that he was adept at using his weapon, a cherished rocket propelled grenade launcher. Recruited into Charles Taylor's National Patriotic Front of Liberia at the age of 14 to "defend his country," Ray had become something of a hero among both his comrades and his foes, even the media. Although it had rendered him near-deaf, Ray was at his happiest when firing his rockets, and never more downhearted than when his daily allowance was used up. In the ecstatic moments following each explosion, he wore the triumphant expression of an Olympic sprinter about to break the tape. One photographer had captured such a moment,

Ray almost in silhouette running towards the camera from a large cloud of smoke produced just seconds earlier by his RPG. The picture appeared on the cover of a special supplement on Liberia published in a Madrid newspaper, brought to Monrovia by a Spanish journalist. Ray probably doesn't receive gifts very often, and I'm sure this testimony to his unsolicited international fame is now among his most treasured possessions.

He hadn't spent much time analyzing his role in the war: "The people I killed, I killed 'cause they wanted to take Monrovia. The people I killed, plenty-oh."

####

Out of this modern conflict conducted with medium-tech weapons emerged much older aspects of Africa: magic, nudity, mutilation, even cannibalism. Fighters wore a variety of "protective" talismans such as cowrie shells and strips of animal skin. Since the beginning of the civil conflict, Liberia's warlords had taken advantage of the widespread faith in such bullet-proofing trinkets to encourage children as young as eight into the frontline. The Butt Naked Brigade, whose leader elicited cheers when seen in public, regularly disrobed in the face of enemy fire as a sign of defiance and invincibility. Other men went into battle decked out in women's dresses, wigs and floral hats. Some said this practice was rooted in the inability of young recruits in the bush to distinguish between female and male attire when attacking the first town in which they had ever set foot.

Juju gear and cross-dressers notwithstanding, there was little to distinguish battle-dress from ordinary street clothes. Combat boots and camouflage fatigues were rare. Charity-donated tee-shirts (Malcolm X was a favorite design), cutoff jeans and flip-flops were more the order of the day.

The prisoner's ordeal was a vicious one. Having been stripped, punched and kicked, his arms would be tied at the elbow behind his back—"to stop him flying away" one captor explained. Not only is this position excruciatingly painful (just try it), it also leads to slow suffocation. But there is rarely time for that process to take its deadly effect.

Looking at the victims, it wasn't always clear whether it was the machete cuts or the bullet to the head that finished the job, but it was often evident that vital organs had been removed before the moment of death. The eating of enemies' innards was a common, if discreet, practice said to imbue the consumer with the strength of the consumed.

"Hey, man, you want some meat?" one fighter asked me at a checkpoint. He held out his hand to reveal half a fresh heart. I couldn't swear it was human, but then again I hadn't seen many pigs around the city. I wondered where the other half was.

Decapitation was also prevalent and dozens of heads in various states of decomposition littered the streets. Fresher ones were prominently displayed at battlefronts, while others were left to rot away in gutters. When fighters from opposed factions called a temporary truce one day in mid-May, they put down their weapons and decided to play soccer. Since no football was available, they kicked around a fleshless skull found nearby.

At least the media had a good time of it. The Mamba Point Hotel was among the very few establishments still functioning in Monrovia. Thanks to some judicious palm-greasing, it had barely been looted. The world's press enjoyed intermittent electricity, fine wines and excellent food prepared by Ming, a Chinese chef who, when asked, as we took cover under a table during a shootout, why he was still in town, said "No money go home."

Among the regulars at the bar were our armed factional protectors, eager to see themselves on CNN.

We felt safe there, even when battles raged just yards away, occasionally sending bullets into the hotel. One of these projectiles entered the owner's bedroom, passing through a closet containing his wife's dresses and leaving a coin-sized souvenir hole in the left shoulder of each.

Of the dozens of journalists who came to Monrovia during the seven weeks of fighting, only one, a French photographer, was injured. A rocket-propelled grenade exploded twenty yards away and its shrapnel broke his leg.

Most of the fighters treated the media with respect and often offered advice as to the safety of crossing roads or venturing down alleys. War-zone veterans said it was the only conflict they had covered where they could cross frontlines in a matter of minutes, often by staying in the same place.

In retrospect it seems foolish to have refused armed demands for money or cigarettes, but at the time, lies such as "I'm broke" or "I don't smoke" came easy. A joke was always enough to defuse tense situations. Of course it took a while to get used to the liberties one could take. A radio correspondent, on his first day out, eagerly handed over his watch to an appreciative militiaman.

"Yeah, that looks good, man," said the young fighter, admiring his new acquisition. "But tell me, man, what time does it say?"

—Anthony Morland

LIBYA

Wrong Place, Wrong Time

Covering a war in a remote place like Chad can lead to some very strange serendipity. It also teaches us that journalists are well-treated but just as likely to be killed or injured as combatants.

In 1979 Chad plunged into a civil war pitting Goukkouni Oueddei and Hissène Habré, the two northern leaders, against each other. In 1982, Hissène Habré seized power and installed his government in N'djamenah, but Goukkouni Oueddei signed a pact with Lybia's leader, Muammar Qaddafi, who sent an army to Chad.

Lybia occupied the north of the country in 1983, causing France to intervene. The country was neatly split in two: the Islamic north (above the 19th parallel) was placed under the control of the GUNT of Goukkouni Oueddei and Lybia, while the animist south was placed under the control of Hissène Habré supported by France and the U.S.A.

In 1986, the rallying of Goukkouni Oueddei helped Hissène Habré fight against the Lybians. In 1987 a cease-fire was decided, and in May 1988 the Lybians officially recognized Hissène Habré's government. Diplomatic relations were restored in October, and Libya agreed with Chad to evacuate the Aouzou Strip, a piece of land between the two countries that it had occupied since 1972. Are you with us so far?

The political situation was not stable for long, though, because of the rebellion of Idriss Deby, former commander-in-chief of the armed forces, and companion of Hissène Habré, in 1990. One more time France was asked to intervene. On December 2, 1990, Idriss Deby, at the head of his FPS (Forces Patriotiques du Salut-Salvation Patriotic Forces), entered N'Djamenah and forced Hissène Habré's National Army (FANT) out. Habré took refuge in Senegal. France eventually decided to let things go and intervene less in Chad.

I am flying into Chad from Tripoli. I have negotiated a trip into the combat zone, and we are taken aboard a C-130 plane along with other journalists and military. We take off from Faya-Largeau and head toward Oumchalloulah and Abeche, where the battle is raging. The heat on the ground had been intolerable, but the unpressurized, unheated plane soon drops below freezing as we gain in altitude.

As we are on final approach into the airport at Abeche, the cold is the least of my worries. There are strange movements on the tarmac. I climb up to the cockpit to grab some photos in case anything happens. While in the cockpit, the pilots figure out that Hissene Habre's troops have taken the town and the airport, and we are landing in enemy territory.

The strange movements we see are men shooting up at the plane. In the clear air, I can see the bullets and rockets arc toward our plane.

The pilots pull the nose up and give it full power. Slipping and sliding, they try to dodge the bullets, as they make the long trip out of range of the soldiers on the ground.

We land without any damage 20 minutes later, not far from Abeche.

Once on the ground, we realize that we hadn't planned to spend more than an hour in the desert and here we are in the middle of the Sahara with only some soup, rotten camel meat that we bought from a local and dirty water.

We spend the night hoping the enemy soldiers will not find us. The next morning, a Libyan picks us up and returns us to Faya Largeau.

####

Five years later in Kuwait for a summit of African heads of state, I told this story to a soldier from Chad. He recognized the incident and told me he was the leader of the soldiers on the ground that were trying to shoot down the plane. *C'ést la guerre.*

—**Coskun Aral**

PAKISTAN

Along the Northwest Frontier

The border between Afghanistan and Pakistan is one of the most colorful and interesting places for adventurers. In an attempt to interview the taliban, *I ended up being the first North American to meet with them (and set up the world's first TV interview with their leader). I also visited a number of other areas to add some depth and perspective to this classic frontier for adventurers.*

The Northwest Frontier of Pakistan is adventure defined. Men in turbans and robes stroll hand in hand down dusty streets carrying machine guns. *Mujahedin*, spy, separatist and smuggler are considered normal occupations in this high risk border area. Shootouts, bombings, kidnapping and violence are common. This is also the land of the Pakhtun (or Pathan) who live by the code of Pakhtunwali, an unwritten code of revenge against your enemies, hospitality to strangers and refuge to friends (*badal, melmastia* and *nanwata*). The trick is knowing whether you are friend, stranger or enemy. I will travel to Peshawar, in Northwest Pakistan, then travel onward to Afghanistan to meet with the *taliban* army.

I arrive at Green's Hotel in Peshawar. Not upscale, but definitely Western. Walking down the streets of Peshawar it be-

comes quite apparent that I am the only pigeon in town. I
smile and wave, and within 20 minutes shopkeepers, touts,
gawking loiterers and an entourage of kids know me as Mr.
Robert. Peshawar is an interesting city for those looking for
adventure. For years this was the gateway to Afghanistan
through the Khyber Pass by train, road or air. Now the war in
Afghanistan between the *taliban* and the government of Rabbiani has closed the pass. Although not reported in most
Western papers, there are kidnappings, murders, robberies
and other violent acts as life goes on in this dusty, bustling
border town.

Any Westerner in Peshawar is automatically affiliated with
aid organizations, journalism, arms, drugs or spying. Most
yuppies head straight to the mountains and hippies head
straight to the drug markets. The heat has been turned up a
little too high for itinerant adventurers because of the kidnappings and robberies.

Since I do not speak Arabic or Pahktun (Pathan or Pashto
depending on your translation) I will need a guide. Since I
naively assume I will have to travel over the Khyber Pass into
Kabul, I will need a member of the Afridi clan. The wily

Pathans are actually three main groups: the Sarbanni, the Bitanni and the Ghurghush. The Afridi tribe is a member of the last—the typical stereotype of the "wily Pathan" proud, noble as well as treacherous and cruel. The Afridis look like throwbacks to the old testament with their long flowing robes, turbans and long magnificent beards. They are the same men that bedeviled conquerors from Alexander to the Russians along the Khyber pass.

If I am to enter Afghanistan I will also need to find someone who works with another Afridi. Yaqub Afridi is "the man" around here—the largest drug and gun smuggler in Northern Pakistan. His people control all the illicit trade between Kabul, Jallallabad and Peshawar.

Jawing with Jabba

After a few discreet inquiries, I am directed to ascend a rickety spiral staircase above a dusty tourist shop. Here I wait for my host who ascends after I am uncomfortably seated cross legged on a dirt-filled rug and given sweet tea in a dirty glass. My host, who shall remain nameless, reminds me immediately of Jabba the Hut—the rotund, grubby alien of *Star Wars* fame. When my host smiles he reveals a set of black and brown teeth and breath that forces me to sit back a few more inches.

I make it clear why I am here but he is determined to unload some of his faded trinkets before granting my wish. He instructs his sons to bring out Russian bayonets, Russian uniforms, Russian money, Russian field glasses, and then with a conspiratorial wink, a Russian AK-47.

Nope, not interested.

Then a parade of ancient coins, ethnic bric-a-brac, tattered rugs and rusty knives follow.

Nope, don't need it.

Then my host leans toward me and looks around as if the crowd of grubby cross-eyed children blocking the stairs have never heard the word and whispers "hashish?"

His breath is painful, but I wheeze back. Nope.

He sits back and scratches his scrotum under his dirty white shalwar. Frustrated and pensive, he picks his rotten teeth and then burps while he figures out how he will make a little money from me. He puts on a squeaky Tom Waits tape in a stolen Walkman to make me feel at home.

Temporarily freed from reviewing the piles of war surplus and cheap clothing, I restate that my need is only for a trustworthy guide who can take me into the Afghan camps and around the Khyber Pass beyond. Trying to figure how much to gouge me, he probes my intentions (or backers). He asks me if I am a journalist and smiles conspiratorially. Nope. Are you a diplomat? Nope. A spy? I think that this guy has been watching too many Sidney Greenstreet movies. I tell him that I want to meet the *taliban* and he gives me a pained look. "This can be difficult."

He says something to one of his sons who scuttles down the staircase and out into the street. The other sons continue to stare as if they paid admission and want to get their money's worth.

Finally eyeing me after a pregnant pause and flicking something off his toothpick, he says, "I have the man but it will cost you 100 rupees. He will not make trouble for you if you do not make trouble for him."

Not agreeing or disagreeing, I thank him and then figure I should loosen up a little cash so that he will have a vested interest in keeping me alive for further plucking. I tell him that

I am traveling, but I will come back to buy souvenirs of my trip. Invigorated he pushes the pile of rusty weapons, smelly caps and trinkets towards me again. I ask him at what generous price would he sell me these fine ancient coins. We haggle for about 20 minutes until what looks like a bearded gopher sticks its head up the stairwell and introduces himself as Papa. He is introduced to me by Jabba the Hut as "my man." I quickly pay him an outrageous sum of $50 for the counterfeit Greek coins and Russian rubles and push my way down the stairs with my new guide in tow.

A well fed but sprightly man of about 60, Papa is wearing the white Chitrali cap and white robes of the region. He is a Pahktun and he speaks perfect but imprecise English. He worked at the U.S. base in Pakistan and learned his English while being the house *wallah*. He has forgetton much of his English but I promise him I will teach it back to him. Papa struggles to keep up with my stride. He has a long white beard, glasses, a pot belly and a nervous, happy personality that reminds me of one of the Seven Dwarfs. Then I decide it's not a Disney character he reminds me of, Papa looks exactly like the R. Crumb character who keeps on trucking. So we set off down the street with Papa hustling to keep up with me. Papa tugs at my sleeve:

"We have made a bargain, my friend?"

Puzzled as to why he is starting the negotiations anew I ask him what he means

"I have been sent to you to guide you, yes? There are many things I can show you."

"Like?"

He rattles off the list of bazaars and tourist sights and I stop him midsentence.

"I am not here for these things. I am interested in meeting the *taliban*."

After a brief silence and a cinematic look around to see who is listening, he says: "There are many things to see in Pakistan, my friend."

Sensing that my aims are not strictly touristic, he launches into another hushed spiel. "I can take you to a place where we can find hashish, heroin, marijuana."

"Papa, I am here to meet with the *taliban*."

Finally I figure out why he doesn't understand me. *Taliban* means religious student here. It is not directly associated with the Afghan group called the *taliban*.

"You want guns? I can take you to where we can fire many guns, even rockets, many, many rockets. Hand grenades, anti-aircraft, boom boom."

"No Papa."

I wait for the women or young boys pitch but it doesn't come. Papa, who I find out later is devoutly religious, sticks to clean stuff; drugs and weapons. It dawns on me that there will be much to discuss in the days ahead.

We get back to his original topic of discussion, his rate. He explains that he must pay his friend for the referral and asks to borrow 10 ruppees to pay his commission. He runs back and conspiratorially mentions that our deal is now between us and that I should not mention anything to our friend if he asks what we did. The impression is that Papa was to continue the *baksheeh* until we are through.

He asks me what I would like to do. Thinking that I had already failed in explaining exactly what I wanted to do, I say, "Let's go to the Afghan refugee camps." At least Papa would come in handy as an interpreter. He explains that we can go to the market, but that I cannot go into the camps because I would be kidnapped. There are three camps outside of town. Actually small cities complete with mud huts, phone, electricity and a smattering of services. There are about 3 million Afghan refugees who live in Pakistan in camps like these and they are here to stay, something the financially beleaguered Pakistanis don't like. The Afghans handle all the transportation in Peshawar. They also evoke the wild west feel of men strolling around with machine guns. Shootouts enforce *badal* or revenge, and a host of entreprenurial efforts include kidnapping people for ransom.

We jump on a bus to the market and Papa is very nervous. Although the people are cheerful and glad to see me, there is a dark curious look in many of the men's faces. We push past the money changers and kabob houses to the depths of the market. We stop in a simple *chai* house for tea and cakes. Not much to look at. Just a large tent with three wide carpeted tables running the full length. Men sit and sleep on the tables in the midday heat. None are particularly thrilled to see us. I finally figure out what I am looking at. We are surrounded by out of work *mujahedin*. Tough 30 and 40 something men with hard gaunt faces, many of them scarred or limping. They all stare directly and impassively at us. Papa is nervous. I ask Papa who these men are. He replies these are the fighters. I ask them if I can take their pictures. He says no. I acknowledge some of the men. Some nod back, others continue to stare. Papa and I talk about the fighters. He tells me that many men came during the war with Russia for money, but now there is not much work.

After our tea I ask him to take me to the Smugglers Bazaar. Once it was in Landi Kotal at the end of the rail line. Now it has moved to the outskirts of Peshawar. I can tell that Papa is not entirely thrilled with my choice of tourist spots. He asks me if I want to see where they paint the buses. Once again I tell him my purpose. He, once again, is suddenly hard of hearing.

The Walking Dead

We jump off the bus, just before a military checkpoint and end up in a carpet of trash in an area of shade trees. Among the trash are what look like piles of dirty rags. Upon closer inspection they are people. Bearded and blackened with the hard core soot of derelicts, it is hard to tell if they are dead or alive. Since they are not bloated I assume they are alive. Other men with frizzed hair and beards stagger in slow motion. Papa warns me away. These are the walking dead—heroin addicts left to wander and then die in the boulevard facing the market. A sobering sight and not one inclined to induce anyone to buy drugs here, one of the largest drug markets in the world.

It would be unfair to characterize this place as all seedy and depressing. Here shoppers can also buy gold Rolexes, Panasonic radios, and cameras. The fact that you can also buy heroin, hashish, machine guns and rocket launchers is more a result of an enthusiastic retail strategy than anything sinister. At one shop, I intimate that maybe his Rolex watches are the same ones found on the streets of New York—tinny, Chinese made with $5 workings. Insulted, he pulls out an entire tray of solid gold GMT Masters and Datemasters. I shut up. He even offers to buy my battered and faded 25-year-old steel GMT master for US$800. Not a bad deal, but I decline. I give him a Mr. DP sticker for his door and we are friends again.

I mention to Papa that I wish to travel on to Afghanistan and meet with the *taliban* army. He smiles and says "Come with me." We go to the far end of the bazaar and Papa cautions me to walk quickly and not get lost. He also stops and tells me that when we cross into the other side he cannot help me if I am kidnapped or killed. I ask him how much it would cost to pay my ransom. Without pausing he tells me US$35,000.

Through the Door

Papa drops his guard and takes me into a quiet corner. He looks me straight in the eye and asks me: "Are you CIA?" I say no. He asks me: Are you a journalist? I say no, but I write a travel guide to dangerous places. He then asks me if I will make trouble for him. I say no.

Papa satisfied for now says "Come with me."

We wait until the soldiers at the military checkpoint are occupied with a heavily laden truck than we walk quickly but purposely into a compound of shops. Papa smiles conspiratorially and points at the large red on white sign "No Foreigners Past this Point." After a couple of lefts and rights through the shops we walk through a large gate in the high wall. Thinking that this has been far too easy, we turn the corner and run smack into a group of armed men pointing machine guns at us.

Having been asked many times what was my most dangerous moment, I always answer that I really have no idea of when I am in danger or not. But considering that I am surrounded by unsmiling machine gun-carrying Afghans and escorted by a total stranger who for some strange reason, seems to know exactly what kidnapped foreigners are worth, the first few seconds of this experience would rank up there.

Papa pauses briefly and then makes the introductions. It turns out that these are some of Afridi's men. A group of about 10 out of 100 heavily armed men who make about 2000 rupees a month to make sure the drug and contraband business runs nice and smooth. And who should be their long lost friend (or best customer) but Papa. I don't know why, but it seems in this part of the world you always get kissed (twice) by men who were pointing machine guns at you a few moments before.

Welcomed into their simple barracks I am introduced to my brigand friends. Not only are the men carrying well-used SKSs and AK-47s but there are machine guns and ammunition cases lying around the wire cots. They thrust weapons into my hands and urge Papa to take pictures of me. They pose with me and bring me tea.

They chat in Pashto while I smile and hand out *DP* stickers. I run out of stickers as they paste them on their rifle butts. They ask me if I would like to fire the gun. I decline thinking of the armed police not more than 200 yards away behind the sandbagged checkpoint.

We talk about getting into Afghanistan and Kabul. Everyone is coming out of Kabul. Kabul is under siege. No one is going in. They will definitely not let foreigners in. The *tali-*

ban is camped above the hills waiting to attack. I ask if can go in disguise. They laugh and tell me "You can take the bus right from here for only 50 rupees but there are eight checkpoints from here to Jalalabad and one of them is sure to find you." Another development is that Afridi has been asked to get out of Pakistan because of the heat the U.S. government is putting on him. He graciously has moved out of his mansion to another one high in the hills of Jalalabad. He is not about to get into more trouble by inviting some foreigner for dinner and a ride into Kabul. Although his bodyguards are eager, they know I'll be arrested and turned back. They also explain that the *taliban* execute drug dealers and it might not be wise for me to arrive under their protection. It looks like the Khyber is not the way to go.

Papa shows me around the market where piles of sickly looking hashish and heroin are on display. There are piles of well-used weapons and even lethal pen guns that fire one bullet. The merchants watch me with some remorse as I jot down the going rates. Two kilos of hash goes for 5000 rupees, 10 grams is 80 rupees, one gram of injection heroin for 100 rupees and one gram of smoking heroin is 50 rupees. In this market weapons are to drugs as shovels are to farming. I can pick up a slighty used rocket launcher for 30,000 rupees (Rockets are 400 rupees each) hand grenades are 100 rupees, Russian AKs go for 6000, a beat up AK-47 goes for 8000, a "short" Chinese-made assault version of the Kalshnikov is 30,000, 30 bullets go for 300 rupees. A helpful salesman reminds me that the barrel of the Chinese AK doesn't get as hot as the home-made versions.

####

Thinking of the wasted humans outside on the boulevard, I pass on buying anything, even after Papa explains the profits to be made once we cross back inside the gate. Papa excuses himself to do a little shopping while we wander through stacks of hashish and marijuana.

On the way back to town, Papa loosens up. He says he does a little bit of this and that to make ends meet. Besides drugs, (he prefers to buy his drugs directly in Afghanistan, in the region of Mazar-i-Sharif, he also buys stamps for stamp collectors, takes the occasional tourist around Peshawar, but mostly he directs foreigners to where they can buy drugs. He warms to the fact that I have no interest in drugs and seem to be comfortable around his well-armed friends. I tell him that I would like to look around the border areas until I can figure out how to get into Afghanistan. It seems getting to Afghanistan through Peshawar is a bust. There is a Red Cross plane that flies into Kabul now and then but I am told it is always full with supplies. I figure it might be worth trying the more scenic and wild northern borders. I ask him if he wants to go visit the remote mountain areas of Gilgit and the Kalash valley and he agrees.

The North West Frontier

The next day Papa shows up with just a single blanket and a plastic shopping bag with his toiletries. I thought I traveled light, but Papa puts me to shame. We take the postal bus north to Mingora. He mentions in an offhand way that the bodyguards we met yesterday were asked by the Pakistani police to help show the U.S. that they were cracking down on drugs, so Afridi's bodyguards offered Papa 10,000 rupees to bring them people to turn over to the police. I ask if he would have set me up. He smiles in a hurt way and says, "But you are my friend."

It is important to remember that the Afghans are a complex result of their code of honor. They are hospitable to strangers, will invite you into their house, and if you become their friend they will deny you nothing. In fact Pathans hate haggling or coyness and are much happier when you simply state your purpose no matter how far from the legal path it strays. You just never want to be on the wrong side of a Pathan because they will kill you even for the slightest wrong.

Along the way we talk about many things. Papa is amazed at the strange places I have been, and I am equally intrigued with his stories about his home in Afghanistan. He grew up in a small town along the Khyber Pass in a fortresslike house where the only profession was smuggling. Every member of the family must post guard duty in the tower and every house is heavily armed. The tower has peepholes to allow the defenders to shoot back when attacked and the thick mud and stone walls make it cool in the summer and warm in the winter. They fight over goats, women, past wrongs and anything else they find worth killing for. Many villages and clans have been warring for years simply because every new generation must carry on the revenge or *badal* for the continuing seesaw of bloodshed. Papa looks into my eyes and says dramatically: "Mr. Robert, if you kill someone, you come to my village, I will give you house, bodyguard, no problem." I keep that in mind.

As we come out of the hot arid valley we head up the Grand Trunk line into the rugged mountains. We pass the old British forts and wind up and down the tortuous passes. Papa tells me stories of how one Australian named Keith came to his village to make a hollowed out Samsonite briefcase so he could smuggle hashish back home. The trick worked once and the second time he was caught. Keith's girlfriend flew in to get him out of jail and lived with Papa in his house helping him cook and even posting guard duty. An Afghan chief from another town took a fancy to her and one day gave her a black Afghan horse worth about $30,000 rupees. Meanwhile Keith liked it in jail because he got to smoke cheap hash with the other inmates. Finally the girlfriend saved up enough money (Papa wouldn't tell me how she made it) and she bribed his way out of jail and flew back to Australia.

Papa sees the pictures of my twin daughters and exclaims; "I must have these for the chief of the Kyhber's son." He is a fine man and his father feeds 50 people a day! I don't know how I will break the news to my daughters that they have both been betrothed to one of the world's largest drug smugglers.

I Read the News Today... Oh Boy

The Northwest Frontier is a land with bad endings. The Peshawar paper has a story about a young Afghan couple, each from a different village, who were spotted kissing by one of the boy's relatives. The father of the boy kidnaps the girl and a cousin ties them up and pumps 75 bullets into them. Just yesterday in the Smugglers Bazaar a man was shot in the neck three times as he tried to run the checkpoint we had so deftly sidestepped. He was trying to take a stolen car into Afghanistan. The newspaper fills up five pages of murders, shootings and crime. Just another day in Pakistan.

I ask Papa how old he is. He tells me that only rich people pay attention to paper and since he cannot write he has no idea how old he is.

####

We are back on the road in the back of a battered Toyota pickup truck I hired. We talk to pass the time. I tell him I like to cook. He tells me that is women's work. He has no idea how to cook. I joke and tell him that he would starve if he did not have a woman to cook for him. "I cook tea" he replies indignantly. Papa's main interest for coming with me seems to be the disparity between the prices of weapons in the north versus Peshawar. In his village in Afghanistan he can get AK-47s for around 6000–8000 rupees. He figures he can unload them in the northern town of Dir for 12,000–15,000 rupees each. All he needs to do is find a buyer on this trip and he'll be back in a week.

We arrive at Dir that night. The evening air is frigid. I check into a room for 300 rupees. Papa takes the cheap one for 200. I get a straight razor shave for 5 rupees. That night I have a warm shower by plugging in a heating element directly into a bucket of cold water. The lights in the hotel dim and I wonder how may people are electrocuted like this. I shiver all night. Dir is a dirty frontier town. Severed goat heads neatly laid out in rows and all business from tailoring to tinkering is conducted while you wait. Overly decorated and loaded trucks blast through town. The blasting of their air horns and jangling of the steel chains that decorate the bumpers are the only things that interest me.

At breakfast the next day we sit next to a stubbly old man with a pure white beard. Both he and Papa extoll the virtues of Allah and the Koran as they drink their tea. They are shocked when they find out that I have read the Koran and drag me into the conversation. Proselytized to the point of pain, I try to change the subject and mention that the short man has a nice beard. He blushes deeply. Papa tells me that with Allah all things are possible and that it will only be a matter of time before I am converted.

He warns me about the tough going ahead, the cold, the lack of food and even the danger of traveling in this area. I reassure him that I enjoy wild mountainous places and that bathing in an ice cold stream by moonlight is one of my favorite things. I realize that it is Papa who doesn't like the cold and the moutains.

It is October and as we climb higher and higher into the mountains we are getting cold. Papa is shivering and I give him my black Goretex jacket newly bought in Frankfurt. He praises Allah for creating such a marvelous garment. Knowing full well that it is a custom to give something that is so lavishly praised as a gift, I say "No Papa, you can't have it." We climb to the summit of the pass at 10,500 feet. Far down below we can see the overloaded diesel trucks that grind and groan up the switchbacks at less than five miles an hour. It is actually faster walking than taking one these trucks. They will continue northward into China along the Karkoram pass loaded with everything from rice to brake pads. Heading down the other side of the pass is unsettling. We descend across 45 switchbacks down to the river below. An armed policeman appears out of nowhere and flags us down. No, we are not in trouble. It seems the government has just put in electricity and the minister will be coming along the other direction. Could we please tell the policemen stationed along the road not to smoke or drink tea? Pakistan is a polite place.

On the truck is a man from the village of Bahrain. He invites us to stay at his home. Although there are a number of new and reasonable hotels in Bahrain we take him up on his offer. His house is a 20' by 20' room with large security bars on the doors. He has a spectacular view of the valley and rushing river that carves through the town. We buy food and fruit and he is embarrassed. He invites his relatives from around the valley to meet me. We eat a large but simple dinner. While his son entertains us by reading out of a primary school English book he confesses that he is a Pahktun separatist and is eager to fight for a separate homeland for the Pahktuns. After seeing the difference between the dark-skinned leather jacketed Punjabi tourists from Lahore and the light haired Afghans it is understandable.

That night something hit me like a train. Lying shivering I had to go to the bathroom, and fast. Maybe it was the fly covered kebab I had in Mingora or the dinner that night but I jumped up and realized I was in a pitch black room with no windows and no idea how to get out. I frantically searched for the heavy bolts that sealed the top and bottom of the doors. Rushing outside the night was brilliant with stars. I couldn't get my pants down in time and for the first time in my life felt like a three-year-old who wasn't diaper-trained.

The panic over, I took my clothes off in the freezing night air and decided to clean myself in a stream or river. As I walked through the orchids along the side of the hill, I punctured my feet with the sharp thorns from the trees. Finally I found an ice cold stream tumbling down the mountain. I began the painful process of washing myself and my clothes. As I shiver and shake under the stars I can't help thinking how funny this is. Papa and my guest find me and they are frantic. I tell them relax, I just came out for a bath. Papa points to me in my nakedness and says "I didn't believe when you told me you like to bathe in mountain streams but now I see that you are made of steel. Allah be praised." My host is less poetic. He tells me that the villagers shoot anyone found walking around at night. And that if I had gone down to the river I would have been killed.

In the morning I tell Papa the real reason I went for a walk in the middle of the night. He doesn't believe me and thinks I am being modest. My host apologizes thinking it is food that has caused it and I feel like an idiot. I don't eat for the next four days.

The Valley of Swat

Shivering from the high altitude we pull into the valley of the Kalash.The Kalash (which means black because of the black garments they wear) are an animist tribe who live in a region sometimes called Kafiristan. The Kalash are considered to be descendants of Alexander's army but have no recorded history. They are known for their colorful festivals, the fact that they leave their dead in exposed coffins and they are in an anthropological timewarp.

It is hard to imagine such a beautiful place in the middle of such desolation. The valleys are lush and green and the people who live in this valley are either touted as the lost tribe of Israel or descendants of Alexander the Great. In any case they are mentioned in many guidebooks as a lost race of peoples rarely seen or visited. Yeah sure.

We make the tortuous trip into the valley along a road that is smashed out of a sheer rock cliff. Coming down from the valleys and moutains beyond are Indian Jeeps with a single 2–3 foot diameter log tied like a battering ram over the cab and hood of the truck. Places where the road has caved in are patched with rubble. Even Papa exclaims "hacha!" as we veer out over the edge of the cliff.

Naturally when we pull up to the main junction there is no primitive scene but instead a huge billboard with all the rules that tourists must follow when taking pictures of the Kalash. Just like a low budget amusement park there is a fee for everything. It seems that the Punjabis come up here in the summer to escape the heat and gawk at the diminuitive white-skinned Kalash. Not only do we pay an admission fee to get in, we pay to bring in my camera. Hard to believe that this valley was just opened up to road traffic in the 70's.

Once inside there are tiny hotels with names like the "Hayatt Hotel" and restaurants that serve "meshed potatoes" or even spagetti. Here we are just a few yards from the Afghan border. As we finally meet the famed Kalash, an old lady not only tells us how much we must pay for their photos (20 rupees), but adds up the fee for every time she hears the shutter click. I assign them to the other Kodak cultures who make their living wearing "authentic garments" and pose for tourists wearing Tilley hats. The dark-haired Kalash look like ethnic Greeks, Macedonians or even Armenians. Now they have the cultural relevance of a cigar store Indian. There is one Punjabi group in the valley who direct the Kalash to perform for their massive VHS recorders. They look like they are having a day at the zoo. Papa mentions that we could take a six hour trip to Afghanistan from here on mules for 80–150 rupees but there are no mules for rent. I see the heavy snow cover in upper valley and remember how cold it was coming over the pass in our thin clothes. I say no thanks, let's try somewhere else. As a bizarre footnote there is a solar eclipse and I can't help but think of Kipling's *The Man Who Would be King*. The only difference now is this time, the Kafirs or kalash do not fall down and worship me, they just want more money because I am using a "big" lens to take their picture.

The Foothills of the Hindu Kush

We head into the mountain town of Gilgit, beneath the snow-capped mountains of the Hindu Kush. Within a 60 mile radius there are 20 peaks that rise above 20,000 feet. Nearby K2 is the most dangerous mountain in the world. The 28,250-ft. high peak has killed an average of every second person who attempts its summit. It is very cold and usually by now the snow in the high passes has cut off Gilgit from the rest of the world. Fokkers can fly out of the 4000 foot high valley by just scraping the tops of the passes but bad weather can lock people in for weeks and once the runway is snowed in you are in for the duration. Gilgit is a one horse town with the spectacular backdrop of Tirich Mir towering above its main street. In the simple hotel there is a Pakistani quiz show on the United Nations.

We walk around the town. In one stall I watch a tailor patiently work on fixing a torn button hole for 20 minutes. He charged his customer 2 rupees or eight-tenths of a penny.

Hobnobbing with the Nawab

Gilgit is the home of two things. One is polo, the other is the Sultan of Swat. Not Babe Ruth but a dynasty that has ruled this remote kingdom for centuries. Technically the Sultan or Nawaab was removed from his position of authority in 1969.

I check out the red brick British fort by the river. Despite the "Do Not Enter" signs, I poke around over the protestations of Papa. The fort looks as if it was abandoned by the British last week with coal fireplaces, rose gardens and hunting trophies of antelope, snow leopard and mountain sheep adorning the balcony. British cannons from 1898 and 1913 still point across the river. Earthquakes have destroyed some parts yet other parts are definitely nostalgic. Turning a corner I am caught trespassing by security guards. I find myself in the presence of a small dapper man in an Eddie Bauer blazer with a small cocker spaniel. It seems I am in the presence of Saif-ul-Mulk-Nasir the Nawab or Mehthar of Swat.

Instead of chastising me, the Nawab (or Nabob in its English form) is pleased to find a Westerner here. He invites me to have coffee at his former home, now a hotel. As we sit on the lawn with bodyguards and aides, he tells me his story.

The kingdom of Gilgit used to control the trade along the ancient Silk Road. It has been overrun and occupied by everyone from the Chinese to the British. The Nawab says his family has ruled the valley since the 15th century. In 1969 Pakistan declared the sultanate dissolved. His father was the last to hold official power and his job is strictly ceremonial. (20 percent of the people in the valley are direct descendants of his dynasty.) His father was one of 16 children. His oldest brother was killed in a plane crash, so it is now his turn to be the Wali.

The hotel is run by a bearded lanky German and I can't help but comment on it. The Wali mentions that his manager was a truck driver from Germany who had studied hotel management. He stayed in Pakistan and has now become a Pakistani national and runs his hotel. He slyly comments that he found out that his trusted hotel manager has local interests of the smoking kind. I noted on the path into the hotel grounds that marijuana plants grew wild along the road.

We spoke of many things. The Nawab likes to hunt and with some sadness pointed to his hunting lodge high up on the mountain behind us. He set up a game preserve to protect the wildlife and now the goverment wardens can be bribed for US$10 and use .22 caliber rifles to hunt deer (which only wounds them).

He is trying to breed cocker spaniels to be bird dogs but is not having much luck. I comment on the fact that the fort looks good in its coat of red paint. He says he painted it that color because it was the cheapest paint he could find. Things will change—the Nawab travels every year to San Francisco to the University of California for medical treatment and he has four daughters. When he goes the dynasty will end.

Polo, With or Without Headless Goats

Since I am in Gilgit I can't skip the polo game. I hang out in the fields by the river with the Afghans who have come to play *buzkashi*. Although polo has been played here for 400 years, *buzkashi* is the real thing. Buzkashi is a very violent game played with a headless goat. It is rough and it is violent and it packs the spectatorsin. Naturally there were none when I was there but during the summer people fly in from the South to watch both *buzkashi* and polo being played.

An Afghan tribe has set up camp and welcomes me. The horses have the skin rubbed down to the muscle in some places and there are scabby bull mastiffs tied to trees. It seems the Afghans get paid the equivalent of 1000 rupees for each game they play. The dog fights are a way of entertaining themselves and making some extra money. The chief offers to let me ride a horse all day for 200 rupees. As we hang around the camp of 20 people I watch the men take the horses out in the field. They ride fearlessly through trees, over broken ground and over brush. They treat their horses brutally yet they never make a false move. Even when the horse rears up in fear they keep pushing it to ride faster.

We talk to the Afghans. They ask us if we want to see a dog fight between their massive Kochi dogs (traveling dogs). They are from Mazar-i-Shariff and will gladly take us to Kabul.

We can can hire pack horses for 300 rupees a day and walk across the pass. We say we want to leave now, but they say we are too late. It will be too cold, the snow will be too deep and the horses will starve or freeze. Why not wait until spring they ask? I don't bother to explain my Western impatience.

Later that day we watch the polo matches. Polo is from 2 p.m. to 6 p.m., timed more by the narrow band of light that the mountains allow into the valley than by a clock. The long field slopes downward and is bordered on the long sides by six foot cement walls. The spectators squat and sit along the wall cheering and yelling. When the horses and riders crash into the wall, mallets flailing, the spectators are ejected like ducks in a shooting gallery. The only thing I could compare it to was the sight of an Indy car going into the railing flicking off spectators in a long ragged rooster tail. When a team charges the open ends of the fields to score a goal, the crowd simply gets run over by the stampeding horses. Finally, a sport that is as dangerous for the specators as the particpants.

The long nose Chitralis are not only good at polo, but they play each game like it is the world championship. Few wear protective gear and many are limping or bleeding afterwards. The ones that do wear gear wear plastic construction helmets tied with string, others wear just the padded Chitrali wool cap. A band plays exotic whiney music to keep the spectators pumped up. When I climb up on the wall to take a picture of the band they suddenly stop. I motion with two fingers towards my mouth to communicate that I want the band to play again. The audience explodes with laughter and the flute player laughs so hard he can't play for five minutes. I had used the symbol for "give me a blow job" to indicate I wanted him to play his horn. So much for cultural literacy.

The game is full of chills and spills. One player hits the goal post so hard it falls over. Horses limp off the field and players are knocked unconscious. Mallets fly and hit both horses and riders. The white wooden ball bounced off the heads of more than a few myopic spectators. Horses were crushed against the rough stone walls and after a while it becomes painful to watch.

Stymied with any attempt to get to Afghanistan, we decide to avoid the tortuous trip back to Peshawar and fly out. We join the crush at the PIA ticket counter. In Pakistan all flights are full but then magically have seats. I pay 650 rupees for myself and 300 for Papa on the exact same flight. It is actually cheaper to fly in Pakistan than drive. Waiting at the airport I gather two oddly striped stones from the river as souvenirs. As he waits for the plane Papa is nervous. I find out it will be the second time he has ever flown.

As the twin engine plane strains to get off the ground I notice that we never actually clear the mountain tops. We are flying in between the peaks. Down below I recognize the long winding mountian passes, ridged fieldings and small villages that took so long to drive through. Despite the spectacular scenery outside, Papa stares straight ahead and prays for the entire flight.

Back in Peshawar

Back in Peshawar, Papa asks to go home to see his daughter and I set out to find the *taliban*. I visit the local newspaper to ask the editor where I can find the *taliban*. He says they have a headquarters in the Afghan market. Stunned by this simple truth I realize I have come full circle. Peshawar, along with Damascus and Beirut is a major center for revolutionary Islamic groups. There was even a university for terrorists here until three months ago. The *New Yorker* had featured them much to the displeasure of the U.S. government who politely asked the Pakistanis to shut it down. The editor rummages through his Rolodex and gives me a local number. He says there should be somebody there who speaks English. Good Luck.

I call the number and ask if anyone can speak English. There is a pause as the person at the other end yells out something in Pashto.

"Hello," an educated voice answers.

"Is this the *taliban*? I ask.

"Who is this?"

I explained who I was and asked if I could ask them some questions to better understand what their goals are.

"Are you a journalist?"

"No. I came here to meet you because no one else in the world seems to know who you are.

"We are in the Afghan market. Just ask anybody and they will bring you to us," he says.

Pleased with my detective work, I go back to the hotel to get Papa to act as translator. Papa is not pleased. It seems that he heard me just fine when I asked him about the *taliban* before.

Papa was dead serious. "You understand that we are going to a place where they can kill you?"

"Yes, but I don't think they will."

"Do you realize we are going to a place where they may kill me?

"Then don't go."

"I cannot let you go alone because then they will kill you and I will be to blame."

"Then come and we will visit the fighters."

We get on a bus and I grab my cameras. I am elated. Papa is quiet.

As I stride through the market past the money changers we ask where the office of the *taliban* is. The men point in a general direction but do not take us there.

As we come across the tracks of the train that goes into Afghanistan, the muezzin calls the people to prayer. "It is time for me to pray," Papa says. "Please wait here."

As I plunk myself down in the shade, I notice two sun-browned men with black turbans sitting eating in the open. Black turbans with long tails and white stripes—the symbol of the religious student. I couldn't believe how blind I'd been—this was the uniform of the feared *taliban*. I nodded in their direction and they just stared back grimly.

Papa comes from washing up and praying and nods towards the fighters. "*Taliban*." I wave as I walk by and ask if should take their picture. Papa says "Please, no." I notice that besides praying, Papa has fortified himself with hashish.

A young boy directs us to a nondescript house with heavy green metal gates. Outside two men with machine guns sit in the shade. I walk past the men and push through the lower half of the green gates. I startle a man behind the gate. I am staring into the face from the first century. The man is dressed in white robes with a white turban. His eyes are piercing and ringed with black eyeliner, a custom rural Afghanis have to keep evil souls from entering their eyes. He just stares. Behind him are a group of men with vicious wounds, some with missing legs others with gashes and bandages. They sit on a pile of dirty blankets 3–4 feet high. Papa is about 8 feet behind me and I motion him forward to make the introductions.

In the courtyard we walk past a battered ambulance and the *taliban's* troop carrier of choice, a well-used white Toyota pickup truck. Black headdresses are hung up to dry. They are over 20 feet long and look like odd mourning flags hanging horizonatally in the sun. The men in the courtyard just stare as we walk up the dusty steps. There are wounded men lining the staircase. At the head of the stairs are piles of cheap plastic sandals. My hiking boots look odd among the piles of dirty brown sandals. I am met by a young man named Abdul Ghafoor Afghani. He is 23 and when asked for his title calls himself the "information person." We are taken into a dingy green room to wait. We sit on the scabby yellow and red plastic mat and take in our surroundings. A ceiling fan is motionless. There is no electricity but the light switches are grubby from many hands.

In various other rooms are badly dressed turbaned men in shalwars who huddle in deep discussions. They do not have the hard look of killers but rather of unwashed country bumpkins. By the hard brown look of their hands and faces many of the men look like farmers not like soldiers. Our host invites us into the main room in to chat with the leader. He is wearing a fully packed bandolier containing an ancient revolver, the white turban of the mullah, and he looks a little pissed at us for interupting his meetings. He asks our host to apologize for the pistol but the market is a stronghold of Hekmatyar and somebody tried to assassinate him yesterday. So he is wearing it just in case they try it again. They also apologize for the armed men outside the door, saying they were put there by the government to make sure nothing got out of hand.

They tell me that this is a staging area for volunteers and bringing out wounded for treatment in the hospitals of Peshawar. Recruits are gathered from the religious schools and the wounded are dropped off at the Chinese hospital. The recruits are sent via 3rd class mini bus to Quetta and then onward to the front by pickup truck. The Pakistanis do not stop the recruits or ask for papers. When the volunteers get to the front they will be given a weapon, ammunition and food supplies. In the double talk of killing, our host explains that there is no recruiting, the men come for *jihad*. This is definitely a low budget war. The dirty faded blankets outside are testament to the fact that the refugees donated their own blankets so that the men would not freeze this winter. He said that during the haj people donated the sales of animal skins slaughtered in the festival and raised 8000 rupees (about US$250) and that even the dingy office we were in was donated by local businessman at 7000 rupees a month. Occasionally they would get 100,000 and 200,000 rupee donations from businessmen to the cause.

He apologized for having no "propaganda" to give me, but he said that the *taliban* was in its formative stages and only a year old.

####

"We the *taliban* wish to rid Afghanistan of robbers, rapists, killers and militia and to create a new Islamic country." He tells stories of how the movement started in October of 1994. In Kandahar there was a brutal warlord who stopped everyone at roadblocks (most of these people would be robbed). But when he began stopping men, having them put makeup on, sodomizing them and killing them, it infuriated the people. The religious students at the mosque got the people together and hung the leader and the gunmen from the barrels of their tanks. From that point on, the revolution was in motion. They now have a radio and television station in Kandahar, but it cannot broadcast very far. So far, they have sent in a BBC crew and an independant TV crew but that is it. I am the first person from North America they have met.

I ask him if I can journey to Kandahar and the front lines or send in film crew to interview the leaders and cover the war. He would like that and I ask him again to make sure he is not just being polite. There is one catch—the leaders of the *taliban* do not allow their photographs to be taken because of the Koran. I explain very carefully that only cowards do not show their faces and that in my culture a man who does not wish to be seen cannot be trusted. He said this is not his decision but I can discuss it with them.

I ask him if they are supported by the Pakistani Secret Police. He looks puzzled. A man from the back of the room booms back in an educated English public school voice.

"Do you see any foreign backing in this room?"

He is an orthopaedic surgeon trained in Britain and volunteering his time to repair the damage of mine blasts. He is mildly pissed since it is obvious even to the blind that the *taliban* are running this operation with one Panasonic phone and little else.

Throughout our conversation my host is painstakingly polite and takes great pains to give full details to my questions. When I ask him how many men they have or other sensistive questions he replies with an embarassed look. "That is a secret. I cannot tell you or our enemies might find out."

He goes on to tell me that they have no designs on neighboring countries and that "after they win the war, they have expressed their desire to communicate with all peace loving countries of the world." As for foreign policy, economics and other items, they will get to that after they win the war. I ask him where all those shiny new tanks and weapons come from if they are just simple students. He smiles and says that when they captured Herat from Hektmatyar they found enough new weapons, vehicles and ammunition to fight Rabbiani for 25 years. I did not get into the fact that all those shiny new toys were actually courtesy of Uncle Sam vs. the Russians via Pakistan. When asked about training he said they have enough people who were trained during the war with Russia. Many were trained by Pakistan with U.S. help. He complained that Rabbiani now has planes and pilots from India and ammunition and weapons from Russia and military advisors from Iran. He said his backers were Saudi and Pakistani businessmen.

There is no trace of artifice, no haraunging, no pat answers. When I ask him to show me what parts of the country the *taliban* control, he pulls out the only reference book in the room. The six inch stack of reports turns out to be copies of the same document. (A well-thumbed 1991 UN report on Kandahar with maps and statistics.) During our conversation, there is a constant coming and going of men who wait patiently outside. The bandoliered mullah excuses himself, goes out and then rejoins us. We drink tea while along the back of the wall about 20 men watch us in silence as we talk. The phone rings throughout our conversation and my host apologizes every time. It seems they are arranging for a Danish Red Cross shipment and are trying to figure out how much to charge them. They are waiting for a fax with the bill of lading which must be sent to a copy shop down the street. The field commanders use a wireless radio to keep in touch.

He invites me to share lunch and, as we eat red beans and flat bread, I am amazed at being in a place where a group of rag tag students are taking over a country. As we share lunch, it is obvious that he is hoping to convince me that they are sincere in their goal. He does not understand why I ask some of the questions. I tell him that it helps me understand the world better and hopefully I can help other people understand as well.

He and some fighters that have joined us insist that I finish the last of the watery broth as a courtesy. It is a humbling experience. After lunch he shows me around the compound and says I cannot take pictures of the men upstairs but that maybe the men downstairs won't mind. He explains they had trouble before with the Russians using pictures to identify and kill people. The men are lounging on the blankets recovering from various wounds. As I lift my camera a man with a deep face wound begins swearing at me. He says that Allah does not like photographs and that I should get a better job than being a thief. I click away while my host and Papa get nervous. Trying to ease the tension, I ask my host to take my picture. He holds my camera up backwards with the lens facing his nose.

The haranguing continues as I tour the compound. I point to the black clothing and ask him if this is the uniform of the *taliban*. He laughs and points to all the men and says "He is *taliban*, he is *taliban* and he is *taliban*. We do not have a uniform."

He excuses himself and I thank him for his time. I remind him that I will be sending in a film crew. That night in the hotel I will call Coskun in Istanbul and tell him that we can have the world's first filmed interview of the *taliban* leaders. They will pass a special fatwah for us to allow us to film them. I tell Coskun of the route I have set up and give him my contact's name. He thinks I'm crazy but he says he will be here as soon as he can.

Out in the bright light of the market, people stare at me. I have my picture taken by an old man with an ancient wooden camera. A crowd of Afghans press around him and never take their eyes off me during the long process. Someone plunks an Afghan chitrali cap on my head. He uses the lens cap as a shutter and then develops the paper negative inside the camera. He then photographs the negative to give me a blurred 2" paper portrait. He hands me the crude, orthochromatic picture. I am a pale eyed Afghan from the 18th century. I am in a time machine and I am holding the proof in my hand.

I sit in the shade while Papa goes to pray in the simple mosque across the tracks. A fighter comes up to me to practice his English. We watch a young boy walking around with a white plastic garbage bag and a handful of wooden splinters and sticks. My new friend sees me looking at the young boy and says, "He does this every day. He will take these things and make a beautiful kite." As I look around at the dirty ancient scene peopled with the hard-faced, turbaned *mujahedin* all I see is the result of centuries of warfare.

My new friend pauses and then says proudly, "He will fly this beautiful kite very high."

—**RYP**

RWANDA
The Slaughter

Coskun has often been a witness to history. In 1994 he was with a group of photojournalists who had heard that there were massacres being perpetrated on innocent refugees in Rwanda. Often what they see is an embarrassment to the human race, and like the dark shadows decayed human bodies leave on the ground, there are also dark memories that never disappear from the human mind.

The apocalypse in Rwanda is too dark and compelling to ignore. In the 20th century, an entire nation is being murdered, while the world sits by and refuses to believe it. If any story needs to be captured, it is this one. We fly to Nairobi. On our arrival, we discover that the jeep we have reserved is not available. It is the height of safari season, and they have rented out four-wheel-drive vehicles for the $250 to $500 a day they can get.

For $20 a head, we take a five-hour minibus ride to Arusha just south of Nairobi. Seeing our massive professional camera, the locals just assume we are tourists. For $5, we can take still photos and, for $20, all the video we want. We pass. We find a 4x4 and driver that will take us on the 13-hour trip to Nyanza, a major staging area for the relief effort in Rwanda. The price is $100, but we have to squeeze in all the locals who want to go along as well. We go through some of the more dramatic scenery of East Africa, but the rough road and long trip make it an ordeal.

We treat ourselves to a three-star hotel when we arrive in Nyanza. There is a U.N. crew, and, wherever there are U.N. people, there are usually pilots around. Naturally, we go straight to the hotel bar to find them. Strangely, not a pilot to be found. The next day we find the pilots eating breakfast. I go to the oldest and ask him if he will fly us to the Ngara Refugee camp. The answer is a definite no. We work on them until finally they agree to take us on. When we let people know that our footage and coverage will support the relief effort, they have a greater desire to help us. As we climb into the Spanish-built *CASA*, we make ourselves comfortable among the crates of medicine and food destined for the refugees.

The 90-minute flight is uneventful, except for the trip over Lake Victoria. From our altitude, I can see tiny islands floating in the turquoise water—they are clumps of bloated bodies. We land on the dusty runway surrounded by a tent city that seems to stretch for miles. A fleet of Land Rovers arrives to collect the supplies and takes us to the U.N. headquarters for the camp. There is a veritable United Nations of relief organizations here—the U.N., the Red Cross, MSF, CARE and the Red Crescent. All of them tell us that they have no room for us. The Tanzanian branch of the Red Cross gives us some simple mats to sleep on and a hot meal.

There are endless lines of Hutus and Tutsi waiting for their daily handout of milk, flour and rice. We shoot some photos and interview the people. There are clusters of children, newly orphaned and wandering around with blank expressions on their faces. There is not much to capture here, other than a sea of gaunt faces. We find a Tutsi chauffeur who, for

$100, will take us as far as the headquarters of the "Rwandese Patriotic Front" about 10–15 km inside the border. We don't bother with a visa, since we doubt there is much of a government left. It takes us an hour to get as far as the Tanzanian border post on the eastern shore of the Kagera River. It should only take 15 minutes, but we are like salmon swimming upstream as we try to make our way through the river of refugees streaming out of Rwanda. The people are carrying the last of their possessions; even the children carry bundles. Old men carry firewood, now a valuable commodity. At this rate, it will take us all day just to get to the headquarters in Rwanda where there are no basic commodities and terror reigns at night.

We decide to try to cross the border the next morning. Our hunch is right. All the refugees are sleeping by the side of the road and the going is easy. We are waved across the Tanzanian border with little fuss. Our exit visas are simply gifts of pens and Camel Trophy stickers, strangely powerful international currency. As we cross the bridge high above the Kagera River, we can see bodies floating downstream. It is strange how their dark skin turns white. One cadaver is caught between two rocks and bobs up and down in the fast moving water.

At the other side, there is no one manning the border posts. Our relief is short-lived. About 50 meters past the bridge, we are stopped by armed members of the RPF. They ask for ID, question our purpose here, and treat us like celebrities when they see our press cards.

Our Tutsi driver does not fare as well. The guards treat him as a deserter and question his ownership of the vehicle. They take him away to a nearby building, despite our desperate protests. We never see him again. Distraught, we come across two old friends—fellow journalists Luc Delahey and James Natchway. We hug each other and exchange information. They have come from Kigali to report on the recently discovered massacre in the village of Nyarubuye 115 km away. They never got there, having all the tires on their vehicles blown when they ran over sabotage spikes laid across the road. They had spent two days trying to find a way out. They had flown in from Uganda, and then were stuck in Kigali by the fierce fighting. They had seen our vehicle and are disappointed that it is no longer here.

We hang around the bridge pondering our situation. When a truck crosses the border, we flag it down and cut a deal on the spot. For $400, we now have wheels. A guard from the RPF rides shotgun in the front with Jim Natchway. Our first dramatic sight is thousands and thousands of rusty, blood-stained machetes confiscated by the RPF from captured Hutus. I immediately think of the piles of glasses, shoes and clothing photographed in the concentration camps in WW II. We drive through burned-out villages and by rows of bodies—most killed with machetes. Among the bodies are stunned survivors searching for relatives. I am struck by the look in these people's eyes. I have seen many, many wars but never one that created so much fear and horror.

The 115 km of horror brings us to Nyarubuye, site of a dark tale we had heard from the refugees inside Tanzania. They told us of hundreds of men, women and children herded into a church and slaughtered like pigs. We smell the heavy stench of rotting flesh long before we come upon the scene. We try to inhale the scent of the eucalyptus trees, but all we can smell is the revolting odor of decay. There are pieces of humans strewn everywhere. Wild dogs had probably been feasting on the corpses. None of us have ever seen anything like this before. Even Luc, Jim and I, who have seen so much, cannot comprehend the horror that we behold. The monastery is surrounded by a brick wall. Inside the wall is a flower-filled garden. Among the flowers are the rotting bodies of hundreds of women and children. The building is a low brick structure built during the Belgian colonial period. There is a simple church adjoining the monastery.

We had all emptied our stomachs when the stench first hit us—a natural and healthy reaction to human decay—but I continue to wretch as nausea comes over me in waves. The people had fled to the church afraid for their lives. They had been taught that the church was the place of last refuge. They were wrong. Men armed with machetes ordered them into the garden and began to slash and cut them. Some tried to escape. One man's upper torso is halfway up the metal ladder on the church steeple. His lower torso and legs hang half a meter below.

Inside the church, a man lies hacked to death at the altar. Piles of bodies lie among the pews. I stare at the dead bodies in the bushes, probably dragged there by the dogs, at the strange grimacing expressions of the contorted faces, as they putrefy.

We return the way we came, knowing that we have captured mankind at its most base. The perverse irony of this sin being committed in a church makes it even more tragic and surreal.

—**Coskun Aral**

Spilt Milk

Many analysts will try to explain what happened and is hap-pening in Central Africa. Lectures on nomadic Nilotes, agrari-an Bantus and forest dwelling pygmies make little sense in an African context. Jack Kramer spent a considerable amount of time in the region and his campfire story says as much about the Hutu/Tutsi/Twa conflict that was to come as any.

I well remember our friend, Gupta, as we sat in this gray light, sipping piping-hot tea from chipped enamelware cups on the Tanzania side of the Kagera. Peering into the mists, he would wonder not just about the identity of the shifting shadows they shrouded, but at the nature of the shroud itself: fog, mist, smoke from a cooking fire, from a land-clearing fire, from a dry-season fire set by lightening, from fire set by poachers to flush game.

This is Karagwe country; it had been a long day, we'd had a decent meal, and, as we pass the plastic Listerine bottle full of *waraki* among us, we feel the spell of the old empires here-abouts. Karagwe, Ankole, Tutsi, have Gupta conjuring punch-drunkenly, straining to glimpse Lord knows what through the mists, as he tells us that an ancient Iron Age city has recently been excavated on the flanks of the Ngorongoro crater on the Serengeti Plain, a highly developed place whose people and whose collapse remains a mystery. He says they had buildings made of brick, which required firing in kilns, which in turn required charcoal. "That mist over there," he says, gesturing toward a cloud that looks like fog to me, "I'm reckoning it's a charcoal mound. What they're doing, you see, is they're digging a pit, lining the bottom with damp leaves and hot coals, filling it with timber, then covering it with dirt, and you're walking about and you're seeing this mound of earth with smoke rising from it, as if the earth itself were smouldering. Well, soon enough they're coming along and uncovering it all, and there you have your charcoal."

He tells us it was also done that way in an ancient empire on the Indian subcontinent called Mohenjo-Davo, and apropos of nothing charcoal, he tells us one of the primal legends of the Watutsi. "As Rwanda's first king lay dying, he summoned his sons, Gatwa, Gahutu and Gatusi. Here's a jug of milk for each of you, he told them. Guard it all night. But Gatwa drank all his, and Gahutu fell asleep, spilling half his jug as he rolled over. Only Gatusi sat up the night, presenting his father with the full jug, and thus Watutsi came to rule the land, Bahutu became serfs, and Batwa were driven from mankind to live in the forests."

—**Jack Kramer**

SIERRA LEONE
RUFing It with the Guerillas

Like most young journalists making their mark, Roddy Scott looks for extreme quests that can earn him those big league by-lines. He was the first and probably only outsider to travel with the RUF rebels in Sierra Leone. Although Foday Sankoh portrayed his people as Muslim freedom fighters, they were destitute and press-ganged tribesmen high on grass and some were eaters of human flesh. Many of their soldiers were 8–14 year-old kids who would torture and eviserate innocent people just to show off to their playmates. Not the best scenario for a journalist who needed to stay alive to get the story out.

The taxi driver wanted $40 for the journey. From Gueckedou, the largest and closest Guinean town to Sierra Leone, to the border was a tricky road, he explained. There are military checkpoints all along the road, not to mention that the road is likely to ruin his precious car with its vast and numerous potholes. I cave in, reflecting as we cruise past the numerous refugee camps en route, that it's a small price to pay if it gets me to my destination without any hassles. Doma refugee camp is right on the border with Sierra Leone and that's where I'm heading to join guerrillas of the Revolutionary United Front (RUF) in one of the nastiest low intensity wars around.

The checkpoints are a breeze, until the dreaded question comes. "Do you have a permit to be in the area," a soldier asks. I try to dodge the issue of permits by telling the driver to say that we're just going to a village up the road and will be back in a couple of hours. That and about $5 seems to satisfy the soldier and we move off, eventually reaching the sprawling mass of mud huts and thatched roofs that Doma refugee camp consists of. Now is the moment of truth. According to my briefing by RUF officials, barely 48 hours earlier in the Ivory Coast, I will be approached in the camp by the RUF contact man who will arrange my passage across the border.

For some time, the only people who surround me are a group of curious, raggedly clad children, who find seeing a white man something of an exotic spectacle. They are soon joined by adults of the camp. Just as my faith in the RUF organizational ability begins to fade completely, I am approached by a young man named Christopher. "Welcome to my Moa," he says, which are the words I have been waiting to hear from my contact since my arrival. In his hut, we discuss how I will cross the border. He speaks in barely comprehensible pidgin English and I struggle to understand his words.

He explains that we will leave the camp in the early morning, but before we can cross the border, I will have to give some money to the Guinean border guards. They supposedly have the key to a small boat that will take me across the river to Sierra Leone.

Even reaching the border poses problems. Some of the villages are inhabited by Guineans, Christopher explains, and if they see us, the alarm will be raised, dashing any hopes of crossing the border. The next hour is chaotic as we run through villages only to find that even at this late hour, there are people colliding with each other in the darkness in their attempts to backtrack and hide before the oncoming invasion. It's like a scene out of "The Keystone Cops" and would be comical except that I am overdosing on adrenaline.

Finally we reach the compound housing the border guards, and by torch light I count out the equivalent of $100 for the captain, who after a cursory examination of my bag, allows us to proceed to the riverbank. It is dark and moonless as my boat sets out from the Guinean side of the border. At the rear of the dug-out tree that serves as our canoe, a Guinean soldier paddles us across the river Moa, which separates Guinea from Sierra Leone. This part of Sierra Leone is currently under control of guerrillas of the RUF, who have waged a five-year war against successive governments, and they are the guerrillas I am clandestinely crossing the border to meet.

There is something surreal about the presence of the Guinean soldier. Just across the border, his compatriots are doing their incompetent best to help the Sierra Leone government defeat the rebels, but he appears indifferent to the contradiction of ferrying a journalist into rebel territory. He gratefully takes the $5 I offer him in local currency. From the far riverbank, a torch suddenly flashes three times and I reply with two short dashes from my own torch.

Three teenage guerrillas are waiting for me on the riverbank. They are dressed in what I will come to recognize as the standard guerrilla uniform of jeans, T-shirts and plastic flip-flops on their feet. Additionally, of course, there are three AK-47s slung casually over the shoulders. It is an hour walk through the jungle before we arrive at the first village. The cacophony of noise the jungle emits is alternately hypnotic and disconcerting. Bar the handful of guerrillas billeted there, the village is deserted. In one of the houses a group of guerrillas listens to raucous reggae music. A bowl of cold, unappetizing rice is provided for me to eat. Wagging his head from side to side to the beat of the music, a guerrilla shouts, "Power to the people!" A little inappropriate, perhaps, as all the locals seem to have taken a rather permanent vacation.

At dawn, I stroll around the village with the commander, Lt. Stanley. The guerrillas, like almost all their ilk, are eager for me to take their photographs, as they hope for a fleeting moment of fame on the inside cover of a magazine. The village is smeared with graffiti: crude drawings of AK-47s grace the walls as well as the usual misspelled slogans, such as "RUF is fighting for [sic] di people." Another building has "Agriculture Committes Office–Dia" written on the wall, but the office is an empty wreck and has probably never been anything other than a few words on the wall.

The following day I receive word that the RUF leader, Foday Sankoh, wants to see me at his headquarters. It will take several days to walk through the bush to reach the leader's camp, says Lt. Marba, into whose care I am entrusted. The daily 30 kilometer trek is exhausting, the breaks infrequent and the fear of government troops constant. During a break, as we sit eating oranges in one of the innumerable burned-out villages, a guerrilla, under the *nom de guerre* of "Rebel 245," rolls up a cigarette with a page from the Bible. I ask if he can read the paper he is using. "Small, small," he says with a contrite grin. "When I smoke through the Bible I become very strong...all the words go up to my head and I become invincible," he boasts. "The Bible is very good."

Others apparently prefer more traditional methods of increasing their strength, or making sure their insurance premium stays at a reasonable level. Noticing that another guerrilla has a series of rectangular cuts on his upper arm, I inquire about their significance. "Bulletproof" comes the slightly embarrassed reply, as if he is fearful (quite rightly) that I won't believe a word of it. "They (the cuts) protect me from bullets," he says, jabbing at his chest with his fingers, then flinging his arms away in imitation of the imaginary bullets bouncing off his body. My suggestion that a proper bulletproof jacket would probably be more effective is met with horrified denials. "No, no, it's African culture…very powerful," he says emphatically. I suspect he means African magic or voodoo, but he can't find the right words. Despite such protestations of faith, however, he churlishly refuses to let me put the power of his protection to the test.

As I join the march again, the Lieutenant hands me lunch, which proves to be lumpy, cold lamb. Gesturing to the jungle path, which has already consumed most of the column, and between mouthfuls of lamb, he asks if I know about antipersonnel mines. With a sinking heart, I admit some knowledge. "Well, then," he says, "the whole of this area is mined and you must make sure you follow exactly in the footsteps of the man in front of you." Amazingly, after two days of jungle trekking, we reach the first of the base camps without incident. The camp is constructed almost entirely from roofing zinc, and now I begin to realize why so many of the deserted villages that we have passed through have no roofs.

The camp mascot is a Strasser, a dog irreverently named for the former military ruler of Sierra Leone, Captain Valentine Strasser, who had recently been deposed by his second in command, Brigadier Julius Maada Bio. Like almost every rebel camp I visit, it resounds to the sound of reggae music as guerrillas relax, confident that the previous day's declaration of a cease-fire will spare them shelling. The strains of Bob Marley and "Buffalo Soldier" emanate from ghetto blasters attached to looted car batteries that have been recharged courtesy of equally looted British Petroleum solar panels.

A guerrilla turns up the music and begins to dance. He is no older than nine or ten, but he handles the Kalasnikov hanging from his shoulder with the confidence of a veteran. In his hand he is holding a book, "Elementary English for Beginners." It is the kind of surreal contradiction that has become all too familiar in Africa—children whose only real schooling in life are lessons in dispensing death. He is joined on the earthy "dance floor" by a woman who loosely holds a Russian-made Tokarov pistol in her hand as she sways, rather fittingly, to the rhythm of "I Shot the Sheriff."

Some days later I set off again to the headquarters in the southeast of the country. By now Foday Sankoh has left the bush for negotiations with the government of newly elected President Ahmd Tejan Kabbah. As we enter one of the many camps en route to the headquarters, I notice a human skull impaled on a stick rising above a cluster of undergrowth. "Enemy's head," says Corporal Chinese Pepper by way of explanation, with a grin. Corpses and skeletons become a gruesome but common sight amongst the shattered remnants of the rural villages. The body of a semidecomposed man, huddled on a pathway, still clad in what looks like a sports jacket, is ignored as we pass by. It is only as I move downwind and the stench of death catches up with me that I, like the guerrillas escorting me, move faster.

In the early evening we arrive at a village where we are met by a platoon that will take me on the final leg of the journey to the headquarters. The senior NCO is decked out in camouflage and white Adidas sneakers—he seems to be the equivalent of a richer cousin to his colleagues from the north. A party is dispatched to find food, a euphemism, I later learn, for raiding a village. If they are unsuccessful, we will eat the standard bush meal of raw boiled bananas and snails. In the meantime, the two platoons relax and chatter in the ruins of the village. Dried tobacco leaves are torn up, and with a piece of paper from notebook, rolled into cigarettes that are passed around. A fire is quickly lit and wet clothes are hung around the flames to dry.

Some hours later, flushed with success, the food team returns carrying large quantities of rice and fried fish. Their leader, improbably named High Firing, confirms that they paid a social call to one of the local villages. They told the villagers that running away is bad form, gave them a lecture about the war and convinced them that the RUF is fighting on their behalf. In turn, the villagers donated food, cigarettes and money to them. It's amazing what an AK-47 does for good PR and mutual understanding.

In the morning we set off again. Trooping through open swamps, we can hear the sound of throbbing in the distance. It is almost certainly a helicopter, but the crucial question is what kind. A guerrilla column caught in the open by one of the newly acquired Mi-24 Hind gunships might, despite the ceasefire, prove too tempting a target for the gunners, and it was with an added urgency in his voice that the commander told us to head quickly for cover. Running toward the closest dense bush, I can hear the click-clacks of weapons cocking, and by the time we reach the bush, the sound of the helicopter is deafening. The density of the foliage around us means that we cannot see the helicopter flying over, and more importantly neither can it see us. Eventually the sound fades into the distance.

On arrival at the Zagoda headquarters I am greeted by the commander in Sankoh's absence, Lt. Col. Mohammed Tarrawally. He is resplendent in a pair of American military jungle boots, combat trousers and Nike-emblazoned sweatshirt. The green beret worn jauntily on his head, courtesy of the Sierra Leonean army, is as good an indicator of his status as anything else. Soft-spoken and small, he is the replica of a little Napoleon as he escorts me to my new quarters. In comparison to the other camps, my accommodation is five star—even including the rare luxury of Lipton's teabags, which like cigarettes, are regularly smuggled in from Guinea.

But even here, far from the front line, the war is never far away. The sound of a jet fighter through the roof of the forest canopy galvanizes guerrillas into frantic action. While they rush to turn over the solar panels that might give away the exact position of the camp, others forlornly seek cover as the jet screams overhead leaving sound waves in its wake, but thankfully, no bombs. "It's just their means of letting us know that they're still around," says Lieutenant Colonel Tarrawally, with a smile, as the camp returns to normal. "The war is not over yet."

—**Roddy Scott**

Diamonds Are a Guerrilla's Best Friend

While young Roddy was humping it in the rainforest below, old hand Jim Hooper was having a much better time of it with the professional soldiers of Executive Outcomes, a mercenary group hired by the Sierra Leonean government to eliminate

the RUF rebels. Jim's account shows the business side of war
and also the ridiculous charades played by army officers. Since
then there have been two coups since Strasser (usually the rul-
ers manage to flee to the UK with full bank accounts) and the
RUF are supposedly part of the new government even though
RUF leader Foday Sankoh is under house arrest in Nigeria.

It's amazing the number of wars I've covered in Africa
where there just happens to be diamonds. Of course, the side
that's dressed in rags and running around in the bush with
guns invariably has an earnest Columbia graduate doing the
Washington cocktail circuit telling any dimwit prepared to
listen that his side is only fighting for democracy and the
rights of the common man. What he doesn't mention is that
there happens to be oodles of diamonds where he comes
from. Or that his side would really like to get their hands on
those babies. Not to mention the gold deposits. And the...
well, you get the picture.

Speaking of pictures, if there is ever one made about Sierra
Leone it will be a surefire hit. Imagine the opening scene as a
4x4 filled with black and white soldiers and one journalist
(that's me, played by Robert Redford for the *gravitas*) noses

into the shabby African village. Cut to: close-ups of narrowed eyes following its progress along the potholed streets. Above the buzz of flies, whispers of "South Africans" ripple ahead. The jeep bumps into the market square and the gathered throng freezes, then approaches timidly, surrounding the car in silence. One woman suddenly shrieks, "South A-fri-ca!" the words becoming a mantra picked up by the others. Children dart in to touch their heroes, racing away in giggling triumph. A woman grabs my arm. "They saved us. They are saints!" These special forces, veterans of the Namibian and Angolan wars, case-hardened tools of the old apartheid regime, cast shy looks at the dancers, then at me. "This happens every time we come here," mumbles the driver. He ducks his head in embarrassment as the wails gather strength. "They really like us."

Now, as a serious war tourist you might be thinking, "So far, so good. Might be fun, but how the hell do I go about getting there?" Okay, imagine it's the middle of the night and your KLM or Sabena flight has just landed in Sierra Leone after a six hour flight from Amsterdam or Brussels. The good thing is, even if you're at the back of the line, you won't wait long to get through immigration. Not many people get off in Sierra Leone.

Immigration may be a breeze, but customs can be a little tricky. Before the officer tells you about his ailing mother and crippled children and asks for a small contribution, say that you're here to interview the Prez and what is the nice customs officer's name so you can mention it to the Big Fella. This will get you a quick and remarkably obsequious "Welcome to Sierra Leone, sir."

Be aware that Lungi airport is separated from Freetown by ten very dark miles of potholes punctuated by kerosene-lit check points, followed by a rust bucket ferry ride, then another 10 miles to your hotel. Outside the terminal, about two dozen shouting taxi drivers will dive for your luggage. Once someone grabs it, you're not getting it back until you're at the hotel and he's demanding 100 bucks, so keep a grip. Your few fellow travelers will be heading in the same direction, so suggest sharing a taxi. Sharing or solo, however, the bone-jarring ride will carry a tariff of at least $50, plus another tenner each for the rust bucket. The best thing about the ferry is the open upper deck and the opportunity to rehydrate yourself with cold beer. Take the opportunity. The flight from Europe may have spanned 1500 miles and six hours, but the 25 mile journey from Lungi to your hotel is likely to take three more.

If you're on an expense account, the only place to stay is the Cape Sierra. The rooms are air-conditioned and, critically important for a hack, there is a well-appointed bar. In the event you're moved to actually file a story, the telephones do work. If your editor is prepared to spring for a C-note a night you're laughing. If you're a freelancer and can't convince any of your various editors to cough up ("We'll be happy to take a look at what you've got when you get back."), then it's down the road to the charmingly named Mammy Yoko. Just across the road from a stunning beach, the rooms were clean- ish when I was there, there wasn't too much fungus in the showers, and the air-conditioning worked— sometimes. Al- though I negotiated down to $50 a night, Mammy Yoko's recently undertook a major refurbishment and may now be less inclined to accommodate journos on a budget.

If you're hoping to be snapping bang-bang photos from your beachside balcony, by the way, you're out of luck; the war's in the interior and you're going to have to get over to army headquarters for an introduction to the South Africans of Executive Outcomes. Bribing your way in isn't desperately difficult, but it may take a while, in which case hire a taxi to wait for you. You should be able to negotiate a daily rate of about $30.

Bribes are definitely part of Sierra Leone's cultural fabric. The aforementioned customs officer, for example, could have been bought off for a couple of dollars. There may well be other instances where the demand will be substantially inflat- ed. An acquaintance found himself under arrest for taking photos of Freetown's landmark baobab tree. For a mere 100,000 Leones ($1000), however, the police were prepared to overlook this open and shut case of espionage. After much haggling, they meekly accepted five dollars. Bribe money should be carried in bills of $1 and $5 denominations. (But never in one wad.)

So what's all the palaver about Sierra Leone, anyway? Un- less you picked up this book because you thought it was about public toilets in Brooklyn, you'll already have guessed they have one of those dinky little wars going on. And guess what? It's all about diamonds. Mountains of diamonds. Not to mention the biggest rutile (titanium ore) mine in the world, serious bauxite and gold deposits, and a good chance of platinum and oil. But it's the same old story: there are a few folks who have it all, and few folks who'd like to have it all. Naturally. The screwy thing is that since independence the haves have turned Sierra Leone into the world's sixth poorest country. Officially. And they were about to lose the whole shebang to the have-nots, until they dialled 911 for outside help.

At the South Africans' base overlooking the Koidu diamond fields a Mi-24 gunship settles noisily. I snap a few photos and fall in with the Belarussian crew, offering to send copies to their families in Minsk. Volodya and Valerii, grizzled veterans of Afghanistan, growl an unmistakable "Nyet!" Valerii slaps a mosquito. "Look, our wives think we're flying cargo. here. If they knew what we're really doing, they'd kill us." He stops alongside Colonel Rudolph van Heerden, the South African commander for the Kono District, and takes the offered beer. "But you can send them to Rudolph and he'll make sure we get them," he says as the former mortal enemies turn to discuss tomorrow's joint operation against the rebels.

The side without the goodies are the rebels of the Revolutionary United Front. Their idea of a good time is a bit of ritual cannibalism in between lopping parts off innocent bystanders. Their head dude is Alfred Foday Sankoh, a 62-year-old former corporal, who a couple of decades ago ended up in the slammer for trying to overthrow the government. Eventually granted amnesty, but still sore at everyone, he headed to Libya for some counseling. A pal at Qaddafi's college for aspiring revolutionaries was warlord Charles Taylor from Liberia, which happens to be right next door to Sierra Leone. Taylor went on to overthrow Liberian President Samuel Doe. Between capturing Doe and putting him out of his misery, Taylor sliced off poor Sam's ears, then sauteed and fed them back to him. One of those cultural things, I guess. I mean, who are we to judge? (Besides, Sam ate his predecessor's liver and inherited his vote at the U.N.) Anyway, when Al Sankoh's time came, Charlie gave him a start with a few guns and thugs to keep the standards up. Oh, and they're fighting for democracy and the rights of the common man. I almost forgot to mention that.

Until recently, the side that did have the goodies was led by Captain Valentine Strasser and his four best chums. Back in 1992 the Boyz From the Barracks, all grumpy lieutenants and captains, marched up to the presidential mansion one day to complain about not being paid for months. Seeing them coming, President Joseph Momoh, ever mindful of his neighbor Mr. Doe's fate, was out the back door like a flash and making tracks for the airport. When the last of the lads' "Hellos?" echoed through the empty mansion, they propped their boots on Momoh's desk and discussed the latest in job opportunities. After flipping coins, 25-year-old Strasser ended up as chairman of the new National Provisional Ruling Council. The others gave themselves the inspired, if not actually prescient, titles of S.O.S., for Secretary of State it's said, and P.L.O., for permanent liaison officer, then shot craps for S.O.S. for Mines, S.O.S. for Treasury, for Defense, for Tourism, Fisheries, Trade and Industry... you name it, then divvied up all the P.L.O. positions. It was tough, but they knew where their duty lay and accepted the heavy burdens of responsibility.

Back in the jungle, the rebel attacks were low key at first: a village for food, a clinic for medical supplies, an everyone-asleep-at-the-wheel army convoy for more guns and ammunition. All straight out of Al's favorite course at Goofy Qaddafi's University, How to Get Your Start in Revolutionary Warfare 101. But with a twist: instead of being nice to the people to get them on your side, which every guerrilla leader since Mao has preached, Al Sankoh preferred chopping off arms and legs and heads. This, according to a RUF defector, was Uncle Al's way of suggesting the survivors join up. As recruiting programs go, it was said to be rather persuasive.

As the rebel attacks moved closer to Freetown a stressed out Strasser & Co. began grabbing kids off the streets, giving them a gun, uniform and a few words on their sacred duty to Sierra Leone, then shoving them into the jungle. The intermittent salaries of $20 and two bags of rice a month, coupled with the prospect of the RUF pouncing on them, convinced a fair number to do a bit of looting, murdering and amputeeing themselves.

There was a certain ebb and flow to the business until Sankoh's Neanderthals grabbed the mines. Suddenly there were no millions flowing into the treasury. Almost as bad was that the diamond smugglers, who paid certain folks good money not to have their bags examined too closely at the airport, had nothing to pay anyone not to look for. And to top it all, the pesky rebels were threatening Freetown itself. It was a vexing moment. Were the boys to do a Momoh and hightail it for the tall and uncut, or bring in some muscle?

In April 1995, Pretoria-based Executive Outcomes, a private security company staffed by black and white former special forces soldiers, signed a contract to sort things out. To the astonished relief of the Boyz, it took less than a week to eliminate the RUF threat around the capital. Before the even more astonished rebels could ask, "Who was that masked man?" EO roared off to recover the diamond fields. That two day operation barely worked up a sweat. As soon as rumors of this reached London, I wangled an invitation, got myself a visa and sprinted for the airport.

Hours after arriving I was sitting on the tailgate of an Mi-17 surrounded by black and white South Africans in all their feathers and warpaint as we skimmed the trees. At Koidu they dragged me off on a jolly op to mortar the bejeezus out of the bad guys. Our nights were spent either under monsoon rains or running back and forth to escape columns of enormous army ants. Two choppers eventually picked us up, then dropped down to a town just captured. Dripping with cameras, I was out the door and down on one knee in my best Hollywood pose, looking for action. I blinked at the sight of the wheel struts lengthening on my helicopter. That means it's taking off, I choked. This is not good. Deafened by the whop-shriek of blades and turbines, I next saw the gunner frantically motioning me to return. Are the bad guys coming? Is someone shooting at us? When the wheels actually left the ground, the determined expression of the professional poser dissolved into near—well, total, actually—panic at the prospect of being left to the mercies of the RUF. (You won't say anything about this to Bob Redford, will you?) This was followed by a leap that left me clinging catlike to the bottom of the door. Hands grabbed my wrists and hauled me inside 100 feet above the jungle. "That'll teach you to get out of my helicopter without telling me," the South African pilot said over a few beers that night. "If you had just stayed there, you silly twit, I'd have come back for you."

Back at Executive Outcomes' headquarters, I leap aside as a shiny 4x4 skids to a stop. Two Sierra Leonean soldiers stagger out under the weight of chromed pistols, shotguns, Bowie knives and hand grenades. One also carries a machine gun and about 50 yards of ammunition belt wrapped around him. The mere weight of it all has this metallic mummy pop-eyed and sweating buckets. The ear protectors perched atop his head are a particularly fetching touch. They are followed by their boss, Colonel Tom Nyuma, universally loved as one of the five coup d'etat-ers back in '92. To the everlasting joy of all Sierra Leoneans, he was recently promoted from captain to colonel, skipping the tiresome ranks in between, and added S.O.S. of Defence of the NPRC of Sierra Leone to his other

S.O.S.s. He held on to all his P.L.O.s for old time's sake. It's rumored that the main requirements for holding the high octane titles are being able to say them without a crib sheet or taking a breath. You probably think I'm joking.

Colonel Tom struts past his bodyguards, the patches on his vest proclaiming him "Ranger," "Airborne," and "Special Forces." Tom is not known to have attended any such courses anywhere in the world. Ever. His clear favorite is a skull and crossbones with the warning, "Mess With the Best, Die with the Rest." Tom, who went from being an impecunious captain with an attitude to a senior government minister with property in England and monthly trips to the U.S., is said to have purchased the patches through *Soldier of Fortune* magazine. Tom is 26 years old. The reader will sleep better knowing he is also in charge of the war.

Inside the operations room Colonel Renier Hugo, EO's operations officer, is briefing the Belarussian gunship pilots and Colonel Tom on another attack. Next to Tom is a Sierra Leonean major whose men have been guarding the diamond fields for Tom since the South Africans chased out the rebels. It should be stated here and now that even though he's keeping a very close eye on the diamond fields, it has nothing to do with him being tight with Tom's sister, or that Tom might have one or two ideas about what to do with those diamonds.

Hugo's pointer taps the map, his tone crisp and professional: The infantry company will advance to this point, another company will be landed here by helicopter, support elements will be placed there, the gunship will orbit over here until.... The pilots listen intently, making notes on their own maps. The major, whose men are integral to the operation, is content with the plan; so content that he's snoring gently. A blinding flash fills the room. Duck! It's Tom's official photographer. Tom bobbies up to the map to explain how the attack should be conducted. Volodya and Valerii's eyebrows lift then meet in bewilderment. The South Africans smile fixedly. Two more flashes for the Freetown newspapers and Tom takes his seat. Hugo carries on as if nothing has happened.

The attack was successful. Of course, Tom and his sister's boyfriend really didn't think it important enough to be at the sharp end with their troops. It was too small an operation for them to be involved, they told me hastily when reports of six wounded were radioed from the advancing soldiers. Consummate professionals, they spent their time studying tactics as revealed in their complete collection of Rambo videos. And no, I'm really not joking this time. But if there ever is a film made, by God you'll split your sides laughing.

—Jim Hooper

SUDAN

Victory in Sudan

Jim Hooper (along wth Rob Krott) knows the Sudan well but this is the longest running war in Africa. In 1997 the SPLA was flush with backing from Western powers and were making gains against the Muslim north.

Koranic verses on the dashboard and plastic flowers round the windshield are legacies of a former driver, but two bullet holes suggest the recent change of ownership has not been amicable. "We are smashing the enemy!" the young rebel officer shouts over the blat of unmuffled engine as the captured truck lurches sideways and two tires drop into a rock-hard rain gully. With a horrible grinding, the new driver finds first gear and puts his weight into the wheel. In the back, half a dozen guerrillas bounce atop tons of mortar and artillery shells abandoned by the fleeing Sudanese army. "Near Yei, we made a big ambush!" the officer yells exuberantly. The truck climbs resentfully out of the gully and immediately pitches the other way on a dirt track that hasn't seen a grader in fourteen years of war. "You will see. It is a very smelly place!"

Barely 72 hours have passed since I returned from a Bosnia update and listened to the telephone message. The Sudan People's Liberation Army has launched a massive offensive against government forces and have already captured Yei, the second-largest town in the south. Do I want to cover it? I swore silently. Just six weeks earlier I'd been in southern Sudan, gambling that, with the end of the rainy season, the SPLA would open a third front against the Sudanese army. In the previous five months the National Democratic Alliance, an unlikely coalition between the SPLA and Muslim parties ousted by Fundamentalists in 1989, had advanced in the eastern part of the country, and were threatening Port Sudan in the north. A desperate National Islamic Front government in Khartoum had declared a jihad and begun drafting high school students to throw pell-mell against the seasoned rebels. With the Sudanese army badly overstretched, military logic dictated that a southern offensive had to be imminent. And indeed my visit had revealed a snorting, bullish SPLA pawing the earth in preparation for a headlong charge. Thousands of new recruits, fresh from months of intensive training, were engaged in large scale infantry and armor exercises; food, ammunition and diesel were being stockpiled; and morale—from senior commanders down to the newest recruit—was stratospheric. It was clear that the biggest donnybrook of the war was gathering force, but my pleas of "When?" received innocent replies of "What offensive?" and I came home in a funk. My editor at *Jane's* was sympathetic and promised a page for my tenuous predictions, but the SPLA had been saying for years that they were on a roll and we can't really justify using much space on maybes, can we? Now it had happened. I picked up the phone.

War comes in different ways, in disparate climates and terrain, at the hands of a rainbow of colors wielding weapons from a rainbow of sources, but its immediate and irreducible end is death. And for those who earn a precarious crust reporting the world's conflicts, each war has a defining image distinct from those past or yet to come.

The road, hemmed by teak forest, straightens and smooths. Through the cracked windshield I see the first burned-out Toyota Landcruiser. Beyond it clusters of scorched trucks and abandoned equipment stretch a mile into the distance. The engine bellows painfully as the driver down-shifts and we pass the first body. "Now you will see," my escort says. "Under just one tree more than twenty enemy." We grind to a halt in a cacophony of hissing air brakes, shaking bodywork and the thud of an ammunition crate against the back of the cab. Here is the "smelly place." Tying a bandanna across my mouth and nose, I step down and glutted ravens fly heavily into the sky. Then the stench penetrates and my stomach rebels as the smaller, darker objects come into focus wherever my eye settles—on the road, the shoulders, deeper into the undergrowth. Bodies, hundreds, lie where they fell ten days earlier, their own eyes long since taken by the birds. Most had died alone, but under a large tree to my left, I see twenty bodies rotted under a blanket of maggots, gunned down as they sought safety in numbers. The gorge rises, I gag and somehow hold it down. Then I shoot them—this time with my camera—and step over an unexploded mortar shell. Just beyond the tree a dry streambed disappears under the road. Two more people, feet and legs protruding from the culvert, had died scrambling desperately for cover. A third lay full length just behind. Click. A few paces more and I see a shriveled form– a white skull and black scalp resting against the warhead of a rocket-propelled-grenade. Pause and...click. I keep walking. Now a fifty-foot swathe of saplings scythed down with another dozen men. I cut around a heavy tree limb chain-sawed off by automatic weapons fire and jerk to a stop, one foot in the air, before stepping back and detouring past three who fell with it. Then I spot a desiccated body, rigidly straight, reclined at right angles to the road, its head broken loose and resting at the ankles. Scattered between and around all of them are piles of small arms ammunition, heavy machine gun belts, mortar and artillery shells—and thousands of Korans. I stoop and pocket an amulet of some sort lying next to a bullet-holed copy. Here and there a page turns idly in the nauseating breeze, but as I lower the camera, the only sounds come from the ravens scolding us for the interruption.

Eight months in the planning, Operation Thunderbolt was a three-pronged attack against government forces along the road between the Ugandan border and Yei. Launched on March 9, 1997, the southern axis took less than an hour to rout the Sudanese brigade headquarters at the border town of Kaya, then began driving towards Yei, 56 miles to the north. The next eight Sudanese army positions, complete with heavy weapons and bulging ammunition bunkers, were taken without a shot, tales of rebel strength having convinced the defenders to grab what they could carry and join the retreat. By now the SPLA's central axis had cut the road twelve miles below Yei, while the northern axis had already struck four miles north of the provincial town. Four days later Yei, a strategic target since the war began in 1983, was in rebel hands. In what would be an incredible stroke of luck for the SPLA, the panicking defenders failed to send a single message that they were abandoning the position. Its impact on the other side would prove catastrophic, for at that moment a column of almost 6000 demoralized Sudanese army and 4000 West Nile Bank Front combatants—a Ugandan Muslim terrorist group armed and funded by Khartoum—was struggling towards the presumed safety of the garrison. Forewarned of its approach, the SPLA commander sent the Yei victors south to join the central axis, which lay directly in the path of the approaching enemy. Outnumbered by almost 2:1, the rebel force would have to rely on surprise and the shock of massed firepower if it were to survive. Tanks and heavy concentrations of anti-aircraft and anti-armor weapons were moved into the forest and hastily camouflaged by newly-blooded infantry, who then filled the gaps and settled silently in their positions. Thirty minutes later the Sudanese and Ugandan column reached the edge of the ambush. Not until the bulk of it had entered the killing zone was the order given to open fire. When it finally stopped, close to 2000 lay dead and more than 1000 had surrendered, the balance abandoning tanks and vehicles and fleeing into the dense forests.

The truck groans to a stop in Yei. The immediate news from Chief of the General Staff Salva Kiir Mayardit is of an attempted government counterattack smashed that very morning 40 miles from the southern capital of Juba. Three enemy battalions had been thrown back with heavy losses. There was now one less obstacle in the way of capturing Juba, the fall of which would be the final step before total victory. My camera trigger finger begins itching. How far from here? Sixty miles.

Can I go there? At the moment it is too dangerous. The enemy has been attacking with gunships and MiGs to cover the withdrawal of their ground forces. Perhaps in a day or two. Okay, then I'll start with the prisoners.

Outside the POW officers' block a depressed Sudanese army colonel accepts a cigarette. Colonel El Tayep El Hussain, who had arrived at Kaya only five weeks before the base fell to the SPLA, speaks passable English, having once attended a U.S. Army munitions course in Savannah, Georgia. Why, I ask, had the NIF closed all churches in the south? "It is government policy to introduce Islam to the southern people," he replies. And the arming of West Nile Bank Front Muslims to murder and mutilate Sudanese refugees in Uganda? El Tayep twists uncomfortably in his chair. "It is government policy," he repeats. What can be done to end the war? "The government must recognize the religious and political rights of the people." The SPLA officers nearby stare stonily at the horizon. They've heard it all before.

Much farther down the scale of prisoners is 18-year-old Yasir Sheik Idris Agib, one of the few surviving members of a self-styled Sudanese *mujahedin* unit. Visibly frightened at being singled out for my questioning, he describes being kidnapped from his high school in Khartoum, given two weeks training and sent to the southern front. What did the instructors teach him? To assemble, load and fire an AK-47. What else? Agib shakes his head. "Only to assemble, load and fire," he mumbles. At the end of the two weeks his class of new holy warriors was addressed by a member of the National Islamic Front, who described the "perfumes of heaven" that would greet those so fortunate as to be martyred in the jihad, whereupon they were each presented with a *hejab*, a tightly folded page of Koranic verses wrapped in cotton, and a key.

The first was to protect them from infidel bullets, the second to unlock the gates of heaven should the first fail. I show him what I picked up at the ambush and he nods: "Yes, that is what they have been given." Hopefully the key was working better than the hejab, for less than half of Agib's classmates had survived. "After they took me from school my parents were never told," he tells me, blinking back tears. "They don't know where I am."

One tire clims a rock and the Toyota pickup leans precariously on its way down the riverbank. "They managed to destroy the bridge here three days ago," Commander George Athor says as we lurch up the other side, "but didn't get any farther." A decomposing body stripped to its underwear lies near the road. "That was the Sudanese battalion commander, a lieutenant colonel," he says grimly. We stop and Athor leads me along the bottom of a ridgeline to where half a dozen bodies sprawl in hastily prepared positions. Athor points to one. "He was too light-skinned to be Sudanese. We're sure he was Iranian or Iraqi." But after three days the bloated corpse has blackened beyond recognition; only the straight hair suggests a Middle Eastern origin. "We captured a Farsi speaker, probably an Iranian, at Mile 40," Athor continues matter-of-factly back in the pickup. "He'd been badly wounded and we tried to save him, but he died. Too bad. He would have been proof that the government is using mujahedin from other countries to fight their jihad."

Ten minutes later we're looking at three burnt-out tanks squatting in earth plowed by explosions and gunfire. Thomas Cirillo, another of the SPLA's young, fighting generals, sweeps his arm across the front line battlefield. "They tried an end play here. Two battalions with armor were sent beyond our right flank as a diversion, then turned west to surprise us. Our tanks were waiting for them. When the enemy passed, we crossed their tracks and hit them from behind." Cirillo hitches his AK sling a little higher on his shoulder as my camera focuses on a turret-less tank and half of a body. Beyond it, dozens more lie motionless under a fine drizzle that has just started. "It was a massacre," he says with professional pride.

Story and photos tucked safely away, I wait next to the 4x4 that will carry me south from Yei to the border. My hosts, ebony giants in battle fatigues, crowd around to wish me safe journey. "You must return when we take Juba," they insist. Looking over my shoulder to wave good-bye, I remember my last question to Colonel El Tayep: Could the Sudanese army hold Juba? A truck carrying cheering rebels towards the front captured his attention and he squinted after it for a long moment, then sighed and shook his head. "I don't think so."

—Jim Hooper

TURKEY

Rocking the Cradle of Civilization

My specialty seems to be tourist spots that hide simmering conflicts or all out raging wars. In Turkey I wanted to lift the carpet to find some dust. I found it. Once again I also tried to introduce a cast of characters to show more than just one viewpoint of this long-running war by the PKK against the Turkish Army.

The road is full of vehicles—tractors, horse carts, sawed-off buses with sagging rear ends, yellow taxis, overloaded motorcycles with sidecars—some carrying entire families with their goats. Everything is square and grey. The road and sidewalks are broken, dirty and patched. Unlike the deathly grey of the towns, the hills beyond are a rich chocolate-brown. The water is a sickly green-blue-black. The sky is the color of slate, with one enormous white cloud stretching off toward the hills in the distance. Acres of cheap boxlike housing sprout from the plains.

DP has come to the cradle of civilization, the uppermost tip of the fertile crescent, now torn apart by ethnic, political, tribal and religious strife. We are determined to get at the heart of this land, in order to understand why so much of the world is a dangerous place.

We stop to buy gas at a new petrol station. The attendant is baffled by our credit card. I run the card and sign the bill for him.

We drive past scattered groves of figs and pistachios. Trucks carry giant pomegranates. We are following the Iraqi pipeline on a highway originally built by the U.S., formally known as the "Silk Road."

Cheap Iraqi diesel, or *masot*, sells for 10,000 TL (Turkish lira or lire) a liter. It is brought from Iraq by trucks fitted with crude, rusty tanks.

As we go east, the fertile soil becomes fields of boulders and sharp rocks. The hills are ribbed and worn by the constant foraging of goats. Not much has changed here in 1000 years.

At Play in the Fields of the Warlords

We drive through the nameless streets of Sevirek, a small town that serves as the center of the Bucak fiefdom. In this age of enlightenment, there are still dark corners in the world where ancient traditions persist. We are in the domain of the

Bucaks, an age-old feudal area in war-torn southeastern Turkey.

As we drive along the cobblestones, we notice that there are no doors or windows in the stone houses, only steel shutters and gates. We ask the way to the warlord's house. Men pause and then point vaguely in the general direction.

We pull up to the Turkish version of a pizza joint. From inside, two men in white smocks eye us apprehensively. The fat one recognizes Coskun and walks out to our car when we call out for directions.

We drive up a narrow cobblestone alleyway just wide enough for a car to pass. There's a Renault blocking the way. Getting out of the car, we notice for the first time that there is a man behind a wall of sandbags pointing an AK-47 in our direction. The large house was built 200 years ago and is lost in the maze of medieval streets and stone walls.

We politely explain who we are and why we have come. We had telephoned earlier and were told that no one was at home—an appropriate response for someone who has survived frequent assassination attempts from terrorists, bandits and the army.

Out from a side door comes a large man with a pistol stuffed into his ammunition-heavy utility vest. He flicks his head at me and looks at Coskun inquisitively. He hears our story. He recognizes Coskun from a year ago, when the photojournalist stayed with the warlord for three days. He smiles and gives Coskun the double-buss kiss, the traditional greeting for men in Turkey. He then grabs me by the shoulders, does the same, and then welcomes us inside. We walk up one flight of stairs and find ourselves in an outside courtyard. We are joined by two more bodyguards. They're older, more grooved, hard looking. Most of one man's chin has been blown off his face; it tells us that we should probably just sit and smile until we get to know each other a little better. We sit on the typical tiny wooden stools men use in Turkey. These have the letters DYP branded into them, the name of the political party with which the warlord has aligned himself.

The bodyguards stare into our eyes, say nothing and watch our hands when we reach for a cigarette. It seems that Sedat Bucak, the clan leader, is out in the fields, but his brother Ali is here. We are offered *chai,* or tea, and cigarettes. The bodyguards do not drink tea, or move, but they light cigarettes. One of the bodyguards sucks on his cigarette as if to suffocate it.

When Ali finally emerges, he is not at all what one would expect a warlord to look like. The men rise and bow. Ali is dressed in shiny black loafers, blue slacks, a plum-colored striped shirt and a dapper windbreaker. He looks like an Iranian USC grad. That he and his brother are the absolute rulers of 100,000 people and in control of an army of 10,000 very tough men is hard to imagine.

A Drive in the Country

Not quite sure why we're here, he offers to show us a gazelle that he was given as a gift by one of his villages. The gazelle is kept in a stone enclosure and flies around the pen, leaping through doors and windows. We ask if we can visit with Sedat. Ali says, "Sure," and repeats that he is out in the fields.

Realizing they would be embarking outside of their compound, they bring out an arsenal of automatic weapons from another room. Ali and his bodyguards get in the Renault and drive down the streets with the barrels of their guns sticking out the windows. Strangely, nobody seems to mind or notice. Even the soldiers and police wave as they drive by.

Following close behind, we are brought to their fortress, an imposing black stone compound that dominates the countryside. It is a simple square structure, each wall about 100 feet long. A central house rises to about 40 feet. The walls are made from *kaaba*, or black stone and are hand-chiseled from the surrounding boulders into squares, filled with special cement to make them bulletproof. One wall is over 20 feet tall.

The men appear nervous when I photograph the compound. This building is intended for combat. For now, it serves as a simple storage place for tractors and grain. From the top, one feels like a king overlooking his land and his subjects, which is exactly what the Bucaks do when they are up here. From this point, we can only see 50 miles to the mountains in the north, but we cannot see the rest of their 200 miles of land to the south and west of us.

We continue our caravan along a dusty road past simple villages and houses. The people here are dirt-poor. They subsist off the arid land. The children run out into the road to wave at us as we drive by.

Ali stops near a field where men, women and children are picking cotton. Cotton needs water, and there's plenty of it. It also needs cheap labor, another commodity of which the Bucaks have plenty.

The people stand still, as we get out of our cars. Ali tells them to continue working, while we take pictures. They resume picking, but their eyes never leave us.

The men decide this would be an opportune time to show off the capability of their arsenal. For one nauseating moment, I have the impression they intend to gun down this entire village. Yet it is target practice that Ali has in mind. Boys will be boys. So we then start plinking away at rocks, using all sorts of automatic weapons. We aim for a pile of rocks about 400 yards away. We are only aware of little puffs of smoke, as we hear the sound of ricochets as the bullets hit the black boulders. Ali is more interested in our video camera, so he plays with that while we play with his weapons.

When boredom sets in, we continue our journey in search of Sedat. We finally locate him about three miles away. We know it's him because of the small army that surrounds the man. His bodyguards are not happy at all to see us. We are instantly engulfed by his men poised in combat stances. Ali introduces us, but we still have to state our case. Sedat recognizes Coskun, but instead of the kiss, we get a Western-style handshake. We introduce ourselves to his dozen or so bodyguards. They do not come forward, so we reach for their hands and shake them. It's awkward, unnerving. They never let their eyes stray from ours.

Ahmed, a chiseled sunburned man who wears green camouflage fatigues, seems to be the chief bodyguard. He appears to like us the least. He wanders over to our car and starts rummaging through the luggage and junk on the backseat. I deliberately put my stuff there so that it would be easy to confirm that I am a writer. He picks up a Fielding catalog and starts flipping through the pages. When he sees my picture next to one of my books, he points and then looks at me.

The Feudal Lord

We chat with Sedat. He is eager to present a positive image to the outside world. We have brought a copy of an interview he had just done with a Turkish magazine. In it, he proposes linking up with the right-wing nationalist party and, together he says, they could end the Kurdish problem. Coskun suggests that such a comment could be taken as a bid for civil war. Sedat says, "Hey, it's only an interview. But I'm still learning." We suggest getting some shots of him driving his tractor. He is happy driving his tractor. But out here there are few other farmers who drive a tractor with an AK-47-armed bodyguard riding behind on the spreader.

Turkey has been at war with the PKK, or Kurdish Workers Party, since 1984. The Kurds want a separate homeland within Turkey, but Turkey insists they possess all the rights they need for now. The Turkish government is correct, but it doesn't stop the PKK from killing, maiming, executing and torturing their own people. The Bucaks are Kurds and the sworn enemies of the PKK, who are also Kurds. The difference is that the Bucaks have essentially carved out their own kingdom and even managed to integrate themselves into the political process in an effective, albeit primitive, way. They use votes rather than bullets to curry favor. They are also left alone by the government. They pay no taxes and have complete control over what goes on in their ancestral lands.

The Bucak family has been in Sevirek for more than 400 years. They are Kurds, but more specifically, they're from the Zaza as opposed to the Commagene branch of the Kurds.

They also speak a different language from the Commagene. They have always controlled a large part of southeastern Turkey by force and eminent domain. Their subjects give them 25 percent of the crops they grow, and, in return, they receive services and are protected by a private army of about 10,000 men. Many other groups have tried unsuccessfully to force them off their land. In times of all-out warfare, all the subjects are expected to chip in and grab their rifles. The Bucaks have wisely aligned themselves with the current ruling political party, the DYP. Realizing that the Bucaks can deliver 100,000 votes goes a long way toward successful lobbying and handshaking in Ankara, the capital of Turkey. Sedat Bucak is head of the clan, at the age of 40. A warrior and farmer by trade, he is now a sharp and shrewd politician. If he's killed, his younger brother Ali will take the helm. Ali is only 24.

Sevirek has long been a battleground. The city was completely closed to all outsiders, including the army, between 1970 and 1980. During this period, there was intense street-to-street fighting between the Bucaks and the PKK. Thousands of people were killed; the PKK moved on to choose easier victims. The Bucaks cannot stray eastward into PKK-held territory without facing instant death.

The countryside the Bucaks rule consists of rolling plains, similar to Montana or Alberta. This is to the benefit of the Ataturk dam project, the fifth-largest dam project in the world.

Sedat can never travel without his bodyguards; neither can Ali. The bodyguards match the personalities of the brothers. Sedat's bodyguards are cold, ruthless killers. They're picked for the bravery and ferocity they showed in the last 10 years of warfare. Ali's bodyguards are younger, friendlier, but just as lethal.

They pack automatic weapons: German G-3s, M-16s and AK-47s. They each also carry at least one handgun as well as four to six clips for the machine guns and three to four clips for their pistols. Ali and Sedat also carry weapons at all times. Their choice of weapons also reflects their personalities. Ali packs a decorative stainless steel 9mm Ruger, and Sedat carries a drab businesslike Glock 17.

Some of the bodyguards, such as Nouri, wear the traditional Kurdish garb of checkered headpiece and baggy wool pants. The *salvars* appear to be too hot to wear on the sunburned plains. One of the guards explains that they work like a bellows and pump air when you walk, an example of something that works. Others wear cheap suits. Some wear golf shirts; still others wear military apparel.

While we are taking pictures of Sedat on his Massey Ferguson, the guards bring out the *gnass*, or sniper rifle (*gnass* is Arabic for sniper). It is an old Russian Dragunaov designed to kill men at 400–800 meters. When I walk down to take pictures, Ahmed, the cagey one, slides the rifle into the car and shakes his head. He knows that a sniper rifle is not for self-defense but is used for one thing only, as they explain to us, "With this rifle, you can kill a man before he knows he is dead."

Many of the men have a Turkish flag on the butts of their clips. One bodyguard offers me a rolled cigarette from an old silver tin. It tastes of the sweet, mild tobacco from Ferat. We both have a smoke. I open my khaki shirt and show him my Black Dog T-shirt, a picture of a dog doing his thing. He laughs: Seems as if we're finally warming up this crowd.

The younger brother of Ali's bodyguard asks me if I am licensed to use guns. He likes the way I shoot. I try to explain that, in America, you need a permit to own a gun and that people are trained or licensed. He looks at me quizzically. It's no use. I doubt they would understand a society that lets you own a gun without knowing how to use it.

We blast off some more rounds. Ali's bodyguards are having fun. We then bring out the handguns. We are all bad shots. Trying to hit a Pepsi can, no one comes close. Then one of the bodyguards marches up to the can and "executes" it with a smile. It is a chilling scene, and I'm glad it's only an aluminum can.

While Ali's bodyguards clown around with us, Sedat's bodyguards never move, or even take their hands off their guns. Nouri has his AK-47 tucked so perfectly into the crook of his arm, it is hard to imagine him not sleeping with it.

After chatting with Sedat and nervously entertaining his bodyguards, we head back into town. There, we're taken to lunch at Ali Bucaks restaurant and gas station. We eat in Ali's office. The bodyguards act as waiters, serving us shepherd's salads and kabobs with yogurt to drink. They serve us quietly and respectfully. They eat with one hand on their guns. The SSB radio crackles nonstop, as various people check in. We talk to Ali about life in general. Can he go anywhere without his guards? No. What about when he goes to Ankara on the plane? They have to put their guns in plastic bags and pick them up when they land. What about in Ankara? They change cars a lot. Does he like his role? He doesn't have a choice. Does he like feudalism? No, but he doesn't have a choice. The government does not provide services or protect their people, so they must do it themselves. Who would take the sick to the hospitals? Who would take care of the widows? Since power is passed along family lines, it is his duty.

As we eat, a storm comes in from Iraq. Lightning flashes and thunder cracks. We talk about politics, baseball cards and America. They are all familiar with America because every Turkish home and business has a television blaring most of the day and night. The number-one show is the soap, "The Young and the Restless," which comes on at 6:15 every night.

Sedat is a soft-spoken man—about 5 feet 6 inches tall, sunburned and suffering from a mild thyroid condition. He wears a faded green camouflage baseball hat, Levis and running shoes, as your neighbor might. He also carries a Glock 17 in a hand-rubbed leather holster. It is unsnapped for a quicker draw. Maybe not quite like your neighbor! He is never more than 15 feet from his bodyguards. Men drawn from his army as personal bodyguards have the lean, sunburned look of cowboys. He comes from an immediate family of 500 Bucaks. They make their money by growing cotton and other crops they sell in Adana.

It is hard to believe that this gentle, slightly nervous man and his forces are the only ones in Turkey who here been able to beat the PKK at their own game.

For now, everything is well in the kingdom. The dam will bring water for crops; the PKK is now concentrating on other areas; the people are happy, and Sedat is now a big-wheel politician. There is much to be said for feudalism. I offer to send him some of my books so that he can read about the rest of the world. He thinks this is a great idea. But he doesn't speak or read English.

We drive from Sevirek to Diyarbakir. The city of Diyarbakier is built on a great basalt plain and has 5.5-km long walls made from this ominous looking black stone. The triple walls and functional look betrays its origins as an ancient military outpost. Today, the 16 keeps and 5 gates have barbed wire, sand bags and machine gun nests. We will pass from a feudal kingdom to a large, bustling city that is the flashpoint for much of the violence that grips Turkey. We realize as we drive down the lonely roads that we are leaving the protection of the Bucaks and will soon be in PKK territory. If we were to be caught with Ali's address, we'd be killed. If the PKK had any knowledge of our contact with the Bucaks, we'd be instant enemies.

The PKK control the countryside and, it is said, the whole of eastern Turkey at night. It is not a particularly large group, perhaps some 8000 soldiers trained in small camps, but they're armed with small weapons—AK-47s and RPGs and a few grenade launchers. They travel in groups of 12 men and can muster a sizable force of about 200 soldiers for major ambushes. Their leader lives in the Bekáa Valley in southern Lebanon, under the protection of the Syrian government. He calls for an independent Kurdistan, which Saddam Hussein has given him by default in northern Iraq. But he wants more. He wants a sizable chunk of Iran and Turkey as well.

Despite the numerous checkpoints and military presence in the area, there has been little success in defeating the PKK. The Turkish Army has set up large special ops teams and commando units that specialize in ambushes, foot patrols and other harassment activities. But once you see the topography of eastern Turkey, you realize that you could hide an army 1000 times the size of the PKK. The terrain is riddled with caves, redoubt-shaped cliffs, boulders, canyons and every conceivable type of nook and cranny. It is easy terrain to move in, with few natural or man-made obstructions.

The PKK go into the villages at night to demand coopera- tion. If villagers do not cooperate, they are shot. In some cas- es, entire families, including babies, are executed. The PKK follow a Marxist-Leninist doctrine and play out their guerrilla tactics similar to the former Viet Cong or the Khmer Rouge. The PKK also likes to kidnap foreigners for money and pub- licity, and they like to execute schoolteachers and govern- ment officials. Special ops teams report to the civil authorities and to the military. Turkey considers the PKK as criminals and is reluctant to use civil law and superficial civilian forces against it.

Turkey has been in a state of war for 10 years now—that being the war the military is waging within its own borders.

The Test Pilot

We decide to spend an evening with a former leader and trainer of special ops teams. Hakan is now Turkey's only test pilot. In Turkey, this doesn't mean flying new prototype planes; it means flying out to helicopters downed by the rebels, making repairs and then flying or sling-loading them out.

Hakan lives in a high-rise building, guarded by three soldiers, barbed wire and fortifications against attack. His apartment is modern and well furnished. There are no traditional rugs, just black lacquer furniture complete with a fully stocked bar. Except for the barbed wire, we could be in Florida, which is where he trained as a Sikorsky Blackhawk pilot.

He has a two-month-old baby and is looking forward to being transferred back to western Turkey. His contempt for the PKK is obvious, having killed many of its members and having many PKK rounds aimed at him. He feels that the PKK is winning in this part of the country, but there will be no victory. The PKK problem cannot be solved militarily. It must be solved economically, by making the Kurds the beneficiaries of government help and giving them a stronger political voice. Killing terrorists is merely his job. He can't wait to get transferred out of Dyabakir. His wife plays with their baby on the floor. The baby never stops smiling and laughing. I think of the barbed wire and nervous soldiers downstairs. He can offer no political insights: PKK are people who he is paid to fight. When he is in Ankara, he will occupy himself with other things.

Eastern Turkey is the poorest and least developed part of the nation. Most educated people come from western Turkey. Most of the soldiers, politicians and professional classes are from western Turkey. The government sends these people to eastern Turkey for a minimum of two years of service. Most can't wait to get back to Istanbul or Ankara. Eastern Turkey has much closer affiliations with Armenia, Iran, Iraq, Azerbaijan, Syria and Georgia. Western Turkey has the ocean as a border. Eastern Turkey is rife with dissension and must deal with its warlike and poor neighbors. Iraqi, Iranian, Armenian and Syrian terrorists actively fight the government and each other. Hezbollah, the Iranian-backed fundamentalist group, hates the PKK. The PKK hates the government. The militia hates all rebel agitators, and the army and police clean up the messes left behind.

The Governor

I decide that we need another point of view. We go to Siirt about 40 km from the Syrian border and directly in the heart of PKK territory. Siirt was once a great city during the Abbasid Caliphate with the remnants of 12th and 13th century mosques. We are definitely in harm's way, since the PKK travel from Syria into the mountains behind us. Just down the road is the military outpost of Erub, designed to control a critical mountain road that leads down toward the Syrian border. There is another reason why we have chosen this tiny town. Coskun was born and raised in Siirt. I suggest that we go and chat up the governor and get his point of view.

Coskun is somewhat hesitant about meeting with the governor of Siirt province because he has a natural (and well-founded) aversion to politicians. But since we will be traveling directly into and through the war zone, we want to be sure that when we get stopped by the military we can drop names, flash the governor's card and ensure at least a moment of hesitation before we are shot as spies or terrorists.

As we pass the heavy security of the Siirt administration building, it seems that the governor is in. His bodyguards are quite perturbed that these strangers have walked right in and asked for an audience. They quietly talk into their walkie-talkies and stand between us and the soundproof door that leads into the governor's office. The governor takes his time to put on his game face and finally invites us in. It is kisses all around, chocolates, tea and cigarettes. We thank him and tell him our business. We are here to see what is going on in Turkey. He is proud to have us in his region. Two of his aids sit politely on the couch. The governor speaks in long, melodious, booming soliloquies that, when translated into English, come out as "We are maligned by the press" or "There is no danger here." Finally, they ask me what I have seen and what I think of their country. I tell them the truth. The people here are extraordinary in their friendship and warmth, but we are in a war zone. He launches into a response that boils down to "It's safe here, and we want you to tell your readers to come to Turkey and Siirt province." He then tells us of the attractions that await the lucky traveler: canyons as deep as the Grand Canyon, white-water rafting, hiking, culture, history, etc. We say great, give us a helicopter and we'll go for a spin tomorrow.

He goes one further. He invites us to dinner that night so that he can spend more time with us. Coskun wants to kick me, as I accept. Later that night we go to the government building for dinner. Joining us will be the head of police, the head of the military, three subgovernors and a couple of aides.

We pass through security and are ushered into the dining room. Sitting uncomfortably, we make small talk while a television blares away against the wall. As we sit down to dinner, we indicate that we are curious and ask the military commander just what is going on. Everyone is dressed in a suit and tie or uniform. Coskun and I do the best we can with our dusty khakis. Either because the room is hot or they are just being polite, they take their jackets off for dinner. The governor carries a silver 45 tucked into his waistband. His formal gun? As the men sit down to dinner, something strikes me as funny. Coskun and I are the only ones not packing a gun for dinner.

The dinner is excellent: course after course of shish kebob, salads and other delicacies washed down with *raki* (a strong anisette liquor) and water. The taste of the *raki* brings back memories of the hard crisp taste of Cristal aquadiente, the preferred drink of the Colombian drug trade. Throughout dinner, the head of police is interrupted by a walkie-talkie-carrying messenger who hands him a piece of paper. He makes a few comments to the side, and the man disappears. Every five to 10 minutes the man returns, the police chief makes a quiet comment, and he goes away.

Meanwhile, the governor continues to extol the beauty of his country—nonstop. He is the center of attention, simply because no one else is speaking. The others nod, smile or laugh. Most of their attention is on the television blaring in the corner. Suddenly, the red phone next to the television begins ringing. The call is answered by the attendant. It is for the colonel. The colonel excuses the interruption and speaks in low tones. The police chief puts his walkie-talkie on the table. It becomes apparent that the base is under attack by a group of PKK of unknown size. Throughout dinner, the conversation steers toward politics as it must. Like many countries, there are two parallel worlds here: the world of administrators, occupiers and government, then the world of the dispossessed—the people who till the soil, who build their houses with their own hands, who bury their dead in the same ground that yields them their crops. Tonight and every night, that world is ruled by the PKK, Dev Sol, Armenian terrorists, Hezbollah and bandits. At dusk, the world is plunged into fear, ruled by armed bands of men that are neither chosen nor wanted by the ordinary people. At dawn, the country is back in the hands of the government, the people and the light. During our conversation, there is no right and no wrong, only an affirmation that each side believes it is in the right.

The red phone continues to ring, and the little pieces of paper continue to be brought up to the police chief. The police chief is now speaking directly into his walkie-talkie. Meanwhile, the governor continues to regale us with stories about Siirt. As we eat course after course, I am offered cigarettes by at least three to four people at a time. Doing my best to accommodate my hosts, I eat, smoke and drink the sharp *raki*, all the time keeping one ear on the governor's conversation and the constant mumbled conversations being carried out on the phone and the walkie-talkie.

The governor is very proud of the tie he wore especially for me—a pattern of Coca-Cola bottles. He brings in his young daughters to meet me. They are shy, pretty and very proud of their English. We chat about life in Siirt, and I realize that they are virtually prisoners in the governor's compound. The governor tells us of a road we should take to enjoy the scenery, a winding scenic road to Lice via Kocakoy. Finally, the colonel is spending so much time on the phone that he excuses himself. The police chief is visibly agitated but is now speaking nonstop on the walkie-talkie. Messages continue to arrive.

The television is now featuring swimsuit-clad lovelies and has captured the attention of the governor's aides and his subgovernors. As the dinner winds down, we retire outside to have coffee. I am presented with a soft wool blanket woven in Siirt. We have a brief exchange of speeches, and I notice that the colonel and police chief have now joined us. I ask them what all the commotion was about, and they mention that it was a minor incident that has been handled. The governor reminds us to tell people of the beauty of this place, the friendliness of the Turkish people and the people of Siirt.

As we prepare to go, they wrap my blanket in today's newspaper. Smack dead center is a full-color photograph of a blood-soaked corpse of a man who has been executed by the Dev Sol terrorist group for being an informer.

The next day, there is no helicopter waiting for us. When we inquire as to its whereabouts, we are told that it was needed to do a body count from the attack the night before. We ask the blue-bereted special ops soldier what the best way is to see the countryside. He assumes that we must be important, and, instead of telling us to get lost, he carefully reviews our options. As for the road we want to take into the mountains, he informs us that it is heavily mined and would have to be cleared before we could attempt a crossing. In any case, we would need an armored car and an escort of soldiers and probably a tank. We ask about the helicopter, which would be safer, but we will need to wait until he can get a gunship to accompany us.

A Place in Time

We figure the only sightseeing we are going to do today is on foot. Coskun reminisces with his first employer, a gentle man who puts out a tiny newspaper with a 19th-century offset press and block type. He has broken his arm, so he apologizes on the back page for the paper being so small. Everyday he laboriously pecks out the local news with one finger using an old Remington typewriter; he then reads his copy, marks it up, and hands it to the eager teenagers who sort through the dirty trays of lead type. He has a choice between two photoengraved pictures that sit in a worn old tray. One is the governor, the other is the president of Turkey. When the type is hand-set, they laboriously run off a couple of hundred copies for the dwindling number of loyal readers. I leave Coskun with his old friend.

Siirt is a dusty, poor Kurdish town, with a history of being occupied by everyone from Alexander to the Seljuks to the Ottomans. Some of the people are fair-skinned, blonde and blue-eyed. Others have the hard Arabic look of the south; while still others have the round heads and bald spots of the Turks. Siirt is a happy town, with the children contentedly playing in the muddy streets. As I walk around the town, the children begin to tag along with me. All are eager to try out their words of English. I urge them to teach me Kurdish. They point at houses, dogs, people, and chatter away, "Where come you from?" and "Hello mister, what eeze your name?" I wonder where I would ever need to use Kurdish. Some visitors say Siirt looks like a poorly costumed bible story. Here and there along the broken streets are ancient houses with tapered walls; many people still use the streets as sewers. Goats, cows and chickens wander the streets. Near the mosque, the less fortunate goats are sold and then slaughtered on the spot. Donkeys sit patiently. Men physically pull me over to where they are sitting and demand that we have tea. I realize it would take me years if I stopped and had tea with everyone who wanted to chat. I begin to respect the delicate but strong social web that holds this country together. Soldiers, fighters, rebels, farmers, politicians, police all offer us hospitality, tea and a cigarette. The tiny parcels of information and face-to-face encounters transmit and build an understanding of what is going on, who is going where and why.

In every shop a television blares. Western programs and news shows constantly bombard these people with images that do not fit into their current world. At 6:10 "The Young and the Restless," dubbed in Turkish, captures the entire population. It is typically Turkish that they would treat the TV like a visitor, never shutting it up and quietly waiting for their turn to speak. I can only imagine that the blatant American and Western European images are as familiar and comforting to the older generation as MTV's "The Grind" is to us. As with all small rural towns around the world, the young people are moving to the big cities. The future is colliding with the past.

They're Your Modern Stone Age Family

We decide not to hang around and wait for the helicopter and the helicopter gunship to be arranged. Instead, we decide to drive into the countryside, where the army has little control. Along the way, we stop in a little-known troglodyte village called Hassankeyf. This was once the 12th century capital of the Artukids, but today, it is a little visited curiousity. Here, Coskun knows an old lady who lives in a cave. This historic area will be underwater when the massive hydroelectric dam is completed. Hassankeyf could be a set from "The Flintstones." The winding canyon is full of caves that go up either side, creating a cave-dwellers high-rise development. Far up in the highest cave is the last resident of this area. The lady claims to be 110-years old. My guess is that she is closer to 80. But it probably doesn't matter, since in this land, she could be older than Methuselah and have seen nothing change. We climb up to chat with her, while down below the golden rays of the sun illuminate the Sassouk mosque. Across the canyon are the ruins of a Roman-era monastery. This was once a remote outpost for the Romans.

She doesn't seem pleased to see us. In a grouchy manner, she invites us into her cave. The lady lives alone with a cat and her donkey. The donkey has his own cave carved cleanly and laboriously out of the soft limestone.

The cave where the old woman lives leads back into a rear cave, where she makes her bed on straw and carpets. The roof is covered with a thick greasy layer of soot from the small fire she uses for cooking. She says she is ill and needs medicine. We have brought her a bar of chocolate but we do not have any medicine with us. We give her some money but realize she is days away from any drugstore and her only method of transport is her donkey or a ride from one of the villagers.

People from across the steep valley yell and wave at us. They do not get many visitors. We take pictures of the lady. She seems happy to have someone to talk to, and, after her initial grumpiness, she offers us some flat bread. It crunches with the dirt and gravel baked into it. We smile and say it is good.

As the sun sets further, the ancient ambience is broken by the loud thumping and hoarse whistling scream of a Cobra gunship returning to Siirt. This was probably our escort, but we are glad to be sitting here in the cool golden dusk in a cave, in a place that will soon be erased off the map.

We have to leave. Travel at night is not safe. The PKK control this area and the military will fire at anything that moves on the roads at night. We must make it to the Christian town of Mardil, or as the locals call it Asyriac, before it gets completely dark. The old lady wishes us well. The Christians who live in the town of Mardil speak the language of Jesus: Aramaic. Strange that we are also in the land of the Yezidi, the religion that prays to Satan. We are told the PKK do not attack Asyriac because of their ties to Assad. Here, we will spend the night with some people who hold the honor of having the most dangerous profession in east Turkey: schoolteachers.

The Most Dangerous Job

Schoolteachers are part of the colonial oppression against which the PKK is fighting. Kurdish children are not allowed to speak the native tongue in school. Teachers in Turkey are assigned to work for four years in East Turkey before they can work in the more lucrative eastern cities of Istanbul and Ankara. Here, they are paid 8 million Turkish lira a month, about US\$220 and about 30 percent more than they would usually make. About 30 percent never do their time in east Turkey and buy their way out of the dangerous assignment. By comparison, soldiers get paid 35–40 million Turkish lira a month.

The teachers live in simple stone houses—one room for living and one room for sleeping. There is no plumbing; the bathroom is an outhouse about 20 yards from the house. But these conditions are not what make this job dangerous. Over the last three years, 75 schoolteachers have been executed by the PKK. Schoolteachers in east Turkey are not raving political stooges of the government who spread torment and hate. They are bright college-educated people who teach reading, writing and math. Many are just starting families and enjoy the work they do. The few who are dragged out of their houses at night, sentenced, and shot in the chest probably wonder what they did to deserve such a cold and uncelebrated death.

We spend the evening with two young teachers, a husband and wife, and their two young girls. They share their simple food and are good company. There is little to do here once the sun goes down. The inside of the simple stone house reminds me of a bomb shelter: whitewashed, cold and damp. The house is lit with a single bare lightbulb hanging down from the ceiling. After dinner, we walk to the homes of the other teachers in this small village. Each family of teachers is happy to meet outsiders. There are two young female teachers who bring us cookies and tea, and there are two married couples, each with a small child. We gather together in their simple homes and talk about life in the war zone. Three days ago, three teachers just northwest of here were rounded up, tied hand and foot, and shot the same way you would kill an old dog.

Many people feel that the teachers were shot because they had weapons in their houses. After the shootings, the teachers from this village traveled to town to talk to the region's military commander and protest the arming of teachers as militia. The colonel instead greeted them as the protectors of the village. Taken aback, they explained that they thought he was the protector of the village. "No," he smiled and said, "it is much too dangerous to have troops out there at night." The colonel offered them rifles and ammunition to give them peace of mind. "After all," he said, "I am surrounded by hundreds of soldiers, barbed wire and fortifications as well as over a hundred trained antiterrorist commandos for backup." He offered the teachers one of each: a "big gun" (a German G-3) for the men and a little gun (AK-47s) for the women. Not knowing how to react, the teachers abandoned their first line of attack and glumly accepted the weapons and boxes of ammunition. They admitted to us they had no idea how to use them and were terrified that the children would find the rifles under their beds. So they kept them unloaded.

As I walked back under a brilliant star-filled sky, I marveled at the ridiculousness of it all. Here we were with eager, youthful young men and women—educated, enthusiastically discussing life and politics, sharing what little they have and trying to make sense of it all, while a few miles down the road sat the PKK training base of Eruh and the Syrian border only 50 km away. The town has been the scene of heavy fighting between the PKK and the Turkish special forces. No one dares go out of the village at night for fear of being shot as a terrorist by the nervous militia.

The people are thankful for their stone houses, as they cower below windows during the heaviest shooting. Here, there is no doctor, no store, no transportation, no facilities of any kind. To think that a beautiful night like this could be interrupted by sudden death is unimaginable.

Tearing Down the Silk Road

Despite our token flirtation with death, we spend a sunny morning playing with the children and then continue on our way to the Iraqi border. I am curious. Just before we leave the village, we are stopped by a group of people. They point to a stinking swamp in the center of the village. They complain that the government came in to build a pond and now it is a sewer. They seem to think that we have some way to restore it. We listen, shrug our shoulders and sadly drive off.

Winding our way down to the main road, we inhale the clean mountain air and stop to take pictures of the sparkling brooks and lush scenery. This can't be a war zone. Down on the main road, the military checkpoints begin. At the first checkpoint 14 km from Cizre, we are quite bluntly asked, "What the hell are you doing here?" The appropriate answer seems to be the most absurd: "Just looking around." Cooling our heels and drinking tea in the commander's bunker, we are given our passports back and smugly told that we have been scooped. A television news crew from "32 GUN" (a Turkish news show) had already made it into Iraq. The commander assumes that we are journalists trying to cover Saddam's big military push to the south. Apparently, the television crew got special permission from the Iraqi embassy in Ankara and is the only news crew in Iraq. Not too bothered by this revelation, we share a cigarette with the sergeant, and more tea is brought out. It appears that our time with the governor and the military commander of Siirt province has paid off. We ask the officer in charge if he could radio ahead and let the trigger-happy soldiers know we are coming.

We should be in the cradle of civilization, between the fertile thighs of the Tigris and the Euphrates. Instead, we are in a hair-trigger war zone, where every man is a potential killer and every move might be your last.

We take a few Polaroids for the officer and we hit the road again. At each blown bridge and sandbagged checkpoint, we stop and chat with the soldiers. Up ahead of us is Mount Kadur, where the Koran says the ark of Noah rests: It sits like a forbidden beacon 3500 meters high. We drive along the Syrian border clearly defined by eight-foot high barbed wire and 30-foot guard towers every 500 meters. We are on a beautiful piece of smooth two-lane blacktop built right smack on top of the "Silk Road." We are not traveling by camel today. I keep the Fiat's gas pedal pressed to the floor, the speedometer spinning like a slot machine. The only time we have to slow down is at a checkpoint or when a bridge has been blown up. The heavy trucks labor toward the west, as we pass burned-out hulks of gas stations. We stop in Silapi, the last Turkish town before the Iraqi border, to get something to eat. Silapi is one of the dirtiest, drabbest holes I have ever visited. Row after row of truck repair shops, dusty streets, and grease-smeared people watching as we drive by.

We pick a restaurant where the secret police eat. You can tell the secret police by their bull necks, gold chains and walkie-talkies. The hotel next door is decorated with stickers from the world's press and relief agencies. The food is good. Outside our restaurant, a retarded man with no legs sits on his stumps. Using blocks to get around, he is black from the soot and grime of the street. He uses an old inner tube to prevent the hot road from burning his stumps. He watches us eat. The people pass him by as he grimaces and grunts, his hand extended. I marvel that this man is still alive in this godforsaken outpost. I go outside and give him some lira. He begins to cry and tug at my leg, thanking me in his tortured way. When I leave him, children begin to crowd around and start to beat him for his money. I go back outside, and another man chases the children away. We tuck the money away, since his spastic hands keep flailing around. When I go back into the restaurant, one of the men at a table next to ours tells us that the beggar will probably be dead tonight, killed for the money he now has. I feel very sad and want to leave this place.

As we blast down the road toward the Iraqi border, I notice that the big guns in the Turkish bunkers are not facing south across the road to Syria, but toward Turkey to the north and the rebel-held hills beyond.

The Angels

Much later, back in Istanbul, I stand in front of the massive Hagia Sophia Mosque. Inside, it is quiet. Two men make their prayers in the serious, hurried style of Islam. The worn carpets and the vast ceiling absorb the whispering and rustling like a sponge.

Outside, it is dark and the rain is cold and heavy, pushed by the sharp wind. The brilliant floodlights cut tunnels of light upward into the low clouds above the softly sculpted building. It is as if the prayers of centuries power this energy, sending the shafts of pure blue light through the clouds and to the stars. High above, I think I see angels. A mysterious low chorus seems to pervade the atmosphere. But alas, the angels are just seagulls and the chorus is a distinct ship horn. And the prayers of a thousand years are lost and rubbed to dust in the aging carpets inside the mosque.

For a brief moment, it was calm and peaceful. The angels had come to answer those prayers. Instead, I know that out in the rolling fields of the east, there will be more death under the Turkish stars tonight.

—**RYP**

Postscript

On Sunday, November 12, 1996, there was a car accident in Susurluk, about 90 miles south of Istanbul. A black Mercedes slammed into a tractor trailer truck killing three of the four passengers aboard. This would not be unusual for a Sunday on the deadly highways of Turkey except the only surviving passenger was *DP's* buddy Sedat Bucak. Although Bucak is colorful in his own right, his now deceased friends are more interesting.

One of the four on board was Abdullah Catli, an accused hit man for the Turkish military, convicted drug smuggler, former member of the extreme nationalist group the Grey Wolves and blamed for a number of arson attacks in the Greek Islands and assassinations in Athens in 1988. He was also accused of selling drugs in Switzerland. In July of '96 he escaped from Swiss prison. Catli was accused of murdering casino operator Omer Lufi Topal. Three policemen were also implicated. These policemen then became part of Sedat's bodyguard. Bucak was accused of trying to grab Topal's assets and to be behind his execution. A search of Catli's body found a false ID card, a badge showing him to be a police officer and a green Turkish passport that only senior civil servants have to avoid visas when traveling.

In the trunk were seven pistols, silencers and ammunition. The registration plates were bogus and it took a while for the government and press to understand exactly what had happened

Mr. Catli's companion in the car was Gonca Us, a former Miss Cinema in Turkey. She was accused of being a Mafia hit-woman under the watchful eye of Catli. He isn't exactly on every girl's crush list. He began his notoriety on March 9, 1978 when he personally strangled seven university students for being members of the Turkish Labor Party. He was wanted by Interpol and was on their "Most Wanted" list.

Catli was also famous for being the man who supplied the gun to the Bulgarian who shot the Turk, Mehmet Ali Agca, who shot Pope John Paul II in 1981.

Sedat Bucak, True Path MP, the head of Bucak clan and leader of a tough anti-PKK army of 10,000 men is still the undisputed lord of the Siverek valley between Diyabakir and Urfa. Although some say his army is only 2000 men, others estimated 8000, he is paid over $1 million a month to fight the PKK. That brands him as a mercenary in the eyes of the PKK. He is also accused of using these men as death squads, smuggling drugs and weapons. They are considered by Turkish politicians as being "out of control."

The fourth passenger was one that started an uproar in the press and government. He was the president of the Erog Police Academy in Istanbul. Although it sounds like a comedy role, Huseyin Kocadag is one of the creators of the Special Teams—groups of civilians who execute suspected terrorists and sympathizers. They too are accused of competing with the PKK to smuggle heroin, launder political donations, sell arms and carry out personal vendettas.

The truck driver who slammed into the car was given a "most respected citizen honor" from a minor leftist party. Around 1000 pro PKK civilians have disappeared in Bucaks region along with 100 people who have disappeared while in police custody. About 23,000 people have been killed in Turkey since 1984 as a result of the conflict with the PKK and the army.

Bucak was seriously injured, and yanked out of the car by his bodyguards who were following behind in a second car. They left the others to die, crushed and bleeding in the wreck. Bucak has recuperated with the assistance of his body-guards who guarded him 24 hours a day.

The parliament finally confirmed the connection between organized crime and the security establishment and some politicians. Unfortunately the generals that really run Turkey are more concerned about the rise of Islamic fundamentalism, a greater threat to the west than the war in the east.

UNITED STATES
Having a Riot

Like most residents of dangerous places, we don't view where we live as particularliy nasty or evil. However when things happen and CNN goes live our friends from around the world call to get a firsthand update. There have always been riots in America, in fact that is how we became a country when a bunch of irate Yanks tossed a load of tea into Boston Harbor. We've also had riots in most major cities. The only difference is most call them a disturbance. The Los Angeles riots occurred less than a five minute drive from my house yet I felt the incident was totally benign. It was only when I compared the incident to some of my other riot experiences that I felt it should be included.

Above Los Angeles, aboard a Delta jetliner that's had to deviate from its approach due to zero visibility, the result of thick black plumes of smoke billowing into the sky, the captain announces to the passenger cabin: "Ladies and gentlemen, the city of Los Angeles is in a state of civil unrest. We will be landing. However, we must urge you in no uncertain terms to use extreme caution in reaching your final destination. Lawlessness and violence exist in many areas of the metropolitan region. A Delta representative will be at the gate to advise you about which sections of the city should not be traveled through under any circumstances."

A petite dental hygienist in 26B turns and says to a long-haired record store manager from Van Nuys in 26A: "So? What else is new?"

####

The scene here is pure Beirut. Pillars of thick black smoke rise straight up in the hot windless afternoon. Looking down from the hill where I live, I see dozens (I counted at least 120) of puffy dark columns rising up from Long Beach in the south to the Valley to the north. Down there, people are looting, burning, killing, maiming and beating each other up. In the air over 20 helicopters circle and swoop like hawks. Onboard are video cameras with new image stabilizers that make your living room feel like the cockpit of a Huey going into a hot LZ. The cameras are in tight. Kids look up and make victory signs as they hustle six-packs, clothes, backyard toys, 19-inch televisions and even mattresses out of shattered storefront windows. Ostensibly, the black community is angered at the "not guilty" verdict in the Rodney King trial. King, a known criminal, was stopped, detained and beaten into submission. Had a neighbor not captured the scene on videotape, Rodney would have been just like any one of L.A.'s petty hoodlums. Today, he is a lucky man. His violated civil rights have elevated him to the level of celebrity and wealthy icon of America's need to punish itself for not doing the right thing.

Because the television viewers can see the expressions of joy on the faces of the looters, we know this is shopping time. These folks are tired of paying retail for the American Dream, and they are going straight for that Friday night Smith & Wesson discount. This isn't necessarily about race nor is it necessarily about anger; it's about maximizing the one benefit of being forced to live in the foul, wasted bowels of one of America's wealthiest cities. It's payback time. Poverty means not being able to buy all the things they sell incessantly on TV. Well, now every looter in South Central L.A. is rich.

Normally, the merchants of the inner city have iron bars, security guards, video cameras, buzzers, 911 autodialers, shotguns taped under counters and fast-draw waist holsters to enforce compliance with their usurious prices. Anyone who tries for a five-finger discount (a stickup) is either gunned down, picked up, or chased down with police helicopters, dogs and car patrols. This day, the balance is out of whack, big time.

Although the police try to put a lid on the initial drunken violence, they are quickly outnumbered. Fearing for their safety, the police try driving by to scare off the first malcontents. When the spectators start throwing beer cans and rocks at the cop cars, they beat a hasty retreat. The police are reigned in by politics and overly sensitive to the violence that must be dealt out to contain the looters. They are prisoners in their stations. When the word goes out over the news that the police are not going in, all hell breaks loose. For the first time since the '60s, America looks straight into the face of its dispossessed and blinks.

Business stops; people dash to their cars and head home. Along with most residents of L.A., the police watch the mayhem live on television and wonder how it will end.

On the street, looters are methodically knocking off first liquor stores, then the big chain stores. The Koreans, the only people tough enough to run the inner-city five-and-dimes, waited a long time for this day. They finally have a chance to use all that German and American firepower they have been practicing with and oiling for years.

Any visitor to L.A.'s shooting ranges can't help but notice the Asian shooters with their black Cordura bags full of expensive and well-oiled weapons. They range from shotguns to 9mm handguns to MAC 10s and AKs, many with full-automatic capability.

As the riot rages, the Koreans luckily never get to use all their ammo and those weapons. The looters think twice and focus on the national chain electronics and camera stores.

The 911 lines are jammed with terrified people who have spotted cars full of "black" men or "Hispanics" in their white neighborhoods. The police inform the people that they are responsible for the safety of their neighborhood, not for the safety of individuals or their private property. Suddenly, people start rummaging in the attic for their old WWII-era Garands, hunting rifles, even BB guns. Gun stores quickly sell out of ammunition, and the city works fast to ban gun sales as they hit record highs. People now sit in their Barca Loungers, watching the news, waiting for the first sign of looters heading into their neighborhood.

As in *War of the Worlds*, people sit glued to their television screens and radios tracking the spread of the violence. Reports come in from Beverly Hills, Santa Ana and Huntington Beach—some false, all inflated, but ominous just the same. The rioters move to the north like locusts. Along the way, some business owners, tired of eking out a miserable existence, clean out their cash registers and torch their own businesses.

Coskun calls me from Istanbul. Always the photographer, he asks, What's it like, are you getting pictures? The world has learned that L.A is in flames and its ethnic population has risen up. I tell him that years of hard knocks have taught me that driving my nice new car into a maelstrom of fire, smoke, bullets, looters and thugs is probably not a wise idea.

Into the night, coverage from helicopters gives us all the amazing sight of hundreds of glowing fires over the Los Angeles Basin.

Once the drinking lets up and the National Guard rolls in, the riots subside. Many proud new owners of ironing boards, car stereos and toasters can't wait to try them out. Driving through the worst hit area is no different from visiting Groxny, Beirut or any other burned-out war zone, except there are no bodies on the street and the curious splatter marks from RPGs and 50-caliber bullets are absent. In the aftermath, the civic leaders pledge to rebuild L.A. and a committee is formed to do absolutely nothing. Most inner-city business owners decide that the snow in Iowa looks a lot more inviting than the white soot that gently falls on their burned-out lot.

When it was all over, there were 52 people dead, 2383 injured, 10,000 arrested, 4500 buildings or homes destroyed and $735 million in property damage.

—RYP

A Night in the Life of Midtown South

Jack Kramer lives in Washington D.C., a place that has the same murder rate as Johannesburg, South Africa. Strangely South Africa gets all kinds of bad PR because it is in "deepest, darkest Africa" yet Washington calls their murder epidemic a crime problem. Jack went to New York to cruise with the local cops and observe through a visitor's eyes. Today New York is becoming safer by the day and any adventurer has to look hard if he wants to walk on the wild side.

Midtown South at 357 West 35th Street, near Eighth Avenue, is the largest precinct house in New York City. For officers Gene Giogio and Charlie Edmond, on the four to midnight shift, the routine this summer night starts with a swing right up Eighth. Both are young and trim, Edmond with light hair, Giorgio, dark.

Some heavy real estate money is betting on Eighth Avenue and the entire Times Square area, which, in fits and starts, is improving. Forty-second street has drifted upward from total decrepitude marked by child pornography, to moderate decrepitude, marked by sex shops that provide shopping carts for men in suits to push through aisles marked "Tickling," "Shoes," "Spanking," "Slaves"...

Eighth Avenue has never been pretty, but beneath its grime there's always been real life and still is. As Giorgio and

Edmond cruise north, they pass an Italian pork store with a 62-cent-a-pound special on pig's toes, a kosher meat market featuring the world's best pastrami, a halal meat market featuring the world's best *basterma* (which not only sounds but tastes like a distant cousin of pastrami), and further up, some totally different meat markets, lounges with three-gold-chain minimums where wise guys from the union go to pick up broads.

At 44th and Eighth is Smith's Restaurant, one of those long-established operations that's open 24 hours for a neighborhood that works 24 hours: a takeout counter, a bar the length of a bowling alley, booths, the kind of place where you can get your pleasure at 4 a.m., breakfast or a tumbler of Irish whiskey and a steak. They get a lot of trade from Midtown South.

"You see those prostitutes over there," says Charlie Edmond to his backseat guest.

"Men," says Giorgio. "Over here on Eighth, most of the prostitutes are men."

The Seventh and Eighth Avenues corridor is not the most dangerous in New York, but it is periodically plagued, and will be so in the weeks ahead. Rapper Tupac Shakur will be shot in a lobby on Seventh, and as summer fades to autumn, a rash of knifings will overtake Eighth Avenue. A victim will be knifed, a few hours later a uniform just coming on duty will scan the report, look into space a second, then inform himself out loud: "I think we got a prior aggrieved party." Finally in October, a rookie cop, Timothy Torres, will make a collar.

As they cruise slowly past what might be a nascent game of three-card monte, an order in the indecipherable language called static breaks over the radio and suddenly we're shooting east across town on 42nd Street a lot faster than I'm used to. The siren wails on, and I look around to see where it's coming from.

"Mugging," says Edmond. "Grand Central. Right in front." By then, we're there. Another squad car had squealed up even earlier, and a large, muscular man, so dirty you can't tell what color he is, wearing hardly any clothes, is lying face-down on the sidewalk, handcuffed. The cops from the other car had just finished stringing their yellow tape, outside of which a crowd is gathering and inside of which there are just "the perp," the other two cops, and two college kids in shorts, looking like they're on the wrong side of the yellow tape. But nobody's asking them to leave.

The victim, an elderly woman who only spoke Spanish, has just been taken away, shivering, they say, in the heat.

The kids look mildly stunned. The front of Grand Central Station, just after dark on a pleasant summer evening, right on Park Avenue, should not be among New York's most dangerous places.

Just like that, it is over, the street is returning to normal, and, as we are getting back into the squad car, through the New York cacophony of honks, shouts and distant sirens, I catch snatches of a conversation a black man in a smartly tailored business suit is having with a liveried black doorman. "*Le probleme aujourd'hui est...*" Haitian, I think to myself, then wonder why this incidental detail in a brutal picture has stood out and induced me to jump to a conclusion. To impress on myself that this is New York? Haitians are in the news, and Haitian refugees are everywhere. But here, these men could be from Martinique, Senegal, the Ivory Coast...

Thus mulling as the lights twinkle by, there's a sudden lurch and I realize we're violating the speed limit again. Back to the West Side. A silent alarm on an office building in one of the side streets between Eighth and Seventh.

"This time of day over there, or I should better put it, this time of night over there, it's real closed up. Dark." It's the driver, Edmond, talking, as we shoot toward the intersection of 42nd Street and Sixth Avenue; the light's red ahead, and I'm hoping that at this time of night up there, drivers pay attention to sirens. "Not long ago, we're just driving around, checking things out, and up ahead we see bales of dresses getting thrown out of a window, maybe six, seven stories up, must have been thousands of 'em. Later we hear it's been going on. Perps ran, but two weeks later, they're collared."

"Thing is, you never know what you're going to run into there," says Giorgio. By now, we're coming up on the block and the siren goes off; we roll down the narrow, deserted side street. In a city where a parking place is a valued commodity, there are more dumpsters strewn along the curb than parked cars. Way ahead, a homeless guy is rooting through one of them. We pull to a stop. One light is on in the lobby, but that's it. We get out. I make a point to stay out of the way (or if you prefer, harm's way.) "Generally, it's a false alarm," says Giorgio, "and, generally, perps in this line of business don't give you trouble."

"Unless sometimes. When they get surprised," says Edmond. It comes back to me: This was a silent alarm.

"Problem building," says Giorgio.

They already have keys. They draw their .38s. After the first floor, the building is dark. At a control panel, they snap on lights, push the elevator button. From above, there's a noise. Floor to floor, along the corridor walls—if there's no one there, it's faintly ridiculous, but then how do you know when it's for real?

False alarm. No actual danger. Just the daily drumbeat of tension.

There are homeless wherever we go, not in great droves, but they're here, thanks to a byzantine system of aid that parks some of New York's poorest people on some of New York's most expensive real estate. In the theater district, they come because the pickings are good. Virtually next door to the Algonquin Hotel where the legendary round table once regularly held forth, a 300-pound woman with an amputated foot now regularly holds forth with her sweet eight-year-old son who lives there with her. They've got an address at the distant end of some subway line, but it's clearly not much, it's hard for her to get around, and this is where the money is. The conversation with Edmond and Giorgio is professional. They're just checking. She knows they can't move her. They know they can't either.

One of the homeless of Midtown South, Carlos Sam, by name, is a computer repairman. Not a former computer repairman fallen on hard times, but a computer repairman now, on the street, with no prior training beyond electronics picked up in an uncle's TV repair shop. He's illiterate, periodically delusional, crippled. He owns a jealously guarded tool box and three canvas mail carts. From discarded computer parts rummaged out of dumpsters, he's taught himself computer repair. Nowadays, he's not only a repairman, but he's in the business. For $15 to $45, you can get a repaired monitor or keyboard. His shop is on the 43rd Street sidewalk between Seventh and Eighth.

By this hour, Carlos Sam is off the street, but this is when the porn shops, now run largely by Indians and Pakistanis, bring in their biggest bucks. "Stuff they sell isn't as rank as it used to be, and on top of that, they're mostly cheap copies, but these guys rake it in," Giorgio informs me.

The porn store is, above all, a business struggle. Landlords who rent to porn shops between 40th and 53rd get $90 to $125 a square foot. If it isn't porn, it only commands $60 to $90. Meantime other landlords are trying to light a fire under the redevelopment that slowly proceeds, anticipating a boom that may already be getting underway...if they can finally get rid of the porn. Disney is spending $34 million to renovate the extravagant, dilapidated New Amsterdam Theatre on 42nd, a 92-year-old landmark that was home to the Ziegfeld Follies. But still there's those rents that can be had from the porn shops. They say one group of landlords actually went to the rabbi of a wavering colleague to help him resist.

There are other ways in which this midtown corridor is less impersonal than it seems. Timothy Torres, the Midtown South cop who collared the Eighth Avenue stabber a couple of months after our cruise through the precinct, was a college dropout, on the force barely two years, wearing the same badge, No. 4049, that his dad, Cesar, had worn as a New York cop before he resigned. Young Torres was on foot patrol the October night he saw the suspect racing up Eighth Avenue on a bike, knife in hand. He jumped the guy, and came out of it bloodied, but with considerable pride for father and son.

Smith's again. Another rapid-fire set of directions over the radio, again indecipherable to me.

"A heavy bleeder," Giorgio translates. "Group therapy session at this hotel, a welfare hotel, a welfare hotel for guys with AIDS actually. Terminal cases. Looks like the group therapy got out of hand, and we got a heavy bleeder."

The dispatcher's voice cracks over the radio again: "All units. Stay off the air unless you have priority. All units."

We brake to a stop, with squad cars from every direction. Cops are all over the place. They're up there for 15 minutes, a half hour. Gaunt, unshaven men in stocking caps stand about in the grim light; beefy young men in stocking caps, also unshaven, come out, an undercover team. There's tension, but when Giorgio and Edmond return, they don't make a big deal out of it.

"If it was serious, they would have had a sergeant over here."

A few minutes later, cruising up Seventh Avenue, we're flagged by a cabbie, Indian or Pakistani. His fare won't pay. Fare is out of the cab by now, a little stocky, substantial, middle-aged guy in a suit, maybe a little tight but not obviously drunk, and meantime he's quiet, even sort of fatherly with the cops, who ask him what the trouble is. He doesn't have the money? Come on, he says. A wad is discreetly flashed. He's getting a little more fatherly. So what's the trouble, sir? Again, fatherly, but no direct answer.

It was going nowhere, except from fatherly to patronizing to abusive. Once they got him to pay, they let it be, but of everything that happened—the mugging, the silent alarm, the 300-pound amputee living on the street with her eight-year-old son, the heavy bleeder at the AIDS hotel—this seemed to get under their skin the most. Perhaps because of its ordinariness—and that it was so unnecessary.

Across the country, about 300 cops killed themselves in 1994; that's more than twice as many as the 137 who died in the line of duty. Over the past decade in New York City, more than 20 cops have been killed in the line of duty; 64 killed themselves.

Columbia University released a study in '94 that showed NYPD officers killing themselves at a rate of 29 for every 100,000. Among the general population the rate is 12. The cops are almost always young, with clean records. The study notes that a virtually standard feature of every suicide is a statement from the department or the family or both that the suicide was personal, the job had nothing to do with it.

Christmas Eve, Timothy Torres, who had brought down the stabber in October and wore his father's badge, pulled the midnight to eight in the morning shift at Midtown South, foot patrol. A little after midnight, he responded to a call on West 43rd, where a man was distraught and raving in the lobby. Torres got him to Bellevue for treatment.

At four, he met up with another cop on foot patrol, and they went to Smith's, the landmark on Eighth Avenue, for breakfast. It was now Christmas Day. Torres shot himself in the head in a booth.

"My understanding was that he went through a divorce six months ago," said a police spokesman.

On the same street that Torres responded to the call about the man raving in a lobby, Carlos Sam is still doing business. He melts plastic spoons to solder the innards of keyboards and monitors. If you want to know if he's really fixed the thing, he uses the swivel chair, which is among his few possessions, to squeak over to a light pole, at the base of which is an electrical outlet. In fact, every light pole in New York City has an outlet at its base, usually sealed. Carlos Sam swears he only uses the ones that are already open.

—**Jack Kramer**

YEMEN

A Matter of Honor

Yemen is a true time warp. A place where kidnappers are gracious and drugs are like Snickers bars. It is a place where if a man does not have a dagger, chew qat *and own a cache of weapons he is considered suspect. Roddy did a little shopping to see what life is like in Yemen.*

There are, would you believe, more guns per capita in Yemen than in any other country in the world. Yemen is one of the poorest countries in the world—with an average per capita earning of US $600 a year, but this does not hinder most of the male population from toting the latest version in automatic fire power. The other favorite, after guns, is *qat*—a leaf that when chewed in large quantities induces a mildly narcotic trance.

Wander anywhere in Yemen after lunch, government buildings (well, not there, they'll all have gone home), local markets or private houses and you'll find most of the male population chewing the proverbial cud, so to speak, with eyes in various states of glaziness. The whole male population goes into a collective trance. And if you want to join in, about $4 will be enough to procure you enough *qat* for an afternoon's chewing.

I decide to visit the north, where Yemen shares a common border with neighboring Saudi Arabia, to the general discontent of both countries. Heading from the ancient capital, Sana'a, I take a taxi for the four hour ride to Sa'da, the provincial capital of the north, an area where tourists are more or less nonexistent.

A few kilometers outside Sa'da, a ten minute journey by car along the single asphalt road, I arrive at the *suq al silah*—the weapons market. It is in these markets that most of the tribal population buy the thousands of weapons sold each year in Yemen. It's an arms dealer's paradise; anything can be sold and everything *is* sold. I am offered an AK-47 for US$300, which I politely decline, (convinced I'm being ripped off). But from the wooden stalls the dealers offer almost anything: alongside the AK's are American made M-16's, G-3's, (an expensive US $1000), Belgium FN's, Rocket Propelled Grenades, (RPG-7's—a mere US $500), warheads, night vision binoculars, fragmentation grenades, flares, pistols—Lugers, Walther PPK's, 9mm Brownings...take your pick, (starting price around US $15), military webbing...even the odd tank is up for grabs! It's everything you'll ever need to start a small war or equip your own private army; and in Yemen, the hundreds of different tribes are little less than private armies.

I watch as wild looking tribesmen stream into the suq to test weapons, although—God forbid—there is nothing as formal as a firing range. Guns are simply taken a small distance from the suq where, hopefully, nobody will be foolish enough to wander around. They're fired before being brought back for half an hour's bargaining over numerous cups of sweet tea. There is a refreshing informality to the scene. There is none of the pedantic questions of the modern western world involved in these happy transactions. No license necessary, no boring ID checks, none of the usual boring questions inquiring if you are of sound mind or are you barking mad to want a 12mm heavy machine gun. Are you a responsible adult? No, have you got a police record? No problem. (Visa cards, though, like American Express are not accepted).

Photographs, however, mine in particular, seem to present something of a problem. They are, I am abruptly told by a passing tribesman, *mamnua*—illegal. For a place where the boys in blue are just a little thin on the ground, (well, nonexistent actually), the idea of something being illegal is intriguing. However, I am feeling distinctly confident about my right to do as I please. In my pocket I have a permit from the local governor which states that I can go anywhere I like. With a triumphant, probably not very nice, grin I tell the tribesman that if he has any problems he can complain to the governor. His reply wipes the smile off my face: "The governor," he says, "has no authority here...this is tribal territory." I look to my guide, Hamid, who is from the governor's office, for moral support. He is squirming with embarrassment, and does not contradict the tribesman. This may have something to do with the fact that Hamid is not carrying an AK-47. But for once I am not alone, and some tribesmen stick up for me, saying that photos are no problem. An argument ensues, and I take advantage of it to slink off in the search for fresh photos hoping that no one will notice that the subject of the argument has disappeared.

You might be wondering if there's a down side to so many weapons floating around: indeed there is, and it comes in the form of blood feuds, which Yemenis seem to covet as if they're going out of style. If you should accidentally kill a Yemeni, the best thing you can do is make a mad dash for the airport. Dialing the local equivalent of 911 will not do a lot of good—even if you can find a telephone. Otherwise, if you're lucky, you'll end up paying blood money to the family—how about $10,000 for the price of a human life? Although it does depend on whom you kill. If you're not so lucky you'll find the deceased's many brothers, uncles, cousins etc., paying a not-so-social call on you.

To gain a better insight into the world of blood feuds I dropped in on a prearranged *qat* chewing session with a local tribal sheikh, (family head). Removing my shoes, I join the other *qat* chewers in a long well-furnished room with cushions set around the edge. Set in each place is the general paraphernalia for *qat* chewing: lots of bottles of Coca-Cola and water pipes. Above each cushion there is a peg where chewers hang, not their coats, but their Kalashnikovs. It is only when I ask my host, Abdullah, about blood feuds that I learn that only a few months earlier his own brother was killed by a member of another tribe. He narrates the events that led to his brother's death with the detached dispassion of someone who has put his grief behind him.

I ask if he knows the identity of the killer. He does indeed, which bodes bad news for someone. "The man who killed my brother has left the area and headed south," he says—which sounds to me like acute common sense. So, what will happen next? He replies calmly and matter of factly: "When this man returns or whenever he is found, whatever is sooner, I will kill him," as if it is the most natural thing in the world—which it is—to personally avenge a brother. I ask, in a typically western manner, about the police. Might he not be arrested? He draws on his large and elegant water pipe before smiling gently, as if amused at the thought of the police doing anything, and says: "The police will do nothing; they will say it is a matter of honor, a tribal affair." And doubtless it will be.

—**Roddy Scott**

NEW FIELDING WEAR!

Now that you own a Fielding travel guide, you have graduated from being a tourist to full-fledged traveler! Celebrate your elevated position by proudly wearing a heavy-duty, all-cotton shirt or cap, selected by our authors for their comfort and durability (and their ability to hide dirt).

Important Note: Fielding authors have field-tested these shirts and have found that they can be swapped for much more than their purchase price in free drinks at some of the world's hottest clubs and in-spots. They also make great gifts.

Back

Front

Back

Front

WORLD TOUR

Hit the hard road with a travel fashion statement for our times. Visit all 35 of Mr. D.P.'s favorite nasty spots (listed on the back), or just look like you're going to. This is the real McCoy, worn by mujahadeen, mercenaries, UN peacekeepers and the authors of Fielding's *The World's Most Dangerous Places*. Black, XL, heavy-duty 100% cotton. Made in the USA. $18.00.

LIVE DANGEROUSLY

A shirt that tells the world that within that high-mileage, overly educated body beats the heart of a true party animal. Only for adrenaline junkies, hardcore travelers and seekers of knowledge. Black, XL, heavy-duty 100% cotton. Made in the USA. $18.00.

Name:

Address:

City:

State: Zip:

MR. DP CAP

Fielding authors have field-tested the Mr. DP cap and found it can be swapped for much more than its purchase price in free drinks at some of the world's hottest clubs. Guaranteed to turn heads wherever you go. Made in U.S.A. washable cotton, sturdy bill, embroidered logo, one size fits all. $14.95.

Telephone:
Shirt Name:
Quantity:

For each item, add $4 shipping and handling. California residents add $1.50 sales tax.
Allow 2 to 4 weeks for delivery.
Send check or money order with your order form to:

Fielding Worldwide, Inc.
308 South Catalina Avenue
Redondo Beach, CA 90277

or
order your shirts by phone,:
1-800-FW-2-GUIDE
Visa, MC, AMex accepted

Order Your Guide to Travel and Adventure

Title	Price	Title	Price
Fielding's Alaska Cruises and the Inside Passage	$18.95	Fielding's Indiana Jones Adventure and Survival Guide™	$15.95
Fielding's America West	$19.95	Fielding's Italy	$18.95
Fielding's Asia's Top Dive Sites	$19.95	Fielding's Kenya	$19.95
Fielding's Australia	$18.95	Fielding's Las Vegas Agenda	$16.95
Fielding's Bahamas	$16.95	Fielding's London Agenda	$14.95
Fielding's Baja California	$18.95	Fielding's Los Angeles	$16.95
Fielding's Bermuda	$16.95	Fielding's Mexico	$18.95
Fielding's Best and Worst	$19.95	Fielding's New Orleans Agenda	$16.95
Fielding's Birding Indonesia	$19.95	Fielding's New York Agenda	$16.95
Fielding's Borneo	$18.95	Fielding's New Zealand	$17.95
Fielding's Budget Europe	$18.95	Fielding's Paradors, Pousadas and Charming Villages	$18.95
Fielding's Caribbean	$19.95	Fielding's Paris Agenda	$14.95
Fielding's Caribbean Cruises	$18.95	Fielding's Portugal	$16.95
Fielding's Caribbean on a Budget	$18.95	Fielding's Rome Agenda	$16.95
Fielding's Diving Australia	$19.95	Fielding's San Diego Agenda	$14.95
Fielding's Diving Indonesia	$19.95	Fielding's Southeast Asia	$18.95
Fielding's Eastern Caribbean	$17.95	Fielding's Southern California Theme Parks	$18.95
Fielding's England including Ireland, Scotland and Wales	$18.95	Fielding's Southern Vietnam on Two Wheels	$15.95
Fielding's Europe	$19.95	Fielding's Spain	$18.95
Fielding's Europe 50th Anniversary	$24.95	Fielding's Surfing Australia	$19.95
Fielding's European Cruises	$18.95	Fielding's Surfing Indonesia	$19.95
Fielding's Far East	$18.95	Fielding's Sydney Agenda	$16.95
Fielding's France	$18.95	Fielding's Thailand, Cambodia, Laos and Myanmar	$18.95
Fielding's France: Loire Valley, Burgundy and the Best of French Culture	$16.95	Fielding's Travel Tools™	$15.95
Fielding's France: Normandy & Brittany	$16.95	Fielding's Vietnam including Cambodia and Laos	$19.95
Fielding's France: Provence and the Mediterranean	$16.95	Fielding's Walt Disney World and Orlando Area Theme Parks	$18.95
Fielding's Freewheelin' USA	$18.95	Fielding's Western Caribbean	$18.95
Fielding's Hawaii	$18.95	Fielding's The World's Most Dangerous Places™	$21.95
Fielding's Hot Spots: Travel in Harm's Way	$16.95	Fielding's Worldwide Cruises	$21.95

To place an order: call toll-free 1-800-FW-2-GUIDE
(VISA, MasterCard and American Express accepted)
or send your check or money order to:
Fielding Worldwide, Inc., 308 S. Catalina Avenue, Redondo Beach, CA 90277
http://www.fieldingtravel.com
Add $4.00 per book for shipping & handling (sorry, no COD's),
allow 2–6 weeks for delivery